Research Project

Pippa Riley

Viva Books

New Delhi | Mumbai | Chennai | Kolkata | Bengaluru | Hyderabad | Kochi | Guwahati

First Indian Edition 2011

VIVA BOOKS PRIVATE LIMITED

- 4737/23 Ansari Road, Daryaganj, New Delhi 110 002
  E-mail: vivadelhi@vivagroupindia.net, Tel. 42242200

- 76, Service Industries, Shirvane, Sector 1, Nerul, Navi Mumbai 400 706
  E-mail: vivamumbai@vivagroupindia.net, Tel. 27721273, 27721274

- Jamals Fazal Chambers, 26 Greams Road, Chennai 600 006
  E-mail: vivachennai@vivagroupindia.net, Tel. 28290304, 28294241

- B-103, Jindal Towers, 21/1A/3 Darga Road, Kolkata 700 017
  E-mail: vivakolkata@vivagroupindia.net, Tel. 22836381, 22816713

- 7, Sovereign Park Apartments, 56-58, K. R. Road, Basavanagudi, Bengaluru 560 004
  E-mail: vivabangalore@vivagroupindia.net, Tel. 26607409, 26607410

- 101-102 Mughal Marc Aptt., 3-4-637 to 641, Narayanguda, Hyderabad 500 029
  E-mail: vivahyderabad@vivagroupindia.net, Tel. 27564481, 27564482

- First Floor, Beevi Towers, SRM Road, Kaloor, Kochi 682 018, Kerala
  E-mail: vivakochi@vivagroupindia.net, Tel: 0484-2403055, 2403056

- 232, GNB Road, Beside UCO Bank, Silpukhuri, Guwahati 781 003
  E-mail: vivaguwahati@vivagroupindia.net, Tel: 0361-2666386

Published by arrangement with

BPP Learning Media Ltd.
BPP House, Aldine Place
London W12 8AA

This edition is for sale in the India, Pakistan, Sri Lanka, Bangladesh and Nepal only. Not for export elsewhere.

ISBN : 978-81-309-1768-9

Published by Vinod Vasishtha for Viva Books Private Limited, 4737/23, Ansari Road, Daryaganj, New Delhi - 110 002.

Printed and bound by Raj Press, R-3, Inderpuri, New Delhi - 110 012.

Contents

Introduction   (v)

Study Guide   (vii)

1   Introduction to the research project   1
2   Research philosophies, methodologies and ethics   35
3   The research proposal   63
4   The literature search   105
5   Methods of data collection: primary and secondary sources   131
6   Data analysis   187
7   Project presentation   235

Bibliography   281

Index   285

Introduction

Viva-BPP Learning Media's Business Essentials range is the ideal learning solution for students studying for business-related qualifications and degrees. The range provides concise and comprehensive coverage of the key areas that are essential to the business student.

Qualifications in business are traditionally very demanding. Students therefore need learning resources which go straight to the core of the topics involved, and which build upon students' pre-existing knowledge and experience. The BPP Learning Media Business Essentials range has been designed to meet exactly that need.

Features include:

- In-depth coverage of essential topics within business-related subjects

- Plenty of activities, quizzes and topics for discussion to help retain the interest of students and ensure progress

- Up-to-date practical illustrations and case studies that really bring the material to life

- A full index, with key terms highlighted in bold

Each chapter contains:

- An introduction and a list of specific study objectives
- Summary diagrams and signposts to guide you through the chapter
- A chapter roundup, quick quiz with answers and answers to activities

Titles in the Series

- Accounts
- Business Decision Making
- Business Environment
- Business Maths
- Business Strategy
- Economics
- Finance: Management Accounting and Financial Reporting
- Human Resource Development and Employee Relations
- Human Resource Management
- Management: Communications and Achieving Results
- Management: Leading People and Professional Development
- Managing Finance
- Marketing and Promotion
- Marketing and Sales Strategy
- Marketing Principles
- Organisations and Behaviour
- Research Project

Study Guide

This Course Book includes features designed specifically to make learning effective and efficient.

- Each chapter begins with a summary diagram which maps out the areas covered by the chapter. There are detailed summary diagrams at the start of each main section of the chapter. You can use the diagrams during revision as a basis for your notes.

- After the main summary diagram there is an introduction, which sets the chapter in context. This is followed by learning objectives, which show you what you will learn as you work through the chapter.

- Throughout the Course Book, there are special aids to learning. These are indicated by symbols in the margin:

Signposts guide you through the book, showing how each section connects with the next.

Definitions give the meanings of key terms. The *glossary* at the end of the book summarises these.

Activities help you to test how much you have learned. An indication of the time you should take on each is given. Answers are given at the end of each chapter.

Topics for discussion are for use in seminars. They give you a chance to share your views with your fellow students. They allow you to highlight holes in your knowledge and to see how others understand concepts. If you have time, try 'teaching' someone the concepts you have learned in a session. This helps you to remember key points and answering their questions will consolidate your knowledge.

Examples relate what you have learned to the outside world. Try to think up your own examples as you work through the Course Book.

Chapter roundups present the key information from the chapter in a concise format. Useful for revision.

- At the end of each chapter, there is a **chapter roundup** and a **quick quiz** with answers. Use these to revise and consolidate your knowledge. The chapter roundup summarises the chapter. The quick quiz tests what you have learned (the answers often refer you back to the chapter so you can look over subjects again).

- At the end of the book, there is an index.

Chapter 1 :

INTRODUCTION TO THE RESEARCH PROJECT

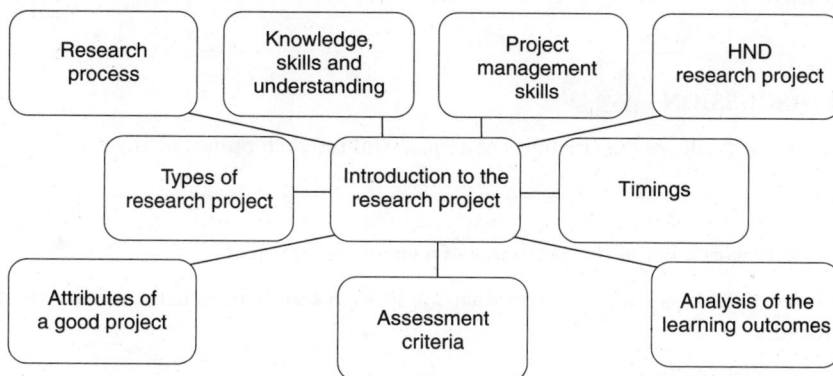

```
┌──────────┐  ┌──────────┐   ┌──────────┐  ┌──────────┐
│ Research │  │Knowledge,│   │ Project  │  │   HND    │
│ process  │  │skills and│   │management│  │ research │
│          │  │understan-│   │  skills  │  │ project  │
└──────────┘  │  ding    │   └──────────┘  └──────────┘
              └──────────┘

      ┌──────────┐   ┌──────────────┐   ┌──────────┐
      │ Types of │   │Introduction  │   │ Timings  │
      │ research │   │to the        │   │          │
      │ project  │   │research      │   └──────────┘
      └──────────┘   │project       │
                     └──────────────┘
   ┌──────────┐    ┌──────────┐     ┌──────────────┐
   │Attributes│    │Assessment│     │ Analysis of  │
   │of a good │    │ criteria │     │ the learning │
   │ project  │    │          │     │  outcomes    │
   └──────────┘    └──────────┘     └──────────────┘
```

The requirement to undertake a research project is a feature common to many courses of higher education. The successful completion of such a project demonstrates many key qualities, such as the ability to organise, prioritise and communicate.

This chapter introduces the concept of management research, and explains the requirements of the HND Business Unit 8 Research Project. Although we make frequent reference to the HND research project requirements, the points made apply equally well to any other form of research project.

Your objectives

In this chapter you will learn about the following:

(a) What makes a good research project

(b) The types of research

(c) The research process

(d) The implications of research for your personal development

(e) The requirements of HND Unit 8

1 THE ATTRIBUTES OF A GOOD PROJECT

1.1 Introduction

Obviously, you must achieve the objectives laid down for your project and we will discuss the HND learning objectives and assessment criteria later in this chapter. However, whatever the specific requirements of the qualification scheme you are pursuing, you should also aim to satisfy widely accepted opinion about the general attributes of good research. This will improve your work and add to its overall credibility.

FOR DISCUSSION

What do you think are the attributes of a successful research project of any kind?

1.2 Jankowicz's list of the attributes of a successful project

Jankowicz (2000) lists six concepts that apply to research in general, at any level of qualification.

    (a) Originality
    (b) Generality
    (c) Pragmatism
    (d) Balance
    (e) Quality of evidence used
    (f) Ethical issues

Originality

Originality, in the sense intended by Jankowicz, is only required at PhD level. We mention it here partly for the sake of completeness, but also because two aspects of this quality are, in fact, relevant to research at lower levels.

First, you will be expected to carry out research that will **add to your professional development**. This means that you should contribute something new to the debate on your chosen subject area, even if it is just looking at something from a different angle.

Second, you **must avoid plagiarism**. Plagiarism is passing off another person's work as one's own, or using it without attributing it. Plagiarism can be both deliberate, by copying someone else's work, or unintentional. Unintentional plagiarism can occur when there is a failure to acknowledge and reference sources properly. The appropriate referencing conventions are described in Chapter 4.

Generality

Jankowicz (2000) describes generality as

    '.......a relevance beyond the situation and setting in which the data were gathered.'

Project work should have relevance not just to the specific context under investigation but also to a wider degree.

Jankowicz says:

> *'If your conclusions apply only to this year's accounts; if your recommendations about employee participation address just one office or one part of a department; if your marketing plan ignores a closely related group of products to the product on which your findings are focused, then your project is unlikely to be successful. Your project will be acceptable to the extent that its recommendations can be extended to different times, locations, markets, departments and so forth.'*

Pragmatism

If we describe a project as pragmatic, we are saying that its recommendations and its tone as a whole are realistic and practical. For example, concluding a project with a recommendation that a company should immediately relocate its accounting and other administrative functions to an Asian base may be completely unrealistic in the context of the company, its staff, its product and its markets.

When coming to conclusions, you should use your common sense. For example, the tourism industry in the United Kingdom has suffered following poor weather and terrorism in the mid-2000s. As a result you should think carefully therefore before recommending a course of action for an airline or a freight forwarding company which assumes a significant growth in the numbers of transatlantic passengers or volume of cargo.

Balance

As you will see in Chapter 3, one of the key aspects of your work at the start of your project will be choosing and refining your objectives and research question. While doing that, you will start to get a feel for the range of possible outcomes. Obtaining balance in your research project means that the outcomes will be equally valuable whether your expectations are confirmed or negated (Jankowicz, 2000). Either outcome could be regarded as a valid contribution to the subject area. If the results of your research are a foregone conclusion, and results at one end of the spectrum are unlikely, then the subject would be unbalanced, and the research would not be of such a high calibre.

EXAMPLE

Your project involves research into the effect on sales of breakfast cereal companies' practice of providing free gifts related to recent film releases. If your research establishes a correlation and can attempt to quantify it, that would be a very interesting and significant finding, of value to both types of company involved. However if your research indicates that there is no such correlation, or that the link is in fact very weak, that would also be of interest, as it would indicate that a change of policy should be considered.

Quality of evidence used

There are two broad categories of data.

    (a) **Primary data** are data you have collected yourself and analysed and interpreted for your own specific purposes. An example would be the results of a questionnaire, designed by you for the purpose of your research.

    (b) **Secondary data** are data initially collected by other people for their own purposes or yourself for another purpose, but which are also relevant to your research.

You are likely to collect a mixture of primary and secondary data in the course of your research. Primary data are of good quality when they are directly relevant to your research objective. Secondary data can be of good quality as long as you bear in mind that they may not give you the whole story, may be biased and may not be directly relevant to you. You will have to show expertise in recognising and demonstrating the relevance of secondary data to your own argument (Jankowicz, 2000).

Jankowicz (2000) also says that

> *'The balance between primary and secondary data can make the difference between a good and a poor project.'*

The use of the right mixture of good quality, reliable primary and secondary data will add to the impression given by your Project.

The characteristics of data are covered in detail in Chapter 5, on data collection, and also in Chapter 6 on the analysis of quantitative and qualitative data.

Ethical issues

Ethical considerations are of fundamental importance in management research, and it is vital that you are seen to be taking them into account. Business research usually involves people and working relationships. From an ethical perspective, you should treat the people involved in your research with respect, tact and diplomacy. From a practical viewpoint, good people-handling skills are likely to be reflected in the quality of the data you gather as well as in the efficiency you achieve in completing your project.

There are two particularly important ethical considerations in business research.

    (a) The way you portray your role to the research population
    (b) The way you interpret and use the research findings

EXAMPLES

1   For many years in the UK, businesses selling double glazed windows would telephone potential customers with their sales pitch. This approach proved extremely unpopular so the window companies now approach the potential customer under the guise of doing some market research.

Clearly, your research should not be a means of providing a business with a cover for gathering sales information.

2   A researcher's project involved determining the reasons why a company performed more poorly in a certain consumer market. In addition to conducting a consumer survey and running several focus groups, the company tried unsuccessfully to persuade the researcher to interview rival companies that were doing well in the market without fully explaining his role.

Remember that you will be performing research as part of the process of completing a Project. You must not involve yourself in anything that might be considered as industrial espionage.

If you are carrying out research within an organisation, you may well be operating at the management-employee interface. You will need to be careful that you behave ethically in relation to both parties.

(a)   Be careful not to play management and employees off against each other.

(b)   Remember to maintain your fairness and objectivity. If your findings are critical of any person or group of people, try to handle it with tact and sensitivity. It might be a good idea to refer it to the people concerned and you may be able to write it up in a constructive and diplomatic way.

(c)   Avoid leading people on and be careful that you do not raise people's expectations regarding what your research might be able to achieve. Jankowicz (2000) maintains that the ethical issue that you are most likely to encounter is that of people's expectations. If research is carried out into problems experienced at an organisation, the expectation arises that some remedial action will be taken as a result. It is wrong to allow people to continue to hold this misconception, if that is what it is.

Ethics in management research is an important topic. We will consider it later in this chapter and there is more material in Chapter 2.

2   TYPES OF RESEARCH PROJECT

2.1   Pure and applied research

In your reading into the nature of management research, you will see references to **pure** and **applied** research. It is important that you understand the difference between them.

Pure research, which is often also called basic, academic or fundamental research (Saunders *et al* 2000) is research that seeks **to understand** the process and outcomes of business and management. Sharp and Howard (1996) describe it as the development of theory without any attempt being made to link it to practice. The principal aim of pure research is the advancement of knowledge.

Applied research is directed towards producing results which are of direct relevance to managers and which form the basis of **recommendations** upon which they can act. It will often involve the finding of a **solution to a problem**.

In practice, most research includes elements of both pure and applied research. For example, a project could include empirical investigation; this, fundamentally, is pure research, but if it is aimed at solving a given problem, it would count as applied research.

2.2 Purposes and forms of research

Saunders *et al* (2003) suggest that there are three main reasons for conducting research.

(a) To provide findings that advance knowledge and understanding

(b) To address business issues

(c) To devise a process for solving management problems

At a personal level, the satisfaction of your own intellectual curiosity can be regarded as a valid and worthy purpose of your research. The extent to which your research topic addresses your own intellectual needs is likely to influence your motivation and commitment and ultimately the quality of your work.

Business research projects can also be classified slightly differently in that they usually take one of three forms.

(a) An **empirical investigation** of a management or organisational practice, justified and supported by detailed reference to relevant theories and concepts from the literature: this would be pure research.

(b) The **empirical testing and development** of an existing **management model** or the development of a new model, with data contributing to the conceptual aspects of this model, justified and supported by detailed reference to relevant theories and concepts from the literature: this would be pure research.

(c) The application of relevant theories and concepts to the **solving of a managerial or organisational problem**, where practical recommendations arise from the interactions between theories and concepts from the literature and the data collected: this would be applied research.

In later chapters, we shall reference the relevance of different research methods to each type of research project.

2.3 Empirical investigation

Empirical means based on experience or observation. Jankowicz (2000) defines empirical data as 'the results of new observations made in order to check out the assertion'.

If you intend to carry out empirical investigations, your research is likely to be carried out into one organisation only, focussing on a specific practice. However, it is possible that your work could go as far as comparing or contrasting the implementation of a practice across a small number of organisations within the same industry.

EXAMPLE

One unpublished undergraduate dissertation investigated the system by which commissions payable to salesmen were calculated. It was an **exploration** into how different reward systems were being used and could be used to motivate sales staff and sales performance, contribution and ultimately the profit of the company.

Other examples could include:

- The **impact of the decision** made by many large employers to close their final salary pension schemes

- The **impact of a particular marketing practice**, such as the move by car manufacturers to target women in their advertising after decades of ignoring them

- The **impact of adopting policies** which are specifically designed to be environmentally friendly, for example the newly introduced policy of Waitrose Supermarkets in the UK to sell only eggs from hens which are not intensively-reared

Saunders *et al* (2003) set out numerous examples of possible research topics in one of the appendices to their book, *Research Methods for Business Students*. One such example is

'An evaluation of the extent to which language training equips managers to better understand foreign business cultures'

This is an example of an empirical investigation that would necessitate your looking at a selection of companies, rather than just one.

You can use both primary and secondary data for such an empirical investigation.

It is likely that you will use a combination of data. In the example cited above, of a dissertation analysing the calculation of sales commissions to the sales force and its impact on motivation, mainly primary data would be used. A research topic such as an investigation into the marketing strategies of motor manufacturers, also suggested above, would involve the collection and use of more secondary data.

As we will discuss later, the issue of access to data can be very problematic. Therefore, your process of selecting and refining a project topic should include an assessment of what primary or secondary data you intend to use.

2.4 Empirical testing and development of a management model

If you select this type of dissertation, you will be looking to the **future** rather than reviewing the impact of something in the past. You will be contributing in some way to a new development, and moving the existing body of knowledge on the topic forward.

Saunders *et al* (2003) look at it in a slightly different way. They see it as a process of exploring the way in which different organisations do things in different ways. They maintain that the purpose of such research is to discover and understand better the underlying processes in a wider context, thus providing greater understanding for practitioners. The testing and development of the management model can be achieved by looking at it in different contexts.

7

The management model in this context can be one of the well-established and well-known models that you have already studied such as Maslow's hierarchy of needs or Porter's Five Forces. Alternatively, it could be a model that has developed in a particular organisation by virtue of management practice within that organisation, for example combining certain management roles.

EXAMPLE

The Times of 28 January 2002 contained a supplement on MBAs. An article on recent research at the Imperial College Management School discussed the results of research indicating that companies with one person as both chairman and chief executive outperform those that have those functions performed by different people.

Research such as that would contribute to current thinking about models of management structure, and could assist in the development of a new model.

Saunders *et al* (2000) include in their list of possible topics the title

Is personality testing a valid tool in the recruitment and selection process?

You would analyse the use of a recruitment model in order to see whether your conclusions contributed to the thinking in this area. In the field of HR you might wish to explore the use of popular management tools such as teamworking styles questionnaires and leadership styles questionnaires and their role and use in organisational development.

FOR DISCUSSION

Is it appropriate for the established scheduled airlines and national carriers to target their marketing almost exclusively at the business traveller?

2.5   Management problem solving

Perhaps the main characteristic of this form of research is the fact that it will involve making a recommendation.

The problem could either be very broad, affecting an industry or a sector of the economy, or it could be a specific problem facing one organisation alone.

EXAMPLE

In the late 1990s a soft drink called Sunny Delight was introduced into the UK. It had previously been very successfully marketed in North America. It initially experienced rapid growth in sales and was popular as a healthy alternative to traditional fizzy soft drinks. However, sales plummeted when it was found that it contained the same proportion of sugar as traditional fizzy drinks, it contained minimal quantities of fruit juice and had a lot of additives. Sales hit rock bottom when there was widespread publicity about a case involving a child turning orange having drunk a litre and a half of Sunny Delight a day.

In that situation, the problem to be solved would be that of overcoming such a marketing challenge and devising a new marketing strategy, applying marketing theories and concepts.

Other examples of this type of research could include:

(a) The application of theories and concepts to devise a strategy for the turnaround of a retailer that has lost sight of its core markets and the needs of its customer base

(b) The application of theories and concepts to ascertain whether it is a wise diversification for a supermarket to offer financial services products, culminating in a recommendation one way or the other

(c) The application of theories and concepts to try to improve the poor profit performance of an airline and recommend a change of strategy.

(d) The application of theories and concepts to restructure and re-engineer the working practices of a service group that is perceived by its customers to be fragmented or not very 'joined-up'.

In management problem-solving research, secondary data may well emanate from the subject organisation itself. Generally it would be wise to negotiate access to such data, as they are likely to add value and quality to your findings and recommendations. These may include previous market research carried out, results of focus group meetings, sales reports, productivity reports, staff surveys and management accounts.

2.6 Choosing the right type of project

This should not be a significant problem, as it is probably not something that you will find yourself consciously doing. It is better to focus on something that you find interesting and follow the guidance in Chapter 3 on how to choose and refine your topic. You are then likely to find that the title you have devised fits into one of the three categories.

You could do the procedure the other way round (ie choose a type of project and then fit a topic to go round it). For example, you may be particularly keen on problem solving, or you know that you will feel happier using only secondary data. At this stage, that is a judgement that you probably cannot make.

3 THE RESEARCH PROCESS

3.1 Introduction

Hussey and Hussey (1997) suggest that whatever type of research or approach is adopted, there are several fundamental stages in the research process that are common to all scientifically based investigations. Similarly, Saunders *et al* (2003) state that most textbooks represent research as a multi-stage process that you should follow in order to undertake and complete your research project.

3.2 Recommended process

This book describes a research process which is tailored to the requirements of the HND Research Project Unit, but also recognises the importance of the role of project management and the need to set up all the necessary administrative aspects properly.

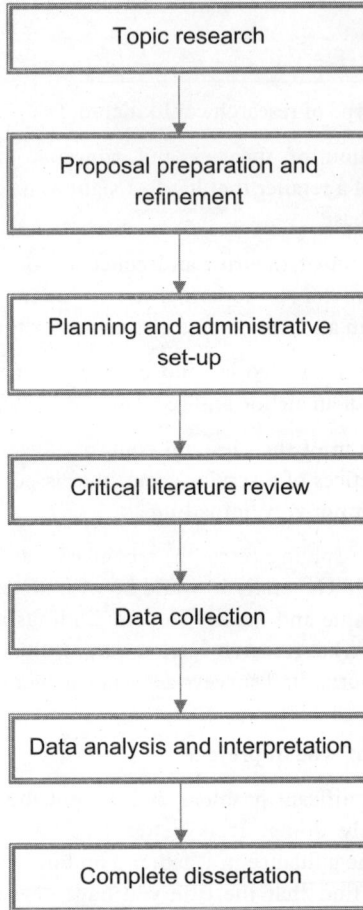

Figure 1.1 The research process

Sources: Author's experience; Hussey and Hussey (1997)

Gill and Johnson (1997); Sanders *et al* (2000)

The recommended research process is depicted in the diagram shown above. A brief description of each step is provided here, but fuller coverage will be provided in later chapters.

The steps shown in the diagram will be covered in greater detail in later chapters.

3.3 Topic research

This is a key step as it will determine what you will be doing over the life of your research project. You may already have some idea about what you would like to work on for your project. On the other hand, like many learners, you may still have an open mind.

A key element of this initial stage will be assessing the feasibility of alternative topics. Factors to consider might include personal interest, career relevance, time required, access to information and cost.

Topic research will be covered in detail in Chapter 3.

3.4 Proposal preparation and refinement

Once you have selected a project topic you would like to pursue, then comes the task of writing your proposal and getting it approved.

Proposal preparation will be discussed in more detail in Chapter 3.

3.5 Planning and administrative set up

Having had your proposal approved you will be standing on the threshold of doing your research work. As we suggested earlier in the chapter, you should avoid just diving in feet first. Instead, you should develop a clear project plan, which of course you will be free to modify as you progress.

To improve your chances of completing your research project both efficiently and successfully, there are several areas that are likely to need advance planning.

    (a)   Determining logistics for completion
    (b)   Negotiating necessary access
    (c)   Setting up administrative systems
    (d)   Establishing milestones and timetable
    (e)   Preparing personal financial plans
    (f)   Setting up physical work space arrangements
    (g)   Discussing and negotiating key personal relationships and support

The technical aspects of your project will present substantial challenges; you should therefore avoid making your life more complicated through lack of organisation.

3.6 Critical literature review

Saunders *et al* (2003) explain that a **critical review** will form the foundation on which your research is built. Gill and Johnson (1997) suggest that whatever its scale, any research project will necessitate reading what has been written on the subject and collating it in a critical review. This demonstrates some awareness of the current state of knowledge on the subject, its limitations and how the proposed research aims to add to what is known.

Gill and Johnson (1997) also caution that the literature review takes place early on in the research process and therefore it is important to keep abreast of the literature on the topic throughout the duration of the research.

Literature review will be covered in detail in Chapter 4.

3.7 Data collection

Robson (2000) states that collecting data is about using selected methods of investigation. Doing it properly means using these methods in a systematic, professional fashion.

There are many methods of data collection, because there are many research techniques (Hussey and Hussey, 1997). Data can be collected in a variety of ways, in different settings and from different sources (Sekran, 2000).

Data collection will be dealt with more fully in Chapter 5.

3.8 Data analysis and interpretation

Saunders *et al* (2003) highlight the importance of considering the **validity** and **reliability** of data you intend to use (these terms are explained later in this chapter). They also emphasise that of equal importance to consider are the appropriateness and suitability of the analysis techniques you decide to use. According to Hussey and Hussey (1997) 'the tools of analysis you use will depend on whether you have collected quantitative or qualitative data'.

Data analysis techniques are explored in Chapter 6.

3.9 Complete the dissertation

Most textbooks on research methodology describe writing-up as a separate, culminating phase of the research process. However, Hussey and Hussey (1997) provide the sensible guidance that you should start writing up your research in draft as soon as you start the early stages of your project, and continue to do so until it is completed.

We recommend that, given the flexibility to cut, copy and paste provided by word processing software, you should consider setting up a skeleton of your project report at an early stage of your research. You can then make entries directly into your prepared format as you go along, knowing that what you have recorded can be edited later on, as and when necessary. The usual file saving and back-up procedures will of course need to be observed. Periodic hard copies might also be useful if your computer were to crash completely or be stolen. The approach should help you to work in an orderly and efficient manner.

The writing up of your findings will be covered in detail in Chapter 7.

4 KNOWLEDGE, SKILLS AND UNDERSTANDING

4.1 Introduction

The various taught units of your degree or diploma course should provide you with the basic knowledge and understanding you are likely to require in order to undertake your research project.

However, 'research requires a number of **qualities** and **skills**, some of which you already have; others you will need to develop during the course of your research (Hussey and Hussey, 1997). From a practical perspective, it would be useful to break skills down into personal skills and management skills.

Activity 1   **(15 minutes)**

Using the space provided below, have a go at trying to identify the personal qualities, personal skills and management skills that will help you to complete your Research Project successfully. Try not to look at the list provided below until you have attempted your response.

Personal qualities	Personal skills	Management skills

4.2   Personal qualities

Personal quality	Role
Self-awareness	Self-awareness is the most fundamental of all the qualities and requires you to be aware of your strengths and weaknesses. It can be described as being able to see yourself as others see you. Your quest to advance knowledge will also be a journey of self-discovery.
Motivation	Motivation is a key ingredient in any endeavour. You need to analyse what it is that drives you. Here are some possibilities. • Learning within a management course • Personal development • Organisational problem solving • Intellectual challenge • Social pressures • Fulfilling creative roles • Increasing personal employment opportunities (Hussey and Hussey, 1997 and Easterby-Smith *et al* 2000)
Analytical mind	You will need to analyse information with a critical mind. You need to cultivate a willingness and ability to analyse things down into component parts.
Creativity	An element of creativity will help you to make progress as well as add quality to your work. Creativity can influence all the processes of completing your research, from the initial search for a topic to the ultimate writing-up of your findings.
Independence	Your course so far will probably have provided you with a fairly structured learning experience. By contrast, you will have a great deal of independence in your work for your research project.
Flexibility	Business research can be complex and even messy: you may need to amend your planning and methods as your research progresses.
Emotional maturity	Philips (1984) describes several problems affecting researchers, including isolation, boredom and frustration. There may be setbacks such as problems of access or difficulties in collecting data. You will need to keep a level head and press on, remembering the ultimate goal of gaining your qualification.

4.3   Personal skills

Personal skill	Role
Active listening	Listening is a key skill and affects your relationship with all the people involved in your research, including your supervisor.
Communication	Communication is a fundamental life skill that is important in all aspects of business work. Good communication skills will help you to conduct effective research.

Personal skill	Role
Persuasion and influencing	As a researcher, you are likely to need the co-operation of people who do not report to you. You will need to be able to persuade and influence people at all levels in order to achieve your research objectives. This is a vital skill to develop for business life generally, since you will frequently have to deal with people such as colleagues, organisational superiors, customers and regulatory authorities.
Problem solving	Problem-solving requires you to be open minded and capable of both generating possible solutions and evaluating them objectively. A solution-oriented approach is important to overcoming the many stumbling blocks you are likely to encounter during the course of your research.
Relationship building	Relationship building is a key competence sought by modern business organisations. Not everyone you will be working with on your research will be naturally friendly and helpful. You will need to handle your contacts with skill and find enough common ground to ensure that your work progresses smoothly.

4.4   Management skills

Management skill	Role
Interviewing	Interviewing will be important if you are carrying out a survey. However, there will be other situations when you will need interviewing skills in obtaining information even if it is a one-to-one discussion.
Negotiation	Dealing with objections to your plans and reaching compromises if necessary are likely to be very important to your research.
Project management	Any research activity is likely to display the characteristics of a project and therefore will benefit from the application of project management techniques to organise and control activities, recording and problem solving. You will need to control your activities on an overall basis. Managing your project will also mean managing your contacts with the people who will be involved in your research. This is part of treating people in an ethical way.
Team working	This is another key business skill. Good skills in working with other people will contribute to a more efficient and effective research effort.
Time management	You will probably have to work to tight deadlines, depending on your college, so managing your time properly is imperative.
Change management	Business research is seldom conducted in a vacuum. You will need to understand the impact of your findings on the organisation sponsoring your research. Academic rigour and commercial credibility should go hand in hand in your research.

Management skill	Role
Report writing	The written report is the outcome of your research and what your sponsors and supervisors will base much of their judgement on. You must ensure that your report does justice to your research.

5   PROJECT MANAGEMENT SKILLS

Your research project will probably be the largest academic project you have undertaken so far. As already noted, project management skills will help you to plan and carry out your work effectively. You will probably not need to make detailed use of sophisticated techniques such as network analysis, but you may well find that an application of basic ideas will be of great help to you. For example, an awareness of dependencies and interactions will help planning your activities and the use of a simple chart will help you to keep abreast of what you should be doing as time passes.

Project management skills are covered in detail in Chapter 10 of the BPP Learning Media Business Essentials Course Book, *Business Decision Making*. You should refer back to that Course Book in order to refresh your memory as to the skills required.

6   THE HND RESEARCH PROJECT

Edexcel's own 2010 specification for Unit 8, the Research Project, is reproduced in the Annex at the back of this book. We will look at some of the general features of this specification in this section and go on to a consideration of the learning outcomes and assessment criteria in Sections 7 and 8.

6.1   The aim of the unit

The stated aim of Unit 8 is to 'develop learners' skills of independent inquiry and critical analysis by undertaking a sustained research investigation of direct relevance to their higher education programme and professional development'. There are three important elements to this aim.

(a) **Development of skills of independent inquiry and critical analysis.** You can expect guidance and advice about your project, but if you are to develop skills, you will have to do the work yourself. Also, observation and recording will not be enough: you will have to think about what you observe and reach some conclusions about it.

(b) **Sustained research.** This is going to take quite a lot of time. The only Edexcel guidance on time estimation is a statement in the specification for HNC and HND that a 15 credit unit implies 150 learning hours: Unit 8 is a 20 credit unit. Draw your own conclusions.

(c) **Relevance to higher education and professional development.** Any properly conducted business research will satisfy the higher education part of this requirement, but you should give a moment's thought to the idea of furthering your professional development and what this implies for the topic area you choose. A topic of general business interest, such as an aspect of customer service, would be appropriate if you do not yet have any clear plans for the way you see your career developing. However, if you have a reasonable idea about the area of business you will probably specialise in, this may help you to decide on your general research topic.

(i)   You may decide to study some aspect of your chosen area. Someone working in banking, for example, might decide to study an aspect of credit-worthiness.

(ii)   Alternatively, you might choose to widen your horizons. Someone aiming for a role in human resources management might decide to do research into a marketing topic, for example.

It does not really matter which of these approaches you take, or even if you take a compromise route with elements of both, but you must give some thought to this requirement and be prepared to justify your choice.

You will have to produce a research proposal (or at the very least an outline of your plans), which should be approved by your tutor before you start work. A proposal that is irrelevant to your continuing education and development is not likely to be accepted. Your tutor will also monitor the progress of your research project to ensure that you are working within the Unit 8 specification and towards agreed objectives.

6.2   The unit abstract

The unit abstract is a general overview of the nature and purposes of the research project. It amplifies and extends the brief statement of the aim. An important feature of this item is what it omits: it does not say that you are expected to produce a ground-breaking piece of research. There is a statement that your research should make a positive contribution to your area of interest, but the main assumption behind the unit abstract is that the principal intended beneficiary of your research is you, yourself, not the wider academic or business research community.

Thus, the abstract speaks of your becoming confident in the use of research techniques, of understanding the theory that underpins formal research, of the context of your area of learning and the focus of your interest.

6.3   Links to other elements of your studies

The unit description does not suggest any specific links to other areas of your studies, apart from Unit 49, which is work-based experience. If you undertake Unit 49, the logical progression would be to do your work placement first and then carry out your research project in the same organisation. In more general terms, by the time you reach the point at which you will start to think about and plan for your research project, you are likely to have made progress with other units and areas of study. You may be considering (or even have completed) one of the specialist unit pathways and it should be a natural progression for you to go on and research some aspect of it in more depth.

You can refresh your memory of the other modules by looking back through your study material, but here are some suggestions as to topic areas, in very broad terms.

(a)   Change, transformation and renewal
(b)   Strategy and structure
(c)   Conflict within organisations
(d)   Human resources
(e)   Organisational cultures

(f)   Personality and behaviour
(g)   Interpersonal communication
(h)   Cultural differences
(i)   Leadership
(j)   Negotiation

The development of the research idea and the writing of the proposal are covered in detail in Chapter 3.

7   THE LEARNING OUTCOMES

7.1   Introduction

Regardless of the type of degree or diploma for which you are studying, there will be stated learning outcomes or objectives (LOs). Learning outcomes for a course of study provide a succinct summary of its purpose and coverage in terms of what you have to achieve. In the case of Unit 8, they also provide you with a working framework that should help you to structure and complete your research effectively.

For the HND research project, the learning outcomes are as follows.

1   Understand how to formulate a research specification
2   Be able to implement the research project within agreed procedures and to specification
3   Be able to evaluate the research outcomes
4   Be able to present the research outcomes

Generally, you will have to achieve all of the LOs set down for a course to achieve a pass: this is certainly true for HND Units.

7.2   LO1 – a problem of terminology

Unfortunately, we are faced with an immediate problem of terminology when we consider LO1. This is because the LO uses the phrase 'research specification'. Generally, this phrase is used in the context of **research commissioned from consultants**. Commissioned research is common in the public and not-for-profit sectors, where charities and government bodies often require detailed information but do not have the technical resources required to carry out the necessary research. They therefore contract with experts to do the research for them. In order to retain substantial control, they set down **specific requirements to govern the scope and conduct** of the research project. Thus, the British Educational Research Association says:

*The commissioning process is set in train through a **specification** or **brief**, normally in writing (though with very varying degrees of steering and/or elaboration), that sets out the research/evaluation remit in the form of objectives, outputs and timeline. Many specifications also define the features of the preferred design and methodological approach, and some even specify particular methods.*

(http://www.bera.ac.uk/commissioning-and-consuming-research-in-education/the-processes-of-commissioning-research/)

When a research specification has been issued, researchers who are interested in the project then bid for the work; each bid, or tender, will include a **research proposal** that explains how they propose to carry out the research. This will include as a minimum, an explanation of the research philosophy and methodology; a detailed timeline; a full budget and an explanation of how the results of the work will be disseminated.

Thus, in this context of commissioned research, we would have these two documents, possibly rather similar in content, but profoundly different in purpose. From our point of view, the essential message here is that a research specification would not be prepared by **the person proposing to do the research**; it would be prepared by **the person for whom the research was to be carried out**.

However, as we have seen, LO1 employs the phrase 'research specification' in the exact opposite sense, using it to mean a research *proposal* as described above. (It is interesting to observe that the previous version of the Unit 8 specification, issued in 2004, spoke in terms of a 'research proposal'; the term 'research specification' has been introduced in the current Unit 8 detail, issued in 2010.)

Here is how we shall deal with this discrepancy.

This book, while based on the requirements of HND, is intended to have wider application and to be useful to students undertaking research projects for other qualifications. We shall therefore use the terms 'research specification' and 'research proposal' in the widely-accepted senses described above. We will only use the term 'research specification' in the sense it is used in LO1 when we are quoting directly from the Unit 8 research project documentation. When we do this, we will put the term in quotation marks thus: 'research specification'; and will include notes as necessary to resolve any potential for misunderstanding.

7.3   LO1 – Understand how to formulate a 'research specification'

LO1 is provided with four sub-outcomes called research formulation, hypothesis, action plan and research design.

(a)   **Research formulation** is concerned with aims and objectives, literature review and resource implications. A key part of the planning phase of your project will be to develop a suitable research strategy that will help you to complete your research successfully within the organisational setting you have chosen. Saunders *et al* (2003) suggest that your research strategy will in effect be a general plan of how you intend to address the research question(s) you have set yourself. Such a plan is likely to involve:

(i)   Clear objectives

(ii)   Statement of data sources

(iii) Identification of constraints, eg access to data, time available, location, finance and ethical issues.

(b)   **Hypothesis** introduces an important aspect of the philosophy of research, which is the choice of an **inductive** or a **deductive** approach. These alternatives are described below.

(c)   Your **action plan** will lay down a timetable for the various activities contributing to your project, including the processes of review and analysis and will set out a series of deadlines for the completion of the various stages.

(d)   Your **research design** will be concerned with the types of research and analysis you will undertake, such as quantitative and qualitative research,

19

statistical analysis, the use of primary and secondary data and so on. Available management research strategies include experiment, survey, case study, action research, grounded theory and ethnography. A sound grasp of the available strategies will facilitate your formulation of the best strategy for your Project. This may rely on one of the strategies stated above or you might prefer to use a mix and match approach

7.4 Deductive and inductive research

The two principal approaches to research are **deductive** and **inductive**.

The deductive approach

Deductive reasoning works from the general to the more specific: it is a 'top down' method. In using a deductive approach, you would begin by developing a predictive statement called a **hypothesis** and then proceed to gather data to test it. In effect, you would try to **disprove** your hypothesis. The wording of LO1, with its emphasis on hypothesis, effectively **requires that you conduct deductive research**.

EXAMPLE

You work for a glassware manufacturer that is experiencing a high level of breakages. After a review of the existing production records, you notice that the breakage rate is higher in the afternoon than in the mornings.

Your theory is that this is caused by employee tiredness alone and not any other factors such as variable machine performance or the bosses going off to play golf in the afternoon.

You might begin your research by setting up more detailed records for each hour of the working day to provide evidence to support your hypothesis.

In addition, you might then organise an experiment where shorter shifts are worked to confirm that fresher employees are less likely to cause breakages.

The inductive approach

Inductive reasoning works upwards from the specific to more general conclusions. With the inductive approach, you carry out data collection and analysis and then develop a theory on the basis of the work you have done. The theory follows the data.

Activity 2   **(20 minutes)**

Imagine that you work for the same glassware manufacturer, discussed above. How might you apply an inductive approach to the research instead?

The complexity of human behaviour means that in business-oriented research, the inductive approach is likely to lead to conclusions that reflect the way the people involved **perceive** and **feel about** the problem. Such conclusions are therefore unlikely to apply to other circumstances. Contrastingly, the conclusions from deductive research are more likely to be widely applicable.

Both deductive and inductive research have strengths and weaknesses. Deductive research gives hard numbers to look at whilst inductive research may provide deeper findings because the approach gets closer to the people involved.

Of course, the two approaches are not mutually exclusive and it is likely that any research programme will contain episodes of both. A deductive phase testing a simple hypothesis might indicate that it had some value but was not sufficiently developed. Further research on an inductive basis might well produce data that would allow the hypothesis to be developed to a more satisfactory state. This developed hypothesis would then be tested during a further phase of deductive research.

7.5   LO2 – Implement the research project within agreed procedures and to specification

LO2 has three sub-outcomes: an over-arching outcome of implementation and two more specific outcomes of data collection and data analysis and interpretation.

(a)   **Implementation** of your project must be according to the method and design you have agreed with your tutor: you must not make it up as you go along. This sub-outcome specifically requires the testing of a research hypothesis, emphasising once again the necessity of carrying out deductive research. It also introduces the terms **validity** and **reliability**; these are two of the three essential characteristics of good data, the third being **generalisability**.

Saunders *et al* (2003) say that **validity** is concerned with whether the findings are really about what they appear to be about. Are they valid (and therefore relevant) in the context of the objective of the project?

Reliability is a measure of whether one could expect similar circumstances to yield the same results on different occasions, or if observed by different observers (Easterby-Smith *et al*, 2001). The subjectivity or bias of the observer can threaten reliability.

Generalisability is described by Saunders *et al* (2003) as **external validity,** ie the issue of whether your findings may be equally applicable in other research settings. This is not usually a problem. If you think that your results are not relevant elsewhere, limit your work to a study of the specific organisation or study you are looking at. This is much the same thing as the *generality* described by Jankowicz (2000) and discussed earlier in this chapter.

Validity, reliability and generalisability are important concepts for research generally and all are as relevant for the credibility of research findings overall as they are to the integrity of basic data.

The three issues of validity, reliability and generalisability are explored in detail in Chapter 2.

(b)   **Data collection** will be a major activity in any research project and the methods used must be carefully considered. Proper consideration must be given to **data recording** and to the avoidance of **bias**.

A research method is a systematic and orderly approach taken towards the collection and analysis of data so that information can be obtained from these data (Jankowicz, 2000).

Remember that your primary objective is to complete your project to the satisfaction of the assessors at your college. Naturally, if you are conducting your research within an organisational context you must be aware of its needs and expectations. Your challenge is to make an accurate assessment of the prospective academic and organisational needs and then design your research methods to satisfy those needs. You may, of course, have to apply some negotiating skills where there are competing and conflicting needs.

EXAMPLE

A manufacturer gathers feedback from time to time from retailers on perceived consumer attitudes to the manufacturer's goods.

The manufacturer recently launched a new product line which has failed to meet expected sales targets. Your research is intended to establish and explain the reasons for the failure of the new product line.

You would like to target your research on consumer perceptions of the product using a structured questionnaire and consumer discussion groups, whereas the company would prefer you to speak to the retailers.

Whilst the retailers would no doubt provide valuable insights into customer behaviour, data collected from actual customers is likely to be more valid.

You will therefore need to apply some negotiation and persuasion skills to open the way to your conducting your preferred research.

Generally, a research project is unlikely to be successfully completed using only intellectual skills. Bear in mind that you will have to apply excellent **personal skills** to help you gain access to people and information as well as build consensus to facilitate the way forward with your research.

Personal skills are also likely to feature heavily in your working relationship with your supervisors. Whatever the travails and frustrations you are almost certain to experience as you work through your Project, always remain positive and maintain a cordial and constructive working relationship with your supervisor.

Methods of data collection are covered in Chapter 5

(c)   **Data analysis and interpretation** techniques will be vital to you if you are to produce good results from your research. A wide range of methods and techniques is available and part of your task will be to select the most appropriate ones. An important concept introduced in this sub-objective is the **data transcript**. A data transcript may be thought of as a summary or 'hard copy' of any kind of potentially volatile data. The most basic form of transcript is simply a written record of spoken words. You will probably produce transcripts of this type to record the details of interviews, where you may produce a verbatim transcript from an audio recording or an abbreviated record in the form of responses to a questionnaire. Other examples of data transcripts are printed summaries of email exchanges and summary sheets that form the initial stage of aggregating basic observation data.

7.6   Overview of data analysis

Analysis is the process of breaking down data and classifying it into its component parts (Saunders *et al* 2003). Synthesis is the process of arranging and assembling various elements so as to make a new statement or plan or conclusion – a unique communication (Rowntree, 1987).

Quantitative (or numeric) **analysis** of data can be very simple or highly complex, with methods ranging from, for example, presenting your results in a table, to sophisticated statistical modelling involving, for example, cluster analysis or factor analysis.

Quantitative analysis is likely to involve three important techniques.

(a)   **Operationalisation** entails setting up a measurement scale, in order, for example, to rank an attribute between 1 and 10 with 1 for poor, 10 for excellent

(b)   **Measurement** applies a scale to the actual data: for example, respondents might be asked to assess a hotel's service quality.

(c)   **Analysis** involves breaking the collected data down in order to approach parts.

Qualitative analysis is the analysis of data in a non-numerical way.

EXAMPLE

The data consists of comments made by participants at a meeting. The analysis entails exploring not only what transpired but why people said what they said but also how the people reacted to it and how they felt about what went on. No attempt is made at quantification of any aspects such as how many times the chairman summed up or perhaps a certain participant interrupted.

There is not a standard way of analysing qualitative data in the way that there is for quantitative data. Qualitative data often has to be classified into **categories** before it can be meaningfully analysed, through the creation of a conceptual framework (Saunders *et al* 2003).

The choice of analysis technique is likely to be driven by what you would like to find out. So if you are trying to discover how the relationships within a board of directors might be affecting a company's performance, it is probably more useful to know whether they like, hate or tolerate each other and how they go about making decisions rather than trying to count which director said what how many times. On the other hand, it might be appropriate to use a quantitative approach to measure how well, in the eyes of employees, information is shared within a business.

Both quantitative and qualitative analysis techniques are described in Chapter 6.

7.7 LO3 – Be able to evaluate the research outcomes

When carrying out research, it is all too easy to become narrowly focussed on the detail of data collection and analysis. Any researcher must, at some stage, stand back and take a hard look at how the project is turning out and what its overall value is. This is the process of **evaluating the research outcomes**; it is a very important part of the researcher's task and must not be relegated to an afterthought. The process of outcome evaluation provides invaluable learning opportunities for the researcher while simultaneously indicating the necessary scope of future research on the same and similar topics. LO3 reflects these purposes in its two sub-outcomes: the first deals with the process of evaluation, while the second extends it into consideration of implications for the future.

(a) **Evaluation of outcomes.** The main outcomes to evaluate are those that relate specifically to the purpose and objectives you have chosen for your research project. However, there is a wider field for consideration. This relates to the nature of HND Unit 8 as a whole and to the progress of your own personal development.

(b) **Future consideration.** Considerations for the future should flow naturally from your evaluation of outcomes, though not all of your conclusions about outcomes will necessarily have implications for the future.

7.8 Evaluating your research.

Earlier in this chapter we discussed the various purposes and forms of research. Your project planning should have led you to define both a clear **overall purpose** and some very specific **detailed objectives** for your research. These will form the basis of the first stage of your research evaluation, which should be concerned with the **extent of its success as a research project**. Measuring your research against its stated objectives should be followed by a wider consideration of its qualities. We have discussed the characteristics of good research in some detail earlier in this chapter and you should review that discussion as part of your review process.

One of the features of good research that we spoke of was **balance**, which means that the outcomes will be equally valuable whether your expectations are confirmed or negated. If you have not designed your research to achieve this kind of balance, it will be more difficult for you to assess its value should your results tend to be negative. Look carefully for the banal, predictable kind of finding that adds little to knowledge of your research topic.

You should also consider the **validity** and **reliability** of your research in formal terms. Review our earlier discussion of these qualities in order to be able to do this.

It may be possible for you to achieve the overall purpose of your research even if you fail to achieve some of the more specific objectives that support it. This is because there are likely to be significant links between those objectives and it may be that a convincing result in relation to one objective will more than outweigh less clear-cut results in relation to another.

7.9   Assessing specific features.

You will probably be able to produce a fairly brief summary evaluation of your research in terms of its success or failure in achieving its purpose and objectives and the extent to which it displays the features of good research. You might even grade each of these variables on a suitable scale. This would be a useful exercise, though probably you would not wish to publish such a simplistic evaluation.

However, a proper evaluation will go deeper than this, in that you must also consider the detail of what you have done. You will have designed your research methodology in the way that seemed most appropriate at the time: experience may lead you to wish you had chosen differently. You must review your design and your choices of approach and technique in the light of your experience while carrying out your project and identify those areas where your ideas worked well and those where they did not. You should be very specific about this, since this is hard practical experience that you should not forget. The real question here is this: do you wish you had done anything in a different way? This includes consideration of things you both did but probably did not need to do and things you did not do but perhaps should have done.

Here are some examples.

- Were your samples large enough? Were they usefully structured?
- Did your questionnaires display any unexpected ambiguity?
- What proportion of your samples refused to answer questions?
- Were your coding methods appropriate?
- Were you able to keep to your time plan?

7.10   Reassessing your objectives.

So far we have been concerned with the basic evaluation of **outcomes** against **intentions**, which you may recognise as the basis of all feedback control systems: a central heating system monitors actual room temperature and switches on or off according to whether it is too low or too high; a system of financial control monitors actual costs and revenues against the requirements of the budget. By examining your achievements in the light of your objectives, you are undertaking a very similar process.

More sophisticated systems of control make provision for a further process, which is **reconsideration of the original target itself**. This allows for the detection and amendment of intentions and plans that are **impractical**, **inappropriate** or **inconsistent**. You should incorporate this process into your research evaluation and reassess the purpose and supporting objectives you set for your research in these terms.

(a) Was your research project **impractical** in terms of the resources required? Consider the following.
- Time available
- Library and Internet service availability and extent
- Co-operation and support from your chosen organisation
- Financial costs

(b) Was your research project **inappropriate** in terms of your wider objectives; the concerns of your chosen research organisation or your employer; the extent and complexity of the research techniques required; or its social and legal setting?

(c) Was your research project **internally consistent and coherent** in that the detailed objectives supported the overall purpose and your chosen strategies were effective in achieving the objectives?

Clearly, this kind of reassessment would be valuable at earlier stages of your research project and you should be prepared to reassess your overall plan whenever it seems appropriate during the life of your project.

7.11 The wider evaluation.

You are undertaking your research project for at least one very clear reason: you wish to pass HND Unit 8. Perhaps you see HND as something of a hoop to jump through for employment progression and a bare pass in Unit 8 may be all you want. Alternatively, you may have ambitions to build on both the HND qualification and the experience of research in future academic and professional endeavours. Or your motivation may lie somewhere between these extremes. Whatever your motivation, you should undertake a **wider evaluation** of your work for Unit 8.

Notice that the concept of reassessing your objectives, discussed above, is equally applicable to this phase of your evaluation

7.12 The objectives of Unit 8.

First, ask yourself if you think you have achieved the stated objectives for Unit 8. The discussions in this chapter should help you with this. Start by thinking about the overall aim.

(a) Do you think the project has led to any development of your skills of 'independent inquiry and critical analysis'? Notice that there are two elements to this. They are linked, of course, but it would be possible to achieve greater development in one of these areas than in the other.

(b) Did you manage to carry out 'sustained research? Was this a practical objective in terms of the demands it placed on your time?

(c) Was your research relevant to higher education? You can probably accept your tutors opinion here; presumably you would not have been allowed to proceed if your project were not appropriate.

(d) Was your research relevant to your professional development? This might be difficult to assess if you have limited awareness of where your career is going or what demands your professional development will place upon you. This is an area where a discussion with a trusted and intelligent manager in the organisation you researched might be helpful. We will return to this topic later.

7.13   The learning outcomes.

Consider the four stated learning outcomes and the detailed unit content items that support them (we called these items 'sub-outcomes in our earlier discussion). This could be a time-consuming process to carry out in detail, so it may be appropriate to use the unit content listing as an *aide-memoire* to help you to recall impressions formed during your research. However, if you are taking the idea of research seriously, it would be difficult to go into too much detail here.

7.14   Your personal development.

Personal development extends beyond academic achievement and professional competence. It is now widely accepted in both professional and academic education as being fundamental to learning and to general progress. An important feature is that it is not limited to a given course of study such as the one you are following. It does not end at graduation or qualification; it should be a **life-long process**. You will recall that the overall aim for Unit 8 includes an element of broader professional development.

You should conclude your evaluation of your work for Unit 8 by considering its contribution to your wider, longer-term personal development. To do this properly, you will have to deploy some self-knowledge, at least to the extent of considering your personal ambitions and your strengths and weaknesses. Think hard about the following questions.

(a)   Do you have a clear idea of what your ambitions and intentions are for the future?

(b)   Has your work for Unit 8 helped or hindered your development of this vision and has it brought you colder to achieving it?

(c)   Are you aware of your own strengths and weaknesses? You could assess these under a range of headings, such as academic, professional and social competence, communication skills and people skills. Be particularly honest in assessing your weaknesses.

(d)   Has your work for Unit 8 led to improvement in any of these personal qualities? Earlier in this chapter, we emphasised the importance of communication and project management skills: how do you think you have done with these and do you think you have made any improvement as your research has progressed? What about creativity, time management and negotiation?

7.15   Future considerations.

The second sub-outcome for LO3 is concerned with the future. You should consider the implications of your research for yourself and for others.

(a)   Do your conclusions lead you to make any recommendations, either to the organisation concerned for possible action, or generally about further research in the future ?

(b)   If you intend to continue taking an interest in the topic you have researched, do you have any ideas about how you will proceed?

(c) Has your experience given you any insights into how you should conduct your own personal development in the future?

(d) Are you able to offer any comments to your college or your tutor that might help students in the future?

7.16 LO4 – Be able to present the research outcomes

Presentation of your findings will be the culmination of your research and constitutes an important part of your research project. The specification of LO3 is very brief. The single sub-outcome is self-explanatory but covers a great deal of ground:

Format: professional delivery format appropriate to the audience; use of appropriate media.

Generally, research would be presented in written form, which might be called a thesis (at doctoral level), a dissertation (at lower levels) or, simply, a report. However, the wording of LO4 would also cover an oral presentation using a wide variety of presentation aids and media.

You are likely to have two main audiences for your presentation.

(a) The assessor (and possibly second marker) at your college

(b) People within the organisation you have researched (which may be your employer, of course).

You may therefore have to produce two reports, one for your college and another for your employer or subject organisation. This extra burden may be eased in three ways.

(a) Planning the structure and content of your academic report so as to facilitate the spinning off of the second one

(b) Maintaining close contact with both your academic supervisor and the relevant business managers so that you fully understand their requirements and how they differ

(c) Intelligent use of word processing software

The presentation of your research, both in writing and orally, is covered in detail in Chapter 7.

8   ASSESSMENT CRITERIA

8.1   The nature of the assessment criteria

We have seen that each of the four main LOs is supported by one or more sub-outcomes that provide extra detail to guide your efforts. The LOs are also linked to **assessment criteria**, which are reproduced in the Annex. The assessment criteria describe the standard of achievement you must demonstrate against each learning outcome in order to pass Unit 8. Note that the wording of the assessment criteria is intended to indicate the **minimum standard** for a pass. Merit and distinction grades are subject to more demanding criteria. Essentially, these criteria will be determined by your college, but they should be based on the grade descriptors published in the general specification for HND.

8.2   The need for clear vision

There is a consensus of opinion that you must maintain focus in your work. You must constantly think in terms of what you are trying to achieve, and how you will be judged on it. This means referring frequently to the assessment criteria. Sharp and Howard (1996) say that

'As far as possible a clear and unambiguous vision of what will be needed should be sustained throughout the research.'

This may be difficult to achieve once you are immersed in the critical literature review and the detailed analysis of your findings. To ensure you keep sight of the overall objective as you work through the minutiae of your project, you will need a clear perception of the two things this chapter has been about so far.

(a)   The general characteristics of a good research project

(b)   The specific requirements of the Unit 8 assessment criteria

8.3   What the assessor will be looking for

A typical outline scheme for evaluating research projects is given below.

(a)   Purpose of the work

(b)   Approach

(c)   Contextual evaluation

(d)   Reasoning and critical thinking

(e)   Conclusions

Purpose of the work

There should be a clear statement of the **objectives** of the work. As well as stating these in the introduction to the research report, you should reiterate them wherever it might be helpful to the reader. For example, at the point when you analyse the data you have collected and move on to drawing a conclusion, it is helpful if you restate your objectives, so that the reader can relate them to the information obtained without having to refer back to the beginning.

The assessor would also expect to see that you have identified the **boundaries** of your work and justified your choice of subject matter in terms of academic or organisational importance

Approach to the work

You should explain your approach, in order to justify it. In general terms, you should explain three things.

(a)   How you obtained the facts and opinions you make use of

(b)   How you collected your objective data

(c)   What thought you gave to the issues of validity, reliability and generalisability

Validity, reliability and generalisability were discussed briefly earlier in this chapter, and they are explored in more detail in Chapter 2.

The assessor will also expect to see you **justify the approach** you have adopted your work. This will require you to explain three things.

(a) How your approach relates to the overall stated objective of the work

(b) The choices you had to make in adopting your approach and how you responded to the constraints under which you were working (such as time, funding and access to information)

(c) The limitations of the approach you have adopted

Contextual evaluation

The assessor will be looking for evidence that the work you have done is set within the **wider context** of academic knowledge on the subject. This will involve consideration of factors such as those listed below.

(a) A theoretical framework

(b) An evaluation and interpretation of earlier academic work on the subject

(c) Proper academic referencing, ideally using the Harvard system (which is the style adopted throughout this book)

(d) Evidence of non-academic sources such as trade journals and newspapers if appropriate

The conventions and techniques of referencing are explained in detail in Chapter 5 on literature and search skills.

Reasoning and critical thinking

The assessor will want to see that your reasoning and critical thinking are **structured** and **coherent**. In particular, your work must show evidence of four intellectual processes.

(a) Analysis
(b) Evaluation
(c) Synthesis
(d) Substantiation (in that the evidence justifies and supports the conclusion)

The assessor will also expect to see evidence of **linkages**, for example between your findings and the wider academic context of the work. This brings us back to the original idea of stating your objectives at the outset and then always keeping them in sight throughout the presentation process.

Conclusions

The assessor will want to see a final drawing together of your key themes and findings and their implications. You should summarise your findings, and present the summary initially in the **executive summary** at the start of your report.

You should state what you consider to be the meaning, implications and limitations of your findings. Generally, it will be appropriate to make recommendations linked to the objectives of the work at this stage. Also, at some point, you should also discuss the approach you adopted (which can now be done with the benefit of hindsight).

The format of all of the sections of the Project, including the conclusion, is discussed in Chapter 7.

9 TIMINGS

9.1 When should I do the Project?

We anticipate that you will carry out your research project in the final stages of your studies, although this may be subject to the constraints of your college timetable.

The topic you choose for your research may fall within the subject matter of the other elements of your studies. It may therefore make good sense not to rush into an early proposal. Instead, you might prefer to make a start only when you have developed a sense of confidence that you have a strong level of academic knowledge and business awareness. This will provide you with a platform on which to build a good project that will stand up to a rigorous assessment process. This approach is likely to help you in selecting and refining your topic, as well as in the eventual analysis of the data you collect.

9.2 How long will it take?

We have already mentioned the time implications of the fact that Unit 8 is a 20 credit unit. In terms of start and finish dates, the time taken to complete a project like this can vary enormously, depending on a variety of factors.

(a)   The topic chosen, its complexity and the challenges you may face in accessing information

(b)   The demands of your other academic studies and any outside commitments

(c)   The type of research you are undertaking and the extent to which you need the co-operation and support of third parties

As a general guide, most projects of this scale are likely to last between three and six months from start to finish. However, in practice, the actual time it will take to complete will depend on a myriad of practical as well as personal issues.

Activity 3   **(10 minutes)**

Do you think you have an idea what these issues might be? Have a go at jotting down your thoughts of practical and personal factors that may be relevant.

The actual time taken will depend on many factors. Awareness of these factors will help you to both measure and manage the progress you make, as well as helping you to achieve your study goals.

9.3 Volume

Most educational establishments indicate the expected maximum number of words for a thesis or report, but the Edexcel specification does not do so. We suggest that you aim for about 5,000 words. That volume would enable you to produce a well-structured report, describing in detail your research processes, analysing your results and then concluding and recommending on the basis of the work done.

Your tutor will give you further guidance on this.

Chapter roundup

- A good research project will display six characteristics.

  - Originality

  - Generality

  - Pragmatism

  - Balance

  - High quality evidence

  - Conformance with ethical standards

- Projects may be classified into pure and applied research. They may also be divided into three groups.

  - Empirical investigation

  - Empirical testing and development of an existing management model

  - Application of theory to problem-solving

- The research process may be regarded as having seven stages.

  - Topic research

  - Proposal preparation

  - Planning

  - Literature review

  - Data collection

  - Data analysis and interpretation

  - Writing up

- A wide range of personal qualities, personal skills and management skills is required for the successful completion of a research project.

- The HND Unit 8 research project aims to develop skills of inquiry and analysis through sustained research of relevance to higher education and professional development.

- The Unit learning outcomes are

  1   Understand how to formulate a "research specification"

2   Be able to implement the research project within agreed procedures and to specification

3   Be able to evaluate the research outcomes

4   Be able to present the research outcomes

- The detail of the first learning outcome implies a deductive approach. This is based on collecting data to test a hypothesis. The alternative, inductive, approach, is based on theorising after collecting data.

- Validity of research depends on whether the findings are really about what they appear to be about. Reliability means that the findings can be expected to be reproduced on other occasions. Generalisability means that findings are equally applicable in other settings.

- Each learning outcome is linked to assessment criteria that define the standard needed for a pass.

- In assessing your research, the assessor is likely to look at five things

  ° The purpose of the work

  ° Your approach to the work

  ° Contextual evaluation

  ° Reasoning and critical thinking

  ° Conclusions

Answers to activities

1   Here are the qualities and skills which this book suggests are likely to influence the progress and success of your dissertation.

Personal qualities: Self-awareness, motivation, analytical mind, creativity, independence, flexibility and emotional maturity.

Personal skills: Active listening, communication, persuasion, problem solving and relationship building.

Management skills: Interviewing, negotiation, project management, team working, time management, change management and report writing.

(Source: Author's own experience; Easterby-Smith *et al* 2000 and Hussey and Hussey, 1997)

2   With an inductive approach you might being by interviewing a sample of the shopfloor staff and their supervisors. Their responses may well indicate that tiredness is a key factor influencing the level of breakages sustained. However, during your discussions, you may also learn other factors which you would not have arrived at if you had started with a formal theory and a hypothesis, eg

(a) Employees might be going out for a drink at lunch time

(b) The machinery might be unreliable and stoppages might lead to rushed working later in the day

(c) Supervision itself might slacken in the afternoon

(d) It might get darker in the afternoons and this might cause the employees to get more careless

(e) The machinery may become more unreliable later in the day because of duration of usage

3   Here are some factors; you may well have thought of some others that are just as valid.

Practical factors: Volume of literature to be surveyed, accessibility of literature, complexity of topic, access to key people, nature of research method, technical demands of analytical process or statistical tools used and access to computing software or hardware and availability of support.

Personal factors: Level of motivation and interest, practical experience, target grade and quality desired, interpersonal skills, level of personal organisation, writing skills, competing personal commitments, personal goals for completing the Project.

Chapter 2 :

RESEARCH PHILOSOPHIES, METHODOLOGIES AND ETHICS

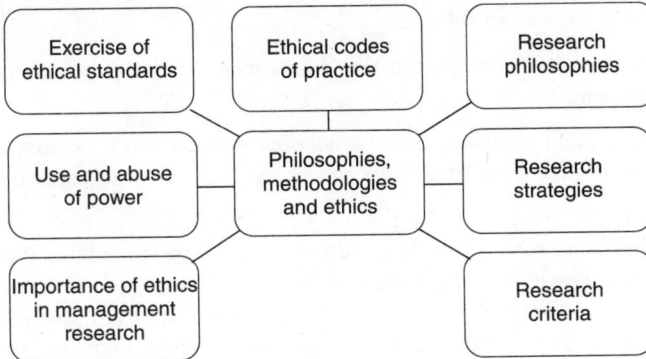

```
┌──────────────┐   ┌──────────────┐   ┌──────────────┐
│ Exercise of  │   │ Ethical codes│   │  Research    │
│ethical stand.│   │ of practice  │   │ philosophies │
└──────────────┘   └──────────────┘   └──────────────┘

┌──────────────┐   ┌──────────────┐   ┌──────────────┐
│ Use and abuse│   │ Philosophies,│   │  Research    │
│  of power    │   │ methodologies│   │  strategies  │
│              │   │  and ethics  │   │              │
└──────────────┘   └──────────────┘   └──────────────┘

┌──────────────┐                      ┌──────────────┐
│Importance of │                      │  Research    │
│ethics in mgmt│                      │  criteria    │
│  research    │                      │              │
└──────────────┘                      └──────────────┘
```

Your objectives

In this chapter you will learn about the following:

(a) Research philosophies

(b) Research strategies and their advantages and disadvantages

(c) The key research criteria of validity, reliability, and generalisability

(d) The nature and importance of ethics in research

1 RESEARCH PHILOSOPHIES

1.1 Epistemology

Hussey and Hussey (1997) explain that **epistemology** is concerned with the **study of knowledge** and what we accept as knowledge. Jankowicz (2000) suggests that it is to do with your personal theory of knowing. He argues that this effectively renders down to two matters.

(a) What counts as knowledge?

(b) Once you have decided on the above, what counts as proof or evidence of knowledge?

For example, you might consider that if a business cuts its administrative overheads it will increase its profits. You find it easy to accept that this is something worthy of research.

However, recruitment consultants may advise prospective candidates that employers tend to reject men wearing brown or green suits or women with red nail varnish or large earrings. Whether you believe these views, feeling and perhaps even prejudices of people to be a valid area of knowledge will depend on your **epistemological outlook**. This in turn will drive your search for a research topic.

If you are being sponsored by an organisation you may need to be aware of its epistemological outlook. If the organisation has a 'hard nosed' remuneration driven approach to staff management, you are unlikely to make much progress if you would like to research 'touchy-feely' issues such as staff development or motivation.

1.2 Positivism

If you have a **positivistic** epistemological or philosophical outlook to research, you are likely to believe that only **phenomena that are observable and measurable can be validly regarded as knowledge** (Hussey and Hussey, 1997).

The key idea of positivism is that the social world exists **externally**, and that its properties should be measured through **objective methods**, rather than being **inferred subjectively** through sensation, reflection or intuition (Easterby-Smith *et al*, 2000).

A key characteristic of the positivist philosophy is that the **observer is independent** of what is being observed. You would maintain an arm's length distance from the people involved in your research.

Remenyi (2000) observes that under positivism, the **research is independent of and neither affects nor is affected by the subject of the research**. It is assumed that there are independent causes that lead to the observed effects, that evidence is critical, parsimony is important and that it should be possible to generalise or to model, especially in a mathematical sense, the observed phenomena.

Parsimony is the principle that an explanation of what is observed should be as simple as possible. Parsimony is said to lead to a **reductionist approach** to research, in that the number of variables considered is reduced to a bare minimum.

EXAMPLE

Research into employee performance is based on the impact of only two variables, employee remuneration levels and the effect of supervision.

The reductionist approach is criticised on the grounds that it over-simplifies complex phenomena.

(a) It is impossible to treat people as being separate from their social contexts and they cannot be understood without examining the perceptions they have of their own activities.

(b) A highly structured **research design** imposes certain constraints on the results and may ignore more relevant and interesting findings.

(c) Researchers are not objective, but part of what they observe. They bring their own interests and values to the research.

(d) Capturing complex phenomena in a single measure is, at best, misleading. For example, is it possible to assign a numerical value to a person's intelligence?

A positivist research philosophy is broadly related to a deductive research approach.

1.3   Phenomenology

If you were disposed to a **phenomenological epistemology** or philosophy, you are likely to believe that the world and reality are not objective and external, but they are socially constructed and given meaning by people based on their personal experience (Husserl, 1946).

Phenomenology as philosophy started when Edmund Husserl introduced the term in his book *Ideas: A General Introduction to Pure Phenomenology* (1913). Phenomenology describes the structures of experience as they present themselves to consciousness, without recourse to theory, deduction or assumptions from other disciplines such as natural sciences.

Phenomenology is a qualitative approach that emphasises the **subjective** state of the individual. It stresses the subjective aspects of human activity by focusing on the **meaning**, rather than the **measurement** of social phenomena (Hussey and Hussey, 1997).

The phenomenologist believes the world can be modelled, but not necessarily in a mathematical sense. A verbal, diagrammatic model could be acceptable (Remenyi, 1997).

EXAMPLE

You are considering the factors that influence the performance of your department.

Using a positivist research approach you develop a theory and hypothesis that link performance to variables such as remuneration and supervision and you might develop a mathematically oriented statement along the lines that performance is a function of remuneration and supervision.

Eg, Performance = (a x remuneration) + (b x supervision)

Where

However, if you were adopting a phenomenological perspective, you would look at the problem more subjectively, being less structured and perhaps more descriptive. For instance, you might adopt a jigsaw puzzle type of model, where performance was the overall picture and all the motivational factors were pieces of the jigsaw. Your approach would be holistic rather than parsimonious/reductionist.

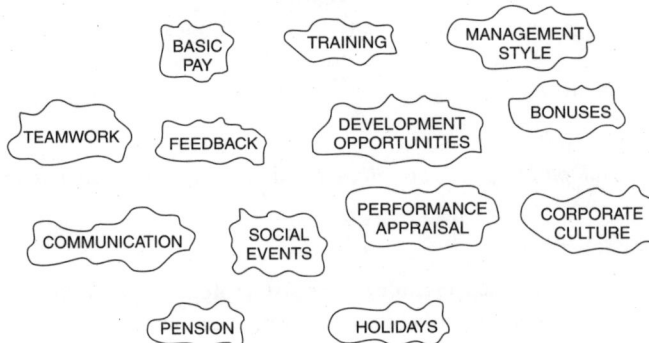

BASIC PAY   TRAINING   MANAGEMENT STYLE

TEAMWORK   FEEDBACK   DEVELOPMENT OPPORTUNITIES   BONUSES

COMMUNICATION   SOCIAL EVENTS   PERFORMANCE APPRAISAL   CORPORATE CULTURE

PENSION   HOLIDAYS

1.4   Pragmatism

There is obviously a debate between the supporters of positivism and phenomenology as to which approach is 'better'. This conflict has been labelled the 'paradigm wars'.

A **paradigm** is a philosophical and theoretical framework within which theories, laws and generalisations, and the experiments performed in support of them, are formulated by particular scientific school or discipline.

Saunders *et al* (2003) suggest that the rivalry misses the point as each philosophy is better at doing different things. As always, which is 'better' depends on the research question(s) you are seeking to answer. Business and management research is often a mixture of the two, often using what in some books is referred to as a **pragmatic** approach.

Pragmatism is a philosophical position with a respectable, mainly American, history (Robson, 2002). The characteristic idea of philosophical pragmatism is that of **efficiency in practical application** – the issue of 'which works most effectively' is of primary importance.

Remenyi *et al* (2000) provide a good summary of the pragmatist position by saying that the researcher should draw on whichever method and approach is appropriate in a particular situation, so as to **triangulate** and validate the findings, even within a single research project.

2   RESEARCH STRATEGIES

2.1   Surveys

The aim of a survey is to obtain information that can be analysed in order to extract patterns and make comparisons (Bell, 1999).

Denscombe (1998) states that the use of a survey is a research **strategy** rather than a research method. Many methods can be incorporated into a social survey. The strategy may be depicted by the following diagram.

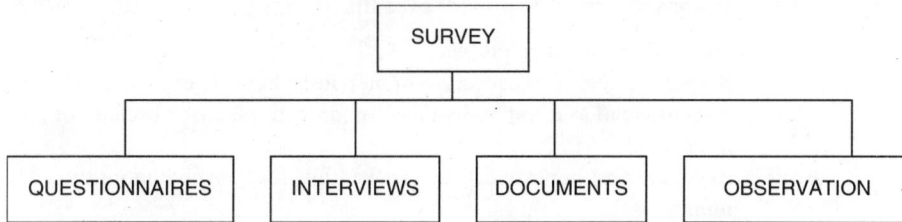

```
                          ┌──────────┐
                          │  SURVEY  │
                          └──────────┘
      ┌──────────────┬──────────────┬──────────────┐
┌──────────────┐ ┌────────────┐ ┌────────────┐ ┌──────────────┐
│QUESTIONNAIRES│ │ INTERVIEWS │ │ DOCUMENTS  │ │ OBSERVATION  │
└──────────────┘ └────────────┘ └────────────┘ └──────────────┘
```

Surveys can provide answers to the questions 'What?', 'Where?', 'When?' and 'How?', but finding out 'Why?' is more difficult. Causal relationships can rarely, if ever, be proved by the survey method. The main emphasis is on fact-finding, and a survey, if well structured and piloted, can be a relatively cost efficient way of gathering information (Bell, 1999).

Denscombe (1998) identifies the advantages and disadvantages of using a survey strategy.

Advantages

- (a) Empiricism
  - (i)   The emphasis is on producing data based on real world observations.
  - (ii)   Information can be said to come 'straight from the horse's mouth'.
  - (iii) Focus on data more than theory (though a good survey does have some theoretical basis)

- (b) Width and inclusiveness of coverage
  - (i)   Copes well with large scale populations or events
  - (ii)   Can also cater for small-scale qualitative research
  - (iii) Facilitates breadth of coverage of data sought
  - (iv)   Usually provides good foundation for generalisation

- (c) Produces data that are amenable to quantitative analysis

- (d) Ease of analysis
  - (i)   The structure of the survey can be planned so as to make analysis easier.
  - (ii)   Experienced researchers will be aware of how best to align input with outcome.

- (e) Efficiency
  - (i)   Relatively more cost efficient than strategies such as experiment and ethnography
  - (ii)   Costs tend to be more predictable
  - (iii) Results can be obtained fairly quickly

Disadvantages

    (a) Empiricism

        (i)   Attention may be devoted to the data itself at the expense of its implications for relevant issues, problems or theories.

        (ii)   The *significance* of the data can be neglected.

    (b) Data detail and depth

        (i)   The use of questionnaires and sampling may result in a lack of **depth** and **detail.**

        (ii)   However, surveys do provide **breadth.**

    (c) Accuracy and honesty of responses

        (i)   Responses may be inaccurate or not fully honest (even if for benign reasons, such as a respondent's willingness to please or because of poor memory).

        (ii)   Accuracy and honesty can be checked but may involve more time and money.

The use of surveys will be covered in more detail in Chapter 5.

2.2   Experiments

'An experiment is a means of testing the effect of one thing on another, or others' (Marshall, 1997).

Thus, experimentation is typically an aspect of research undertaken using the **deductive** approach

Saunders *et al* (2003) provide a handy guide to the deductive experimental process.

    (a) Definition of theoretical hypothesis

    (b) Selection of samples of individuals from known populations

    (c) Allocation of samples to different experimental conditions

    (d) Introduction of planned change to one or more of the variables

    (e) Measurement on a small number of the variables

    (f) Control of other variable

The advantages and disadvantages of experiments, as identified by Denscombe (1998) are as follows.

Advantages

    (a) Repeatability

        (i)   Procedures are carefully recorded and variables controlled.

        (ii)   Hence, the experiment may be checked by being repeated by other researchers using identical procedures.

    (b) Precision

    Precise measurements can be made of the variables that form the basis of the data.

    (c) Convenience

    Where laboratory experiment is involved, the researcher does not need to spend (too) much time and money.

Disadvantages

    (a) Artificial settings

        (i)   The experiment may not replicate conditions existing in the real world.

        (ii)   Hence the behaviour of the dependent variable may not reflect what might happen in a real setting.

    (b) Deception and ethics

        (i)   Differences in treatment between the experimental group and the control group may entail an ethical dilemma. For example, a hypothesis might propose that improved working conditions improve productivity. It might seem unfair to provide one group with quality office accommodation, new computers and kitchen facilities which are denied to the control group

        (ii)   Sometimes it may be regarded as necessary to conceal the purpose of the experiment. Is such deception ethically cceptable?

    (c) Representativeness of research subjects

        (i)   The experimental group and the control group must both be equally representative of the population under research.

        (ii)   A practical problem here is 'self selection', which arises from people putting themselves forward and hence influencing the composition and character of the groups involved

    (d) Control of relevant variables

        (i)   This may be difficult to achieve in practice. For example, how do you make sure that the bonus scheme under review is the only thing that affects employee performance?

        (ii)   Large groups may be needed if the many variations and ambiguities involved in human behaviour are to be controlled. Such large-scale experiments are expensive and time consuming to set up (Bell, 1999).

2.3   Case studies

Denscombe (1998) states that case studies focus on one instance (or a few instances) of a particular phenomenon with a view to providing an in-depth account of events, relationships, experiences or processes occurring in that particular instance.

According to Yin (1989), case studies have the following characteristics.

    (a) They are an empirical way of investigating a contemporary phenomenon within its real life context.

    (b) The boundaries between the phenomena and the context are not clearly evident.

    (c) They use multiple-methods of collecting data which may be both quantitative and qualitative

    (d) They are particularly valuable in answering 'Who?', 'Why?' and 'How?' questions in management research.

Hussey and Hussey (1997) state that case studies are often described as **exploratory research** and are used in areas where there are few theories or a deficient body of knowledge.

Scapers (1990) describes the following uses of the case study technique.

Type of case study	Overall aim
(a) Descriptive	These are restricted to describing current practice.
(b) Illustrative	The research attempts to illustrate new and innovative practices adopted by particular organisations.
(c) Experimental	The research examines the difficulties of implementing new procedures and techniques in an organisation and evaluating the benefits.
(d) Exploratory	Existing theory is used to understand and explain what is happening.

A case study is sometimes carried out to follow up and add detail to a survey. Alternatively, it can precede a survey and be used as a means of identifying key issues that merit further investigation. However, the majority of case studies are carried out on a 'stand-alone' basis (Bell, 1999).

Remenyi (1998) argues that because of its flexible nature, a case study may be an almost entirely positivistic or almost phenomenological study or anything between these two extremes.

Saunders *et al* (2003) suggest the following benefits of case studies.

(a) They can be a very worthwhile way of exploring existing theory

(b) They can enable you to challenge an existing theory and provide a source of new hypotheses.

The advantages and disadvantages of case studies identified by Denscombe (1998) can be summarised as follows.

Advantages

(a) Focus on one or a few instances enables the researcher to deal with the subtleties and intricacies of complex social situations. 'These processes may remain hidden in a large-scale survey' (Bell, 1999).

(b) The analysis is holistic rather than based on isolated factors.

(c) The case study approach allows for the use of a variety of research methods and fosters the use of multiple sources of data.

(d) There is no pressure to control events.

Disadvantages

(a) Generalisations made from a case study may lack credibility. It is necessary to demonstrate the extent to which the case is similar to or different from other cases of its type

(b) Susceptibility to accusations that the case in question has been chosen because it will yield '**safe data**'; that is, data that supports the researcher's hypothesis. Hence careful attention to detail and rigour must be exercised in the use of this approach

(c) The **boundaries** of the case can prove difficult to define in an absolute and coherent fashion

(d) Negotiating access to case study settings can be a demanding part of the research process

(e) The **observer effect** can come into play. Those being observed might behave differently from the way they would do usually, because they are being observed

2.4 Action research

Hussey and Hussey (1997) explain that action research is an approach which assumes that the **social world is constantly changing,** and the **researcher and the research itself are part of this change.** The main aim of action research is to enter into a situation, **attempt to bring about change** and monitor the results.

According to Somekh (1995), action research rejects the concept of a two-stage process in which research is carried out first by researchers and then in a separate second stage, the knowledge generated from the research is applied by practitioners. Instead, the two processes of research and action are integrated. Elliot (1991) tells us that in action research 'theories are not validated independently and then applied to practice. They are validated through practice'.

The term action research was originally used by Lewin (1946) who saw the process of enquiry as forming a cycle of

(a) Planning
(b) Action
(c) Observation
(d) Reflection   (Hussey and Hussey, 1997)

Denscombe (1998) has refined this cyclical process as reflected in the following diagram.

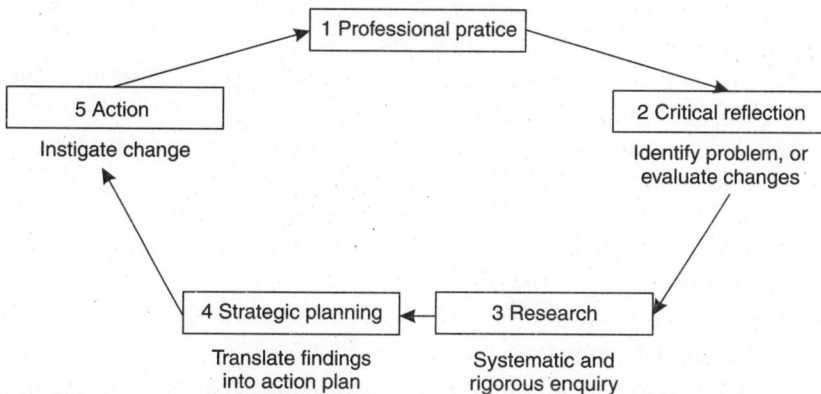

Figure 2.1 The cyclical process in action research

Saunders *et al* (2003) explain that action research is interpreted by management researchers in a variety of ways, but there are three common themes within the literature.

(a) Focus on the management of change as the purpose of the research (Cunningham, 1995).

(b) Involvement of practitioners in research to the extent of close collaboration between practitioners and researchers such as academics and external consultants

(c) Belief that research should have implications beyond the immediate project; the results should inform their contexts

The essentially practical, problem-solving nature of action research makes this approach attractive to practitioner-researchers who have identified a problem during the course of their work, see merit in investigating it and, if possible, in improving practice. There is nothing new about practitioners operating as researchers, and the 'teacher as researcher' model has been extensively discussed (Bartholomew, 1971; Cope and Gray, 1979; Raven and Parker, 1981).

Denscombe (1998) summarises the advantages and disadvantages of action research as follows.

Advantages

(a) It addresses practical problems in a positive way, feeding the results directly back into practice.

(b) It contributes to the professional self-development of the practitioners involved.

(c) It should entail a continuous cycle of development and change for the organisation, to the extent that the action research is geared to improving practice and resolving problems.

(d) It involves participation in the research for practitioners and generally involves greater appreciation of, and respect for, practitioner knowledge

Disadvantages

(a) The need for practitioner involvement can sometimes limit the scope and scale of the research.

(b) The 'work-site' approach affects the extent to which generalisations can be made on the basis of the results.

(c) The integration of research with practice limits the researcher's ability to control important variables since their state and functioning may be operationally determined.

(d) There may be rivalry between researcher and practitioner over ownership of the research process.

(e) Action research tends to involve an extra burden of work for the practitioner, particularly early on before any benefits feed back into improved effectiveness.

(f) The action researcher is unlikely to be adequately detached and impartial in his or her approach to the research.

2.5   Longitudinal studies

A **longitudinal study** is one that looks at changes over a period of time and therefore itself lasts for a long time.

Hussey and Hussey (1997) describe it as a study over time of variables or a group of subjects. The aim is to research the dynamics of the problem by investigating the same situation or people several times, or continuously, over the period in which the problem runs its course. Such studies allow the researcher to examine change processes within a social, economic and political context.

Adams and Schvaneveldt (1991) argue that in the observation of people or events over time, the researcher is able to exercise a measure of control over the variables being studied, provided they are not affected by the research process itself.

Longitudinal studies have the following advantages and disadvantages.

Advantages

    (a)   There is a capacity to study change and development over time (Saunders *et al* 2000).

    (b)   It takes into account the impact of social process and focuses beyond the individual (Hussey and Hussey, 1997).

    (c)   Smaller sample sizes may be used and may make access easier (Easterby-Smith *et al* 1991).

Disadvantages

    (a)   The methodology is very time consuming and data are expensive to collect (Hussey and Hussey, 1997).

    (b)   The complexity of data requires very high skills from all researchers involved (Easterby-Smith *et al* 1991).

    (c)   Over time, there is likely to be some drop-out of research subjects (Hussey and Hussey, 1997).

2.6   Cross-sectional studies

Cross-sectional designs usually involve comparisons between different organisations and contexts during a single research period (Easterby-Smith *et al* 1991).

Hussey and Hussey (1997) explain cross-sectional studies as being designed to obtain information on variables in different contexts, but at the same time. Normally, different organisations or groups of people are selected and a study is conducted to ascertain how factors differ. Cross-sectional studies are conducted when there are constraints of time or resources. The data is collected just once, over a short period of time, before it is analysed and reported.

Remenyi *et al* (1998) describe cross sectional studies in terms of taking a 'snapshot' of a situation in time. This type of research does not attempt to comment on trends or on how situations develop over a period of time.

Advantages

(a) They are relatively cost and time efficient (Hussey and Hussey, 1997.).

(b) They have the ability to describe features of large numbers of people or organisations (Easterby-Smith *et al* 1991).

Disadvantages

(a) It may be difficult to obtain a sample large enough to be representative of the total population (Hussey and Hussey, 1997).

(b) The studies do not explain *why* correlation exists; only whether it does or does not (Hussey and Hussey, 1997; Easterby-Smith *et al* 1991).

(c) It may be difficult to eliminate the external variables that could have caused the observed correlation (Hussey and Hussey, 1997; Easterby-Smith *et al* 1991).

3   RESEARCH CRITERIA

In Chapter 1, we briefly introduced the wider criteria by which research is usually judged. Here we amplify that discussion.

3.1   Validity

Remenyi *et al* (1998) define **validity** as the 'degree to which what is observed or measured is the same as what was purported to be observed or measured'.

According to Hussey and Hussey (1997) validity can be undermined by:

(a) Research errors
(b) Faulty research procedures
(c) Poor samples
(d) Inaccurate or misleading measurement

Under a **positivistic paradigm**, validity measures the extent to which the research instruments set up actually measure what is supposed to be measured (Easterby-Smith *et al*, 1991).

Hussey and Hussey (1997) argue that a positivistic paradigm may emphasise precision of measurement and repeatability at the expense of validity; he danger is that the things measured do not actually reflect the phenomena the researcher claims to be investigating.

EXAMPLE

A research project attempts to demonstrate a cause and effect relationship between publishing typesetters' remuneration levels and error rate. It succeeds in establishing a correlation between the two things. However, the research is flawed because it does not confirm that remuneration drives a typesetter's effort to minimise errors. The higher remuneration may reflect an individual typesetter's work accuracy rather than motivating it. Furthermore, there may be other factors that influence whether one typesetter does or does not make mistakes.

Within a **phenomenological paradigm**, validity depends on whether the researcher has gained **full access** to the knowledge and meanings of informants (Easterby-Smith *et al*, 1991).

Hussey and Hussey (1997) suggest that a phenomenological paradigm is aimed at capturing the essence of the phenomenon and extracting data which is rich in its explanations and analysis. The researcher's aim is to gain full access to the knowledge and meaning of those involved in the phenomenon and consequently validity is higher under such a paradigm.

EXAMPLE

Referring back to the typesetting research, if a phenomenological paradigm were adopted, the research would be likely to focus on subjective feedback obtained from the authors and editors as to the root causes of errors in books.

Colins and Young (1988) advise that there is also a need to feed research field notes or interview transcripts back to respondents for verification to ensure that it reflects their understanding of the phenomenon.

3.2   Reliability

Marshall (1997) defines **reliability** as 'the degree to which we could expect the same results if we or other researchers carried out the study again, using the same methods on a similar sample'.

According to Easterby-Smith *et al* (1991) reliability might be assessed using two questions.

    (a) Will the measure yield the same results on different occasions? (positivist paradigm)

    (b) Will similar observations be made by different researchers on different occasions? (phenomenologist paradigm)

Repeating a research study to test the reliability of the results is known as **replication**. Within a positivist paradigm, where reliability is usually high, replication is very important (Hussey and Hussey, 1997).

Under a phenomenological paradigm, reliability may not be as important, or it may be interpreted differently. What is important is that similar observations and interpretations can be made on different occasions/or by different observers.

Marshall (1997) suggest that the various research methods inherently provide different levels of reliability and offers the following two examples.

(a) **Observation methods.** These are relatively unreliable, since the researcher's own subjectivity plays a significant part in the generation of data

(b) **Postal questionnaire.** These are relatively reliable, because the participants do not come into contact with the researcher

Robson (1993) identifies four generic categories of potential threats to reliability.

(a) **Subject error.** This relates to problems of replication related to the people chosen as research subjects, such as differences in mood and hence response/input, on a Monday morning as compared to a Friday afternoon

(b) **Subject bias.** This relates to situations where the subject tells you what you want to hear or what his or her manager expects him or her to say to the researcher

(c) **Researcher error.** Where there are errors in the design or execution of the research.

(d) **Researcher bias.** Where there is more than one researcher, there may be different approaches to eliciting answers and/or interpreting the replies

3.3   Generalisability

Remenyi *et al* (1998) define **generalisability** as 'the characteristic of research findings that allow them to be applied to other situations and other populations'.

Hussey and Hussey (1997) suggest that if you are following a positivistic paradigm, you will have based your research on a **sample** of the wider population you are interested in. You will need to quantify the degree of certainty with which the characteristics you have established in the sample are present in the wider **population**.

So is generalisability applicable if you are using a phenomenological paradigm? Gummerson (1991) argues that in phenomenological research you may be able to generalise from one setting to another. He makes the case for the applicability of **generalisability** within a phenomenological approach by arguing that generalisation can be understood in two ways.

(a) Quantitative studies based on a large number of observations are required in order to determine how much, how often and many

(b) The other approach involves the use of in-depth studies based on exhaustive investigations and analyses to identify certain phenomena, for example the effects of change in corporate strategy, and lay bare mechanisms that one suspects will also exist in other companies.

4   IMPORTANCE OF ETHICS IN MANAGEMENT RESEARCH

4.1   Definition

Remenyi *et al* (1997) define ethics as a sense or understanding of what is right or wrong. It can be summed up as the sense of doing what is right in the circumstances, or maybe as a moral code.

4.2   Ethical issues

In the world of scientific research, there are many obvious ethical issues that need to be addressed. Here are some examples.

(a)   How far should research on human cloning go?

(b)   To what extent should the scientist explore the development of weapons of mass destruction?

(c)   Should scientific experiments that cause pain and suffering to live animals be carried out?

Ethical considerations in management research may not involve such dramatic problems, but they are no less important.

Remenyi *et al* (1998) acknowledge that ethical issues in business research will be less 'lofty' than those of scientific research but does give some examples of areas of concern in management research.

(a)   Implications of employment of new technologies on those employed in the production function in a factory

(b)   Marketing practices that might impinge on privacy, or which might exert excessive influence or coercion on prospective buyers

(c)   Ways of controlling or manipulating a workforce

Remenyi *et al* suggest that although there are ethical concerns regarding **what** is researched, perhaps of greater concern are questions of **how** the research should be conducted.

4.3   Courtesy

Hussey and Hussey (1997) emphasise matters they refer to as **common courtesy**. These include:

(a)   Thanking individuals and organisations for their assistance with your research, both verbally at the time and afterwards by letter

(b)   Keeping your promises to provide copies of transcripts of interviews or the final report/dissertation

4.4   Researcher's reputation

An aspect which should not be forgotten is your own reputation, which as a professional person should be preciously guarded. A good name, once damaged, will be difficult to repair. This is especially the case where you are conducting research into your own organisation, or one with which it deals.

5 USE AND ABUSE OF POWER

5.1 Power and structure

According to Easterby *et al* (1991) ethics are most frequently discussed in relation to the responsibilities of powerful people to those who are less powerful.

Saunders *et al* (2003) argue that managers will be in a very powerful position in relation to researchers who request organisational access. They suggest that they will remain in a powerful position in terms of the nature and extent of the access that they allow in an organisational setting.

Saunders *et al* (2003) also examine the potential exercise of power at the researcher-research subject interface. They conclude that such situations will 'place the researcher in a position of some "power", albeit for a short time, because they are able to formulate questions including probing ones which may cause levels of discomfort'.

5.2 Power and research approach

Easterby-Smith *et al* (1991) distinguish between the levels of power potentially exercised by researchers under the qualitative and quantitative approaches.

(a) **Qualitative methods**. The researcher has far more control about how the information is gathered, how it is recorded and how it is interpreted.

(b) **Quantitative methods**. Generally, the informant provides the information directly, by completing questionnaires or whatever, and the researcher simply has to accept what is provided by the informant without having much opportunity to question it.

Easterby-Smith *et al* (1991) therefore suggest that the use of qualitative methods may put the researcher in a considerably more powerful position in relation to individuals, hence the additional concern with ethical issues in this case.

5.3 Example of use of power

Easterby-Smith *et al* (1991) provide an example that might illustrate how the assumption of power of a researcher over a research subject can sometimes be turned upside-down.

EXAMPLE

A senior academic interviewed a member of the British Royal Family. At the end of the interview the interviewer offered to have the tape transcribed and to send the Royal personage the transcript for him to delete anything which he did not like. The Royal personage stretched out a hand and said, 'No, I shall retain the tape and I shall let you have the portions I am prepared to have published.'

(Easterby-Smith *et al* 1991)

6   EXERCISE OF ETHICAL STANDARDS

6.1   Areas of concern

There is broad consensus amongst authors regarding the areas where it is important to exercise ethical standards.

    (a)   Informed consent of research participants

    (b)   Approach to likely deception of participants

    (c)   Confidentiality and anonymity

    (d)   Privacy and dignity

    (e)   Integrity of evidence

    (f)   Presentation of findings

6.2   Informed consent

Definition

Marshall (1977) suggests that 'informed consent means that researchers have satisfied themselves that the participants had an adequate understanding of the risks they would incur, before they gave their consent'. They explain that the term 'adequate' understanding is used because for practical purposes, full understanding will not be attainable.

Saunders *et al* (2003) describe informed consent as 'participant consent given freely and based on full information about participation rights and use of data'.

Researcher obligations

Denscombe (1998) argues that 'there is some moral obligation on the researcher to protect the interests of those who supply information and to give them sufficient information about the nature of the research so that they can make an **informed judgement** about whether they wish to co-operate with the research'.

Consent areas

Luck (1999) provides an ethical, legal and social issues (ELSI) questionnaire to help researchers in their consideration of 'matters of ethics, or at least of moral and social responsibility'. Issues of informed consent highlighted by the ELSI questionnaire are as follows.

    (a)   Willingness of participants to be involved

    (b)   Freedom from subtle or unfair pressure to participate

    (c)   Clarity of what to expect as a result of participation

    (d)   Statements of rights and obligations

    (e)   Supply of background information to participants (and the impact of this information on the data collected)

    (f)   Participant is informed of any personal risks (physical or psychological)

    (g)   Participants have opportunity to withdraw from the research at any time without having to provide a reason

Saunders *et al* (2003) have the following points that might be added to the above.

(a) Participants have the right not to be harassed or offered inducements

(b) Recognition that participants have the right to decline to answer a question or set of questions, or to be observed in particular circumstances

(c) Participants retain control over the right to record any of their responses where use of a tape recorder is contemplated. (This might also extend to the use of video recordings, for example in focus group meetings.)

Getting it in writing

So how do you actually go about establishing **informed consent**? Saunders *et al* (2003) discuss the various approaches and related issues.

(a) Exchange of correspondence

(b) Correspondence, supplemented by a more detailed written agreement, signed by both parties

(c) Simple verbal agreement

Researcher behaviour

Sekaran (1992) suggests that it is necessary for the researcher to declare if he or she has any connections or relationships that could in any way be competitive to the informant or to his or her organisation. Thus anything which could remotely relate to a conflict of interest needs to be specifically dealt within advance of any evidence being revealed.

As explained earlier in Chapter 1, you should not use the guise of academic research to infiltrate a competitor organisation to gather commercial intelligence, because this is, in effect, industrial espionage.

As mentioned above, the participant should be free of subtle pressure to participate. In this regard, Robson (2002) refers to 'any overt or covert penalties for non-participation'. The nature of the corporate culture must be taken into consideration in that the glare of management 'expectations' may make it difficult, and a 'non-career advancing move' to refuse to participate.

6.3 Potential deception of participants

Scope for deception

Saunders *et al* (2003) suggest that although research subjects may have agreed to participate in research, they may nevertheless still be subject to deception.

(a) Researchers might misrepresent the nature of the research to the research subjects. This is most likely to occur where experiments are being performed (Sekaran, 2000)

(b) There may be concealment or lack of full disclosure of the purpose and sponsorship of the research (Zikmund, 1997)

(c) Another associated organisation might use the data collected for its commercial advantage

(d) There is a particular problem with **covert observation**. Observation is covert when the subjects are unaware of its nature and extent. Thus, a researcher may carry out a programme of interviews in an office setting, to which informed consent has been given, but also make undisclosed simultaneous observations of behaviour and interactions during the interviews, perhaps using a hidden camera. Covert observation is often used when the researcher considers that full disclosure of the purpose and nature of the research would unduly influence the research subjects and therefore distort the research findings. The technical term for this phenomenon is known as the research subject's **'reactivity'**.

Participant observation

According to Ditton (1997) the use of (covert) participant observation research methods are essentially deceitful. The researcher participates in a situation where he or she is at the same time observing and recording (perhaps later) what has taken place, without the participants knowing.

The view of Denscombe (1998) reinforces this by suggesting that 'when researchers opt to conduct full participation, keeping their true identity and purpose secret from others in the setting, there are **ethical problems** arising from the absence of consent on the part of those being observed, and of deception by the researcher'.

Justification for deception

Saunders *et al* (2003) suggest that the key question to consider is, will this approach be more likely to yield trustworthy data than declaring your real purpose and acting overtly? The answer will depend on a number of factors.

(a) The existing nature of your relationships with those whom you wish to be your participants.

(b) The prevailing managerial style within the organisation or that part of it where these people work.

(c) The time and opportunity which you have to attempt to develop the trust and confidence of these intended participants in order to gain their co-operation.

Where a data collection method involves the use of deception, 'the ethical questions for the researcher concern how much deception in a situation is acceptable, are how far the researcher should go in not betraying the trust of any particular informants' (Easterby-Smith *et al* 1991).

Zikmund (1997) rehearses two typical arguments used by researchers to justify the use of deceptive research practices:

- There is an assumption that no physical danger or psychological harm will be caused by the deception.

- The researcher takes personal responsibility for **debriefing** the research subject of the concealment or deception at the end of the research.

Various authors have put forward the notion that there may be circumstances where the deceit is benign, and argue that a full declaration of purpose at the outset by the researcher might lead to non-participation or problems relative to validity and reliability, if the research subjects alter their behaviour (Bryman, 1988; Gummerson, 1991; Wells, 1994).

Zikmund (1997) expresses the deception dilemma in terms of a 'means-to-an-end' philosophical issue. Easterby-Smith *et al* (1991) proffer the view that one should 'only deceive people as far as it is necessary to get by'. They cite Taylor and Bogdam (1984) who suggested that the researcher, being asked about nature and purpose of his work should 'be truthful, but vague and imprecise'.

Habituation

Dalton (1964) revealed that he was prepared to explain the nature and purpose of his research to most of his participants, and that in the long run, this did not inhibit the majority of his participants.

Saunders *et al* (2003) cite Bryman (1988) in suggesting that 'the problem of **reactivity** may be a diminishing one where those being observed adapt to your presence as a declared observer'. This adaptation is known as **habituation**.

Researcher's responsibility

It is your responsibility to resolve any ethical issues before embarking on your research. Your own ethical position will help you determine how to design your research project (Hussey and Hussey, 1997).

Maybe an approach to adopt is to 'do as you would be done by'; do not carry out any practice in your research that you would not want done to you.

6.4   Confidentiality and anonymity

Participants' rights

Saunders *et al* (2003) refer to the participants right to expect agreed anonymity and confidentiality to be observed strictly in relation to discussions with other research or organisational participants and during the reporting of findings (including from those who gain subsequent access to data). They advise that 'once promises about confidentiality and anonymity had been given, it is of great importance to make sure that these are maintained'.

Areas to consider

The ELSI (ethical, legal and social issues) questionnaire developed by Luck (1999) and mentioned earlier, includes several points relating to confidentiality and anonymity.

(a)   The importance of ensuring that sources of data are protected and not traceable back to particular individuals (or organisations)

(b)   Circumstantial information should not uniquely point to or identify one individual (or organisation)

(c)   Ensuring that participation in your research does not identify anyone as belonging to any social, medical or ethnic group

(d)   Participants do not object to the publication of information about them.

(e)   Participants have the right to deny use or have destroyed, any particular pieces of information if they so wish

(f)   Participants have a chance to confirm that any information recorded about them is factually correct

Easterby *et al* (1991) advise that researchers must exercise due ethical responsibility by not publicising or circulating any information that is likely to harm the interests of individual informants, especially the less powerful ones.

Non-sale of respondent details

Zikmund (1997) warns that organisations might be 'keen to exploit the business opportunities that might potentially exist in any of your survey respondents'. He cautions that it is 'the researcher's responsibility to ensure that the **privacy** and **anonymity** of the respondents is preserved'. You should not pass on the personal details of your respondents, without their permission, to your sponsoring organisation. Nor should you attempt to sell any of this information.

Data protection regulations

Consideration should also be taken of any data protection legislation in your local environment. If you are in the UK, you will need to comply with the relevant provisions of the Data Protection Act.

6.5   Privacy and dignity

Cultural influences

Privacy is a concept that is probably subject to strong cultural influences and hence a researcher will need to be aware of the interpersonal boundaries of the locality or society in which the research is conducted.

EXAMPLE

The individualist culture of Western countries may be contrasted with the more group-oriented culture of Far Eastern countries. In the West, privacy is prized, but in the east openness is essential to foster the trust implicit in a group culture.

Westerners visiting countries with such a culture find it awkward to deal with personal questions concerning such personal details as age, marital status, children, occupation, educational achievement and income.

Nevertheless, these **dominant** social paradigms of West and East may be said to have **back-up** social paradigms: for example, western individualism is complemented by teamwork whereas eastern group orientation operates alongside the importance of personal independence.

Embarrassment and ridicule

Hussey and Hussey (1997) state that 'in research it would not be ethical to embarrass or ridicule participants, but unfortunately this can easily be done. The relationships between the researcher and the phenomenon being studied is often complex'.

Care should be exercised not only in what a respondent is asked but also what a respondent is asked to do, listen to, watch or taste.

EXAMPLE

People may have cultural, religious or humanitarian reasons for not eating or drinking various products such as beef, pork, meat in general, shellfish and alcohol. Care should be taken not to place a potential respondent in an embarrassing position in refusing your request.

Also be careful about asking a potential respondent who has strong views about animal rights to try on a leather jacket, or a fur coat.

Dignity

Dignity refers more to the research subject's right not to be embarrassed or humiliated in any way. In practice, this involves not only the questions a participant is asked or any actions they are required to perform, but also the way they are treated and spoken to.

EXAMPLE

You may need to interview the poorest performing employee in a company, department or group to find out his or her views on their situation. Such a person is probably in a psychologically vulnerable state of mind and will need to be handled with tact, diplomacy and sensitivity.

Sekaran (2000) counsels that 'personal or seemingly intrusive information should not be solicited, and if it is absolutely necessary for the project, it should be tapped with high sensitivity to the respondent, offering specific reasons therefore'.

Activity 3   **(10 minutes)**

It might be a good idea at this juncture to consider areas where potential participants' rights to privacy should be guarded. Jot down areas which you would avoid asking questions about during your research.

Timing of approaches

Saunders *et al* (2003) suggest that 'privacy may also be affected by the nature and timing of any approach which you make to intended participants, say by telephoning at "unsociable" times, or, where possible, by "confronting" intended participants'. Zikmund (1997) describes this aspect in terms of 'Is the telephone call that interrupts someone's favourite television programme an invasion of privacy?'

Zikmund (1997) puts forward a 'society benefits'-based argument in suggesting that 'the answer to this issue – and most privacy questions – lies in the dilemma of determining where the rights of the individual end and the needs of society for better scientific information or citizen preference take over'.

FOR DISCUSSION

Before reading on can you identify times and circumstances when it might be inconvenient to contact individual or organisational participants to your research and thereby infringe on their right to privacy and dignity? Some suggestions appear below.

Personal

    (a) At meal times

    (b) When the potential respondent is busy

    (c) When the potential respondent is not in a state to see you, eg
        (i)   just got out of bed
        (ii)   just about to receive visitors
        (iii)   home is being redecorated

    (d) When the potential respondent is about to go out

Organisational

    (a) In busy periods

    (b) When the people involved are in a meeting

    (c) Generally when they have other priorities

Key message

The key message of this section is well summarised by Sekaram (2000) in suggesting that 'whatever the nature of the data collection method, the self-esteem and self-respect of the subjects should never be violated'.

6.6 Integrity of evidence

Objectivity

Zikmund (1997) emphasises the importance of ensuring accuracy via objectivity. He outlines some examples of behaviour the ethical researcher should avoid.

    (a)   Selective use of data to prove a particular point
    (b)   Misrepresenting the statistical accuracy of data
    (c)   Overstating the significance of the results by altering the findings

Remenyi *et al* (1998) reinforce the above message in warning that any attempt to 'window dress or manipulate and thus distort is of course unethical, as is any attempt to omit any inconvenient evidence'.

Zikmund, *op cit.* explains that it is assumed that the researcher has the obligation to analyse the data honestly and report correctly the actual data collection methods. He warns that 'hiding errors and variations from proper procedures tends to distort or shade the results. A more blatant breach of the researcher's responsibilities would be the outright distortion of data'.

Active v passive honesty

Remenyi *et al* (1998) also explain the importance of **active honesty** as opposed to **passive honesty**. Passive honesty exists when, for example, data that do not support the hypothesis are reported with as much prominence as data that support it. Active honesty exists when, for example, data discrepancies are investigated rather than ignored.

EXAMPLE

You have say five or six research assistants helping you to administer a face to face survey and you find that one of them is producing data which you are not entirely sure about. You are ethically obliged to **actively** investigate the underlying reasons for the difference, rather than accepting the data and incorporating it into your results.

Fabrication of evidence

Remenyi *et al* (1998) provide some sound advice and perhaps a modicum of reassurance regarding the processing of research evidence. They advise that it is 'not a useful or relational strategy to fabricate evidence or deliberately to misrepresent it, as a master or doctoral degree does not rely on the candidate finding or proving a particular result. Even where hypotheses or theoretical conjectures are rejected, the research is perfectly valid and there is no reason why such findings should not lead to the awarding of the degree'.

EXAMPLE

Sir Cyril Burt was a famous British psychologist whose work on the relationship between IQ and genetic factors lead for a time to IQ testing in British schools.

However, after his death doubts surfaced about the statistical reliability of his work and even the existence of his two research assistants.

Unfortunately, he is alleged to have placed his papers into six chests which all got burned.

(Saunders *et al* 2003; Mackintosh, 1995; www.discovery.org/lewis/bettleheim.html)

Retention of research records

The above example highlights the importance of keeping proper records of your research work. According to Remenyi *et al* (1998) 'the original source of evidence, for example, a transcript of an interview, or copies of the original questionnaire, should be kept for a period of time, say somewhere between two and five years, to allow other researchers to access the data'.

Replicability

Earlier in this chapter, we discussed the importance of **replicability**. Marshall (1997, p. 101) suggests that it is 'incumbent on researchers, therefore, to do all they can to facilitate replication of their work by others'.

    (a)   This requires full disclosure of methodology used
    (b)   Findings should be presented in quantitative form, rather than prosaic form
    (c)   The language used should be unambiguous

However, phenomenologically orientated research tends to be less replicable than positivistically based research.

EXAMPLE

Medically it is difficult to graft skin from one person to another because of the problem of rejection, unless certain unusual circumstances prevail, as with identical twins.

In 1974, a Dr William Summerlin, of the Sloan-Kettering Institute of New York announced that he had discovered a 'tissue culture' technique that would lead to successful skin transplants.

He had trouble in convincing the scientific community regarding his technique so he produced two white mice with black patches which were purported to have been transplanted from a black donor mouse. What Summerlin did was to use a black felt tip pen to touch-up the grafts he had made to the white mice.

Unfortunately, scientists were not able to *replicate* the results and eventually the fabrication was uncovered.

(*Medaware, 1996*)

Research trail

When you are working on your research project, it is very important that you maintain a proper set of full working papers that show how you have planned and carried out your work and how it has developed. A research trail must stand up to close academic scrutiny if necessary.

6.7 Presentation of findings

Saunders *et al* (2003) emphasise that the duty of researchers to represent their data honestly extends to the reporting stage of a project and stress the importance of sustaining objectivity.

Remenyi *et al* (2000) reinforce this message and stress the importance of ensuring the results must not be produced in such a way as simply to support the opinions or prejudices of the researcher. They aver that sometimes personal bias is so subtle that it might unconsciously creep into the presentation of findings. They argue an approach for dealing with this is to articulate the bias and leave it to the readers to compensate for it. They cite Gould (1980) when he said.

> *'Science (as well as management) is not an objective, truth-directed machine, but a quintessentially human activity, affected by passion, hopes and cultural bias.'*

In the face of the above, Saunders *et al* (2003) cite the advice given by Trevelyn (1993) that the researcher should try to apply 'disinterested intellectual curiosity'.

7 ETHICAL CODES OF PRACTICE

7.1 Definition

Zikmund (1997) defines a code of ethics as 'a statement of principles and operating procedures for ethical practice'.

7.2 Arguments for and against

In practice there is an ongoing debate as to the desirability and effectiveness of using a code of ethics. Hussey and Hussey (1997) explain that

> *'Some commentators believe that firm ethical principles should be established for business research; others believe that such codes would be too simplistic and rigid.'*

Easterby-Smith *et al* (1991) advance the popular argument that the presence of a code is likely to raise an awareness of the need to consider ethical dilemmas, if nothing else. However, they also cite potential problems relating to attempts to implement a code of ethics on a research project.

(a) Ethical guidelines will not only be too rigid and simplistic to deal with real cases; they also contain the biases that are inherent in one or another ideological position (Snell, 1926)

(b) Ethical codes may very easily be constructed to protect the powerful and provide no particular consolation to the weak. Ethical codes should be used as guidelines for practice, rather than tablets of stone (Punch, 1980).

(c) Ethical codes are essentially pluralistic and depend on the viewpoint of the rule-maker: 'The social investigator must sort his values and obligations and weigh them repeatedly throughout the research process ... he cannot impose one fixed code on multiple conflicting codes' (Dalton, 1964).

Chapter roundup

- There are several different research philosophies of which you should be aware in order to select the appropriate one for your research project. They include, positivism, phenomenology and pragmatism.

- Research strategies include surveys, experiments, case studies, action research, longitudinal studies and cross-sectional studies. You need familiarity with these in order to be able to select the right one.

- Key criteria by which the quality of research is judged are validity, reliability and generalisability.

- Ethics is of vital importance in management research, especially with regard to the use and abuse of power, informed consent and the potential deceit of participants.

- The confidentiality, anonymity, privacy and dignity of participants in your research may be key issues that must be resolved to ensure their participation.

Answers to activities

1 (a) This is probably quite acceptable because a person's selection of bread is not likely to involve privacy issues.

   (b) This is probably unethical because there are many toiletries that are of a very personal nature to either men or women and which they would prefer to select unobserved.

2 You might explore what they think about the product itself, its feel, its scent, its effectiveness, how it compares with other deodorants used and so on. However, you should perhaps avoid asking how many times they use it each day, whether they have a body odour problem, how often they bathe or shower and other very personal questions.

3 (a) Age
   (b) State of health/medical history
   (c) Race
   (d) Family background
   (e) Income
   (f) Sexual orientation
   (g) Family/relational status

Chapter 3 :

THE RESEARCH PROPOSAL

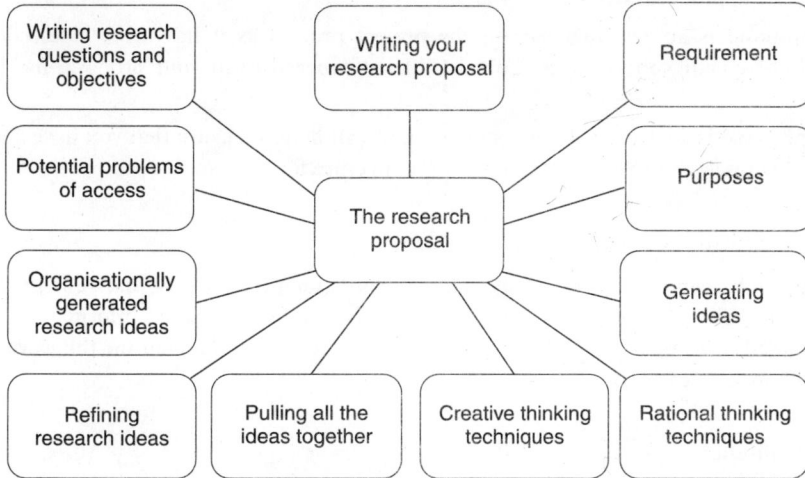

```
┌──────────────┐        ┌──────────────┐        ┌──────────────┐
│ Writing research│      │ Writing your │        │ Requirement  │
│ questions and   │      │research proposal│     │              │
│ objectives      │      │              │        │              │
└──────────────┘        └──────────────┘        └──────────────┘

┌──────────────┐                                 ┌──────────────┐
│Potential problems│                              │ Purposes     │
│ of access      │                                │              │
└──────────────┘        ┌──────────────┐         └──────────────┘
                        │ The research │
                        │ proposal     │
┌──────────────┐        └──────────────┘         ┌──────────────┐
│Organisationally│                                │ Generating   │
│ generated      │                                │ ideas        │
│ research ideas │                                │              │
└──────────────┘                                 └──────────────┘

┌──────────┐  ┌──────────┐  ┌──────────┐  ┌──────────┐
│ Refining │  │Pulling all the│ Creative thinking│ Rational thinking│
│research ideas│ ideas together│ techniques │ techniques │
└──────────┘  └──────────┘  └──────────┘  └──────────┘
```

Your ultimate success in the research project element of your studies could well hinge on the quality of your research proposal. This has to be a very carefully thought-out and constructed document, as it will set the parameters for your subsequent work.

Your objectives

In this chapter you will learn about the following:

    (a)   The value of producing a detailed research proposal

    (b)   Various techniques for generating ideas

    (c)   How to pull all your ideas together to generate a final proposal

    (d)   Problems of access

    (e)   Ideas from within your organisation

    (f)   How to write your research proposal

1 THE REQUIREMENT FOR THE PROPOSAL

1.1 Introduction

The first major step in the production of any research project is to write a proposal. This is important, as it establishes the foundation for the project itself and provides a structure for you to work to. Without it you are likely to flounder and find it virtually impossible to proceed with your research.

The proposal is an essential part of the project process as it has to be assessed and approved by your college tutor. You should not proceed until your proposal has been approved.

Your proposal is a basic working document and will help to ensure that you have a valid and viable research project. It sets out the architecture for your subsequent work.

1.2 Length of the proposal

The research proposal should be about 1,500 words long. It is likely that your proposal will fulfil this requirement: you will see from this chapter that much information must be included in it, including a full justification for the title and a plan for the work that you will do to research it.

1.3 Content

The proposal should include these elements:

(a) **A working title**, which clearly represents the research subject matter

(b) **The background and academic context**: an explanation as to why you have selected this topic and what you hope that your research will achieve

(c) **A statement of the research question and objectives**

(d) Some reference to the **academic literature and authorities** you will read in the course of your research, and an indication of how your proposal will fit into the existing debate

(e) An indication of the **methods** you will use for both data collection and data analysis

(f) A discussion of any potential problems of **access to the data**

(g) An indication of the proposed **timescale**

2 THE PURPOSES OF A RESEARCH PROPOSAL

2.1 The need to organise ideas

You have probably met the type of person who says of any complex plan or idea: 'I carry it all in my head'. Some restaurant waiters pride themselves on their ability to take an entire order for starters and main courses for a table of six people without writing any of it down. You may even be that type of person yourself, and believe that you are quite good at doing this, so that you do not need to write your ideas down. Beware! In the context of your research proposal this is a dangerous game to play.

FOR DISCUSSION

What do you think are the advantages of writing down your research ideas as opposed to organising them in your head?

Saunders *et al.* (2003) believe that **writing** can be the best way of clarifying our thoughts. By writing something down, you can ensure that you fully understand it: this is a technique which you have probably used when studying for your previous exams and assessments. If you fully understand what you are doing for your research project and why, you will be able to communicate that understanding to your audience. You will also then have a solid foundation on which to build.

It does not matter if what you write as part of the thought-clarification process never sees the light of day. For example, you may find it helpful to write down what you understand by the different types of research strategies set out in the Chapter 2 as an aid to understanding the difference between them.

2.2   Establishing a contract

Businesses do not usually enter into any long term research engagement without drawing up a **contract** with the other party involved (Saunders *et al*, 2003).

In your research proposal you set out the key details of what you are going to do and the deadline for doing it. Approval of the proposal indicates acceptance by the other party (in this case your tutor) of those terms. It means that both sides know what is happening, and what to expect from each other. Effectively you will have a contract with each other.

Remember that acceptance of your proposal is not a guarantee of success. It starts you off in the right direction, but you will need further guidance and will have to maintain contact and a good working relationship with your tutor as you progress with your research work.

2.3   The requirements of organisational and academic audiences

Organisational needs

The production of a good piece of research can be of great personal benefit to a student. First, it can provide a sense of **achievement** and boost **self-esteem**; second, it can enhance your **career prospects**. Sharp and Howard (1996) suggest that a project that is closely allied with the student's career aims is better than one that has no obvious relevance.

If you are choosing a topic which is relevant to your career and, more specifically, to the organisation you work for, you may need to consider the impact upon that organisation of your research proposal. As you will see later, access to information can be one of the difficult aspects of carrying out a research project. You may find it easier to obtain access to information within your own organisation if you can demonstrate the benefits to it of facilitating your research. To this end, you may have to write your research proposal with the **needs of the organisation** as much in mind as the needs of the academic audience at your college. In some cases you may need to rewrite a proposal in order to satisfy the precise requirements of the second audience.

EXAMPLE

You work for a large removals and distribution company whose operations are currently restricted to the UK and Ireland. You are considering research on the impact of the single European market on companies that currently deal with only one European country, in order to assess whether they should expand further or maintain their existing trading practices.

Your employer is far more likely to give you access to records that could be quite commercially sensitive if you can demonstrate that benefits such as rapidly increasing turnover may flow from your research. You would therefore stress these possible benefits in the research proposal to the organisational audience.

We suggested in Chapter 1 that personal and management skills will go a long way to helping you succeed in your research. Hence, you are likely to be aware of the need to **actively sell** the benefits of your proposal to your audience rather than just making assertions. During the course of your project you are likely to need excellent persuasion and influencing skills to keep open your lines of access to information.

Academic needs

The other audience which needs to be sure of the value and feasibility of the work you propose to do is the academic audience. This consists of the staff at your college who will assess your research proposal. Effectively, this will be your tutor.

The Edexcel Guidelines indicate that your research proposal for Unit 8 should be approved by your tutor and this applies to the research element of most degrees and diplomas. In reviewing your proposal, your tutor will probably be looking at the following issues.

    (a)   The working title
    (b)   The background and academic context
    (c)   The research objectives
    (d)   The research methods (including any issues of access)
    (e)   research ethics
    (f)   The timescale and resources

Your tutor will consider each of these in depth, form a view as to whether the treatment in your proposal is accurate and identify any areas that require further thought and any additional elements which must be incorporated into the proposal.

Your tutor will be concerned both with the content of your proposal and also the practicalities of your proposed research. As well as defining your research objective and outlining the literature you will read and types of research you will undertake, you must also give a time scale and an indication of ease of access to data.

Your tutor should indicate whether there is some specific aspect of the proposal that must be developed further or clarified. A common problem is an insufficiently detailed description of the literature that you intend to use.

Remember that most degrees and diplomas, including the HND/HNC, are widely recognised academic qualifications and must satisfy the needs of academic rigour. The critical review of literature is a key part of your project as it establishes the positioning of your own works within the overall sphere of prior academic work and defines your contribution to the body of knowledge. From a practical point of view, your review of literature needs to be comprehensive to ensure that you are not researching something which has already been done by someone else.

You will not convince the assessor of the feasibility of your proposal if your main sources of information are back copies of journals published overseas which you have not yet located in the UK, and you plan to produce your project within a period of a few weeks while simultaneously holding down a full-time job.

The assessor must believe (as must you!) that you can genuinely do the stated work within the stated time.

3 GENERATING IDEAS FOR RESEARCH TOPICS

3.1 The two categories

There are two broad categories of thinking technique for generating ideas for a research topic. They are:

(a) **Rational,** being those techniques which are dictated by logic and which involve looking at specific sources of information

(b) **Creative,** being those techniques which involve ideas being 'dreamed up' by an individual or a group, such as 'brainwaves' or moments of unexplained inspiration.

Both types of technique can have an important part to play in the generation of ideas. If you use some examples of both, you are more likely to 'think round' the problem of identifying an area and come to a balanced decision.

4 RATIONAL THINKING TECHNIQUES

4.1 Sources of information

All sorts of pre-existing material can provide a source of inspiration. Sharp and Howard (1996) provide the list below.

(a) Theses and dissertations
(b) Articles in academic and professional journals
(c) Conference proceedings and reports
(d) Books and book reviews
(e) Reviews of the field of study
(f) Communication with experts in the field
(g) Conversations with potential users of the research findings
(h) Discussions with colleagues
(i) The media

From Sharp and Howard's list, you can see that you should not restrict your train of thought merely to books and journals, but should explore some of the numerous other possibilities.

4.2   Past research projects and dissertations

You can look at past research dissertations both to seek inspiration for an area of study and for ideas as to approach and other sources of information used. The lists of references and bibliographies in similar projects are likely to be a very useful source of information for you.

Jankowicz (2000) suggests the very basic approach of a systematic search of past research reports in the library. However, this could be rather like looking for a needle in a haystack and it might be better to identify an area to focus on before starting such a search. The risk otherwise is of your wandering through a selection of report on a wide range of different topics and not really getting to grips with any of them. Also, as Saunders *et al.* (2003) remark:

> *'The fact that a project is in your library is no guarantee of the quality of the arguments and observations it contains. In many universities all projects are placed in the library whether they are bare passes or distinctions.'*

Nevertheless, it would be worth having a look in your college library to see what type of previous projects are stored there.

Additionally, you may be able to gain access to the libraries of universities and business schools located near you, and view examples of degree-standard research projects there.

Rather than look at individual dissertations for sources of inspiration, you could adopt the approach suggested by Saunders *et al.* (2003) and scan a list of past titles, writing down any titles that attract your attention.

4.3   Examination of your own strengths, weaknesses and interests

Luck (1999) suggests that 'being asked to come up with a subject for your research project may either excite you or fill you with dread. You may see it either as a chance to express yourself and realise a dream or a threat to the limitations of your existing knowledge and imagination'.

Saunders *et al* (2003) counsel strongly that a research topic should both interest and excite the researcher. Otherwise the researcher will fail to produce his or her best work. They also stress the importance of selecting a topic in which the researcher is likely to do well and, if possible, have some academic knowledge.

Jankowicz (2000) reinforces the above in suggesting that you will have 'less work to do if you choose a topic which you have encountered and worked on before. Analysis, evaluation and judgement will come more easily, and you'll be more aware of the issues that arise if you've covered the basic ground already'. He advises that 'the best guide here is provided by the marks you have received for the prior work you have done. Choose something you're good at'.

Remenyi *et al.* (1998) explain that the more competence the researcher has in the proposed field of study, the easier it will be to identify a suitable research problem or question. They add that it is 'essential that the candidate feels enthusiastic about the area of research at this early stage as research projects take a considerable amount of time, and enthusiasm may decline over time'. Luck (1999) recommends the choice of a topic then the posting of the question 'Could I become passionate about it?'

This 'safety first' route is appealing. However, the note of caution sounded by Gill and Johnson (1997) might be relevant here. 'Some researchers may have already defined their topics and, while this may at first sight seem ideal, the work may be impractical or have already been done; either way, the inexperienced researcher may not be aware of the position.'

The goal of achieving your academic qualification may well motivate you to pick a really safe topic. However, you should not forget the importance of **self-development,** both in terms of stretching yourself as well as building something new for yourself that could serve as a stepping stone for your next career move. As Jankowicz (2000) says, 'choose a topic which draws on your experience by all means, but also one which helps you grow in a desirable direction. "What sort of topic will assist me in my next career move?" is a very helpful and legitimate question in this context'.

Finally, do not forget **your own epistemological outlook**. If you are a positivistic type of person, you are likely to be more comfortable with deductive, quantitively oriented research, though some mixture of qualitative aspects may well help to give your research a more rounded and deeper feel as well as taking your own self-development into a new dimension. Similarly, a phenomenological approach might derive a modicum of added value through the application of some quantitative techniques, if appropriate.

4.4 Discussions

It is always sensible to talk through any ideas you have for any big project or commitment before you embark upon it. These groups of people can all be invaluable:

(a) Family
(b) Friends
(c) Employer/manager
(d) Colleagues
(e) Fellow students
(f) Tutors

As you are to be engaged in the area of business or management research, your employer or manager is likely to be an early and sensible port of call.

There may be problems that you have identified or something your manager might like to have researched. On the other hand, if you are working for a professional service provider such as a firm of accountants or consultants, there may be clients who have problems that might benefit from some research. Have a chat with your manager to explore possibilities that might be of mutual benefit to both yourself and the organisation.

According to Jankowicz (2000), 'If you're a part-time student following a professional programme, or an in-company-based qualification, your work experience gives you a great advantage, since your topic is likely to deal with your own organisation. The danger is that you choose a project which you would have been covering already as part of your day-to-day responsibilities. While your project should be relevant, it should also have a measure of academic content!.

If you know anyone who has done any form of research as part of an undergraduate or post-graduate degree, chat to them about possible ideas and also about any specific 'do's or don'ts' that they have picked up in their own experience.

Remember to make a note of any ideas arising from informal discussions like these, as it is infuriating to have a brilliant idea and then forget what it is.

4.5 Exploratory review of literature

As we have seen already, Sharp and Howard (1996) suggest a number of sources within literature. These include:

(a) Articles in academic and professional journals
(b) Conference proceedings and reports
(c) Books and book reviews

UK professional journals that might be worth a look include:

(a) *The Economist*
(b) *The Financial Times*

Sharp and Howard point out that you will need access to a good quality **library**, which means being 'good' in terms of carrying a wide stock of books and journals, and also in terms of its ability to borrow your required reading from elsewhere.

Journal articles and reports (whether of conference proceedings or government reports) tend to be reasonably up to date and are published within a short time of the completion of the work. Books, however, especially in areas of rapid change, such as information technology, are sometimes regarded as not being so up to date. They are still invaluable, however, as they can provide a good overview of the current state of affairs in a particular field, and also suggest other sources of information. **Book reviews** are often of use. Sharp and Howard (1996) recommend them as

> '... the reviewers of a book are usually able to evaluate the extent of its contribution to knowledge and can provide a useful service for students seeking ideas for topics.'

Remenyi *et al.* (1998) explain that 'traditionally researchers used paper reference indexes available in the university or business school library as the way of initiating a literature search. However, increasingly this type of paper-based literature search is being replaced by electronic searches. Many libraries now supply their students with access to electronic databases, either over telecommunications networks or on CD-ROM. In addition, there are extensive literature search facilities on the Internet, which is currently available to researchers at a low cost'.

Other sources at the topic generation stage suggested by Remenyi *et al* (1998) include:

(a) Popular press articles
(b) Television broadcasts
(c) Videos

However, they caution that in such cases 'it is important that support for views expressed in these media be sought from experts in the field'.

At this **preliminary search** stage, you are likely to be looking for certain key pieces of information that indicate a **research opportunity**:

(a) What is known in the field and what is still a matter of conjecture (Sharp and Howard, 1996)

(b) Unfounded assertions and statements on the absence of research (Raimond, 1993)

(c) Suitable areas for research and the research methods or approaches that have been traditionally used in this field (Creswell, 1994)

(d)   Contradictions and paradoxes that might suggest that there is an interesting research question to be tackled (Remenyi, 1998)

You should regard the literature search as an ongoing process, so as well as being a means of helping to choose a topic it also should be employed when you are refining the topic into a research project title. If you search for inspiration in the subject matter you have already studied to date, a good starting point for the initial literature search would be the lists of recommended reading.

This initial search of the literature at the proposal stage is not to be confused with the full-scale review of the literature during the project work itself. This latter review is often called the **critical review**, and forms a fundamental part of the work, taking a large proportion of the time spent on the project as a whole.

The critical review is discussed in detail in Chapter 4.

The reason for carrying out this initial review is to enable you to demonstrate in your proposal that you are **aware** of at least some of the literature in your field, and to show how your research project will fit into the debate and discussion already generated. It should outline the key ideas and discuss them briefly. This will then demonstrate to the assessor of your proposal that your research has a foundation in the literature. You might find the following diagram useful in helping you to understand the various phases of literature review during the course of your project.

EXPLORATORY REVIEW

- Broad based, including popular press, television, magazines, talks and lectures

- Purpose to identify interesting research topics

TOPIC SELECTION

- Focus on academically credible literature sources

- More detailed review

- Purpose to identify research questions and to support proposal

CRITICAL REVIEW

- Covers breadth and depth

- Demonstrate awareness of current state of knowledge, and its limitations

- Purpose to position project in context of existing knowledge and how it intends to add to this body of knowledge

ONGOING REVIEW

- Any new literature published

- Purpose to ensure project remains relevant in view of ongoing material published

You should think in terms of citing at least half a dozen books or journal articles in the proposal.

Remember the importance of talking to others. 'Talking through problems and possible topics with colleagues is an essential stage of any plan. Their views may differ from or even conflict with your own and may suggest alternative lines of enquiry' (Bell, 1999). 'The notion that research can be pursued from behind a desk may appeal to some students (and indeed may be all that is expected for a research project), but whatever the field, at research degree level, much advantage may be gained from discussions with others' (Sharp and Howard, 1996).

5   CREATIVE THINKING TECHNIQUES

In the last section, we considered **rational thinking** techniques for generating ideas. These largely involved looking for suggestions within tangible sources, such as past research project titles.

There are many views of what is meant by creativity. It is a word that is freely used in the fields of art, sport and business.

Activity 1   **(5 minutes)**

Jot down what you understand by the word creativity.

FOR DISCUSSION

Fold your arms as you would do normally. Which arm is on top and which arm is underneath? Right over left? Or left over right? Now try it in the opposite way. How does that feel? Uncomfortable? Why?

That was just a little exercise to highlight the fact that we often do not challenge the way we do things. Think over other things that you do or say as a matter of routine without challenge where there is some other way of doing it, eg:

(a)   Which shoe do you put on first: left or right? Do you change this behaviour occasionally?

(b)   What route to do take to get to work/home?

(c)   Do you have favourite foods or drinks? How often do you deliberately try something else?

(d)   Do you predominantly wear a certain colour? Is there any colour you avoid wearing? How would you feel if you went out wearing that colour?

(e)   Do you always say 'salt and pepper' or do you sometimes say 'pepper and salt'? What about 'rice and curry' instead of 'curry and rice'?

(f)   If you wear a tie, do you always do the knot the same way? Do you experiment with other forms of knots from time to time?

(g)   What type of films or shows do you like? Do you try to see and get to know and appreciate other genres?

(h) Do you always take (buy and read) the same newspaper every day and at weekends? Or do you occasionally or regularly have a look at how other titles might present similar stories or see events from a different perspective?

(i) How often do you rearrange your furniture?

The definition given in the answer to Activity 1 (at the end of the chapter) is interesting and helpful because it progresses from the traditional (and not so creative) ways of thinking of creativity as being something which relates only to individual inspiration and genius. It suggests that we can use a process to bring us creativity.

Some people are probably more intuitively creative than others, but others may achieve creativity through an awareness of creativity and by using creative thinking processes.

Activity 2   **(2 minutes)**

Jot down:

(a) A country beginning with the letter 'D'
(b) An animal beginning with the letter 'E'

Hold onto your answers. We shall come back to them later.

FOR DISCUSSION

Your company has completely computerised its operations and gone completely paperless. As a result it has a supply of a million used paperclips which it cannot get rid of by sale, nor will the refuse collection authority take them away.

Can you think creatively of what might be done with the paperclips?

Here are just a few suggestions.

(a) Give them away to a charity
(b) Sell them to a business that uses paper
(c) Melt them down and make a piece of artwork
(d) Make jewellery out of them
(e) Give one a day to each employee to throw away at home
(f) Make them into a chain or chains

Borean (2002) suggests that 'creative thinking involves opening up your mind to find new solutions and new ways of doing things. This involves suspending your judgement and looking for different more inventive solutions. Generally it includes developing a flexible and open mind'.

Have a look at the following nine dots and try to join them using four straight lines.

```
  •      •      •

  •      •      •

  •      •      •
```

Many people will see some things in a situation while others will see something else.

Activity 4 (2 minutes)

OK. Do you think you are becoming attuned to thinking more creatively? Would you like to stretch your mind again?

Jot down:

(a) A country beginning with the letter 'I'
(b) An animal beginning with the letter 'C'

This exercise has hopefully helped emphasise the importance of examining alternatives.

Creative thinking is a little more nebulous. It involves using your mind (or those of other people) and the concepts within it to conjure up ideas.

You may well find that you use a **combination of techniques** to devise your research project title, both rational and creative. This is very much a case of personal preference and character, so do not worry if you find yourself using one type of technique to the exclusion of the other. Just be aware of the range of techniques available, and do not automatically discard one group of techniques because you think they won't be of any use.

5.1 Notebooks

This is probably one of the simplest techniques. All you have to do is keep a notebook available at all times from the point at which you start thinking about your project proposal. Jot down any thoughts about topics that occur to you and the source of the idea if that would help. You can then research the idea in greater depth, probably using some of the rational thinking techniques discussed above when you have the opportunity.

There is nothing more frustrating than having a fleeting idea, which you know could be developed further, but then forgetting what it is, or forgetting some subtle twist to an existing idea and being unable to recreate it. Keeping a notebook during the course of your project proposal work (and during the course of the project work itself) will help to prevent this from happening.

5.2   Use of past projects and dissertations

You can use past projects and dissertations to analyse your own views as to what makes a good research project and what makes a bad one.

Raimond (1993) cited in Saunders *et al* (2003) suggests that you follow the steps given below.

1   Select six projects that you like.

2   For each of these projects, write down your first thoughts in response to three questions:

    (a)   What appeals to you about the project?
    (b)   What is good about the project?
    (c)   Why is the project good?

    Note that it does not matter if your responses for different project are the same, for example more than one project appeals to you because they handle a highly topical or controversial topic, or you think they are good because they contain particularly lucid and cogent argument.

3   Select three projects that you do not like.

4   For each of these projects, as before, write down your first thoughts in response to three questions:

    (a)   What do you dislike about the project?
    (b)   What is bad about the project?
    (c)   Why is the project bad?

    As before, do not worry if some of your answers regarding different projects are the same, or you cannot clearly express them.

You will end up with a concise list, unique to you, of attributes about research projects that **you** consider to be good, and attributes that **you** consider to be bad. This will start to focus your mind on the characteristics of projects that you feel are important. You will also have identified those characteristics that you feel are negative and which you should therefore try to avoid. As Saunders *et al.* (2003) point out, these can be used as the parameters against which to evaluate possible research ideas.

The main problem with past research projects is that of **access**. You may not be able to locate nine or more projects. Try to organise reading rights in a local university or college library. Such a library will probably have a large stock of previous research projects and dissertations in all disciplines.

5.3   Relevance trees

A relevance tree enables you to develop ideas from a basic, fairly broad starting point. The approach suggested by Buzan (1989) is that you should try to generate three aspects from the original basic idea which then fork out as 'branches'. From each of those a further three branches should fork out, and then a further three from each of those, and so on. Keep doing this until you end up with an idea which you find interesting.

EXAMPLE

Globalisation is an issue that is currently highly topical and which many people find extremely interesting. Globalisation as such is so broad that it might be quite difficult to create a relevance tree, but if you narrow the topic down a little it becomes much easier. Restrict yourself to globalisation in the legal and financial sector, and you might come up with something like this:

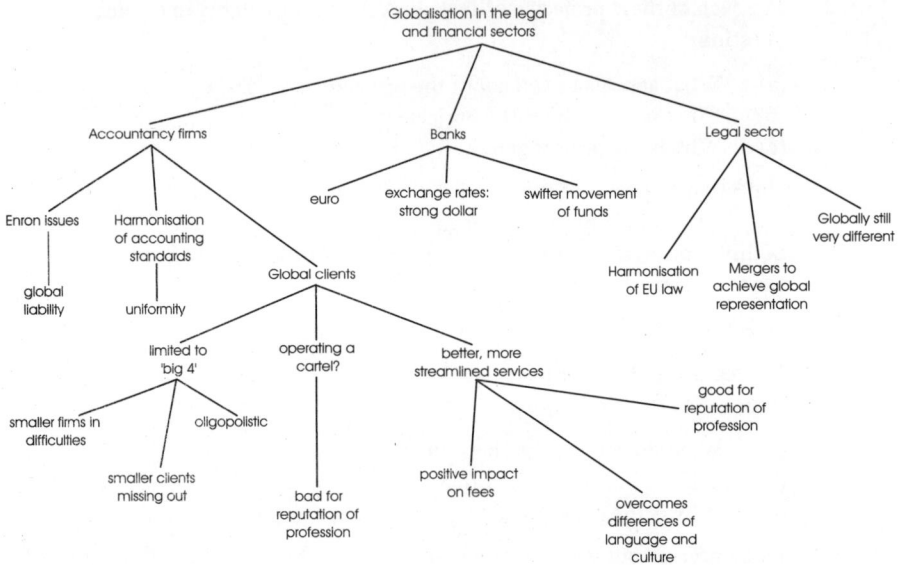

Sharp and Howard (1996) show an example of a relevance tree based on demand for transport which has only two branches stemming from each idea. It really does not matter whether you have two or more: as long as you allow the tree to branch out in sufficiently diverse directions to enable you to think right across the subject.

EXAMPLE

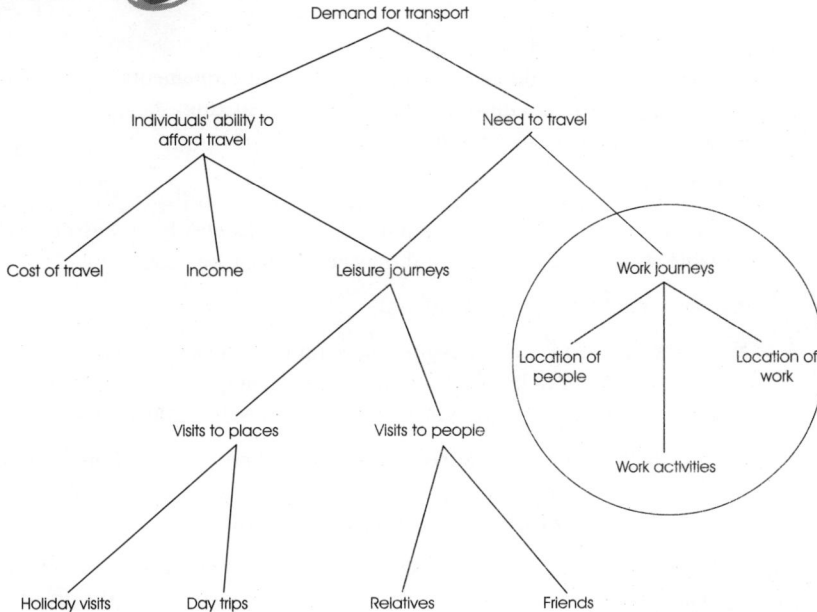

Figure 3.1 Relevance tree
Source: Sharp and Howard (1996)

5.4 Analogy

Sharp and Howard (1996) suggest that the concept of **analogy** may provide a fruitful line of enquiry by applying an aspect of completed research to some other area.

Here are some examples of the use of analogy in topic selection.

(a) Past research found that advanced computer equipment used in the West is inappropriate in developing countries with a less developed technical infrastructure and to whom intermediate technology is better suited. This indicated a research opportunity relating to the implementation of 'intermediate technology' in British small businesses (Sharp and Howard, 1996)

(b) Methodology used to study marketing managers (Grafton-Small, 1985) was helped by analogy with the methods used by Watson (1977) in his study of personnel managers

5.5 Brainstorming

This is a technique which is normally conducted in a group, although Saunders *et al* (2003) suggest that it could be done alone. Done as a group exercise, it means that you can derive the benefit of the ideas of a group of people. Each person's ideas can then be built upon by the rest of the group. A two hour brainstorming session with six participants can generate far more than twelve hours worth of solo thinking time, because of the way in which the thought processes of each individual interact with those of the other participants.

Key characteristics of brainstorming are that:

(a) Group members should be open minded and non-judgemental

(b) There should be a free flow of as many ideas as possible

(c) Cross-fertilisation of ideas is helpful

The stages to follow are these:

1 Try to state the problem or the potential topic as clearly and as precisely as possible, although by definition it may at this stage be quite vague.

2 Ask for suggestions from the others.

3 Note down every idea that anyone comes up with, no matter how ridiculous it may initially seem to be. Don't make any judgement or enter into discussion about the ideas at this stage: just concentrate on writing them down.

4 Discuss each of the ideas to seek clarification and consider how it could be implemented as a potential research topic. At this stage you can engage in critical thinking and effectively 'pull the ideas apart'.

If you are brainstorming alone, the key stages are 1 and 3. You must take the time to state the problems as clearly as you can, and then allow your brain the freedom to wander around the subject. Make a note of anything that springs to mind, but don't start to analyse it at this stage. Allow a little time for your ideas to germinate and then engage in critical thinking, as if you were in a group.

Many practitioners of brainstorming encourage the raising of wild or radical ideas, on the grounds that these are radical but can then be translated into sensible, practical ideas. Of course, in a business you would have to take into consideration any negative publicity if a non politically-correct suggestion was leaked and published by the media.

Activity 5 (10 minutes)

You are the manager of a suburban shopping mall which is experiencing severe graffiti problems. It is costly to remove, as well as being unsightly for shoppers. Take a piece of paper and jot down as many ideas as possible. Let your mind roam without any constraints.

You may well have some wild, perhaps not so socially-acceptable ideas. Write them down anyway; they may be capable of translation into sensible and workable proposals.

5.6 Other sources of ideas for research projects

Various tried and tested approaches to identifying research topics have been explained above.

Luck (1999) provides a handy and user-friendly checklist that you might find useful, if nothing else, as an *aide memoire*.

(a)   A tv/radio/newspaper item which caught your attention

(b)   Something mentioned in a lecture or tutorial which seemed to be unresolved

(c)   A generalisation made by someone outside your field ('Everyone knows that …'. 'What's the point of …?'. etc.) of which you feel suspicious or which you think could do with testing against the evidence

(d)   Something you have always wondered about

(e)   A hunch you've had for a while

(f)   A quotation that particularly stuck in your mind

(g)   A necessity in need of an invention

(h)   A flick through a current journal

(i)   Previous research projects in the department

(j)   A chat with a postgraduate about their work

(k)   A book or poem you read recently

(l)   An article that caught your eye in the popular journal section of the library

(m) A public lecture you attended

6   PULLING ALL THE IDEAS TOGETHER

6.1   Introduction

So far in this chapter, we have considered numerous thinking techniques, both rational and creative, to help you identify topics on which you might like to do your research project. You are likely to have come up with a list of, say, two or three potential topics. You now need a process to evaluate the most suitable topic for you.

6.2   Evaluation criteria

Various authors have suggested a variety of criteria that might be useful in evaluating which topic might be best suited to you for your dissertation.

The criteria put forward by Jankowicz (2000) are summarised below.

(a)   Level of personal interest
(b)   Existing knowledge and experience
(c)   Level of difficulty
(d)   Ease of access to data
(e)   Time required
(f)   Financial cost

And a summarised version of the criteria suggested by Luck (1999) are:

(a)   Broad interest of area
(b)   Specific interest in topic
(c)   Working relationship with supervisor
(d)   Impact of team-working
(e)   Additional financial cost
(f)   Time demands
(g)   Skills requirements

Saunders *et al* (2003) provide a comprehensive list of attributes of a good research project which are summarised below.

    (a) Match between researcher's topic and university's assessment criteria
    (b) researcher interest in topic
    (c) Clear link to theory
    (d) Time availability
    (e) Financial resources
    (f) Ease of access
    (g) Clarity of research question(s) and objectives
    (h) Contribution to advancement of knowledge
    (i) Symmetry of potential outcomes
    (j) Match to researcher's career goals

We have attempted to incorporate these criteria in developing a scorecard which you might find useful in assessing which topic to go forward with. The technique essentially consists of scoring each candidate topic against a list of qualities that are themselves weighted to reflect their desirability to the researcher. The example given below is intended to be indicative; you can tailor it to suit your own particular outlook and needs. You can put in your own evaluation criteria or your own weighting system. It lends itself to being converted to a spreadsheet which you can keep on your PC.

EXAMPLE

A student living and working in the Far East has gone through the processes recommended earlier in this chapter and has identified two potential dissertation topics.

(a)   Consumer attitudes to Western fast food restaurants in Beijing
(b)   Financial structures of small to medium sized enterprises in South-East Asia

The scorecards shown below provide examples of how the student might make the selection.

Potential topic: Consumer attitudes to Western fast food restaurants in Beijing

Evaluation criteria	A	B										A + B
	Weight	10	9	8	7	6	5	4	3	2	1	0	Score
Compliance with HNC/HND learning outcome	7	✓											70
Personal interest	9		✓										81
Theoretical foundation	6			✓									48
Ease of access	8			✓									64
Advances existing knowledge	6		✓										54
Clarity of research question and objectives	7			✓									56
Technical experience required	5				✓								35
Adequacy of personal skills	8			✓									64
Financial support required	6					✓							36
Time required	4			✓									32
Career goal congruence	9			✓									72
TOTAL													612

Potential topic: Financial structures of small medium sized enterprise in South-East Asia

Evaluation criteria	A	B										A + B
	Weight	10	9	8	7	6	5	4	3	2	1	0	Score
HND/HNC learning outcomes	7	✓											70
Personal interest	9			✓									63
Theoretical foundation	6			✓									48
Ease of access	8					✓							40
Advances existing knowledge	6			✓									48
Clarity of research question and objectives	7			✓									56
Technical experience	5		✓										45
Adequacy of personal skills	8		✓										72
Financial support	6		✓										54
Time availability	4		✓										36
Career goal congruence	9					✓							54
TOTAL													586

In this example the consumer attitudes research scores higher than the SME financial structures research, so on this analysis, the researcher might be better off deciding to go forward with the consumer attitudes project instead.

7   REFINING RESEARCH IDEAS

7.1   Introduction

Once you have identified a broad research idea, you must start to be more specific and ultimately move towards a **project title**. The process of refining the title is really a process of refining the project's content (Luck, 1999). You will find that in thinking about the title you will start to think in terms of whether your research idea is really feasible.

Do not despair if this detailed thinking reveals gaps or inconsistencies in your plan. It is better to discover them at this stage and revise your ideas before too much work has been done rather than to come to that conclusion much later, when much more work may prove to have been fruitless.

In this section we cover two specific techniques that you may find useful at this stage of refining the basic idea.

7.2   The Delphi technique

The Delphi technique is a procedure whereby a group of people who are either involved in, or in some way interested in, the research idea discuss it to generate a more specific idea. This might be useful if there is a small group of colleagues who are prepared to invest some time in helpin each other to select their research topics.

The procedure for carrying out this technique as described in Saunders *et al* (2003) can be depicted in the diagram on the following page.

The benefits of using the Delphi technique include:

(a)   Its value in building a team spirit among members of a group

(b)   Its value in bringing out the best in people as they are in a position to help one another.

> **STEP 1**
> Brief the members of the group about the research idea.

> **STEP 2**
> At the end of the briefing, ask them if they need
> clarification or further information.

> **STEP 3**
> Ask each member of the group (including the person whose research idea it originally
> was) to generate up to three research ideas based on the broad research idea
> described. They are to do this independently of each other. They may be asked for a
> justification for their specific ideas.

> **STEP 4**
> Collect the specific research ideas together and distribute a consolidated list to all the
> members of the group. They should not be edited in any way and should not be
> attributed to their originator.

> **STEP 5**
> Go through steps 2-4 again; that is, ask group members if they need further
> clarification, ask them to comment on the new wave of research ideas and ask them to
> revise their own contributions in the light of the comments and contributions of the
> other members of the group.

> **STEP 6**
> Go through this process again until the group is in a position to indicate whether a
> consensus as to a specific research idea has been reached.

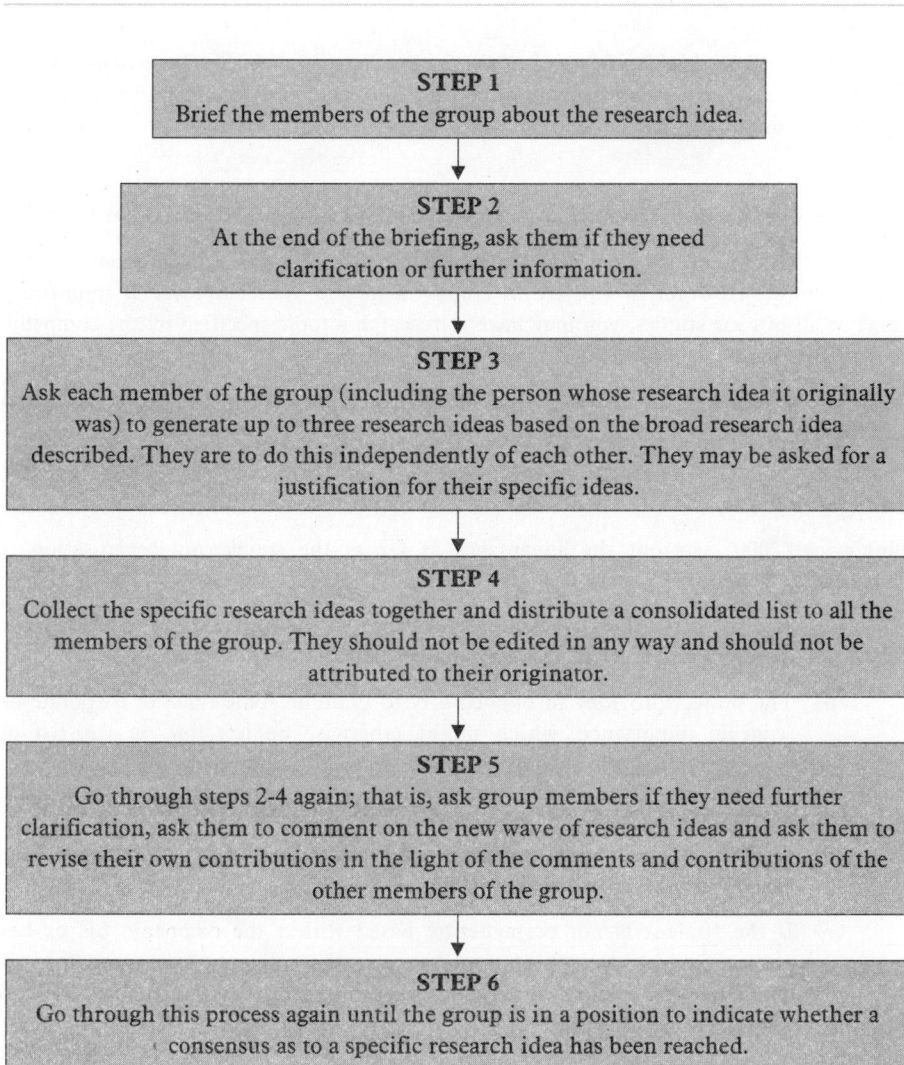

Figure 3.2 The Delphi technique
Source: Saunders *et al* 2003

7.3 Preliminary studies

The preliminary study is described by Saunders *et al.* (2003) as a possible stage in the topic-refining process. It can involve:

(a) An initial review of some of the literature

(b) Informal discussions with other people with knowledge of the research idea or experience of the field

(c) Shadowing employees who might be important in the research

(d) Gaining an in-depth understanding of the organisation or part of it you will be researching

You should still be thinking in terms of the factors considered in Section 6 above on the feasibility, practicalities and logistics of the research idea, and be prepared to revise the idea if necessary.

8   ORGANISATIONALLY-GENERATED RESEARCH IDEAS

So far in this chapter, we have assumed that you will have a free rein in choosing your research topic. However, if you are in employment and your employer is sponsoring some or all of your studies, you may have to research a topic specified by the company, or gain your employer's approval for your choice of topic.

There are advantages and disadvantages to this, both for the sponsoring organisation and for the student.

8.1   Advantages

Jankowicz (2000) sets out the advantages as far as the sponsoring organisation is concerned:

(a) The project tackles an issue of relevance to the organisation (and will not therefore be purely an academic exercise)

(b) The project provides an opportunity to examine some issue of corporate or strategic importance, which might otherwise be left low on the list of priorities in the face of competition from more urgent operational issues

(c) It can form an inexpensive way of conducting a quasi consultancy exercise

(d) If the topic is carefully chosen and refined, it can be of use to the organisational superiors of the student

(e) If the student is not permanently based within the company, his or her engagement in research of importance to the company may mean that an employee who would otherwise be engaged in the research can be released to work on something else.

From the student/employee's point of view, the advantages can include:

(a) Funding and other support provided by the sponsoring organisation

(b) Ameliorating any problems of finding a research project topic

(c) Providing a platform for a move, presumably upwards, within the organisation

8.2   Pitfalls

As far as the company (or other sponsoring organisation) is concerned, the main deterrents to sponsoring a research project would be:

(a) The cost
(b) The lack of any tangible benefit to the company, and
(c) The deployment of the individual on non company-related matters

From the individual employee/student's point of view, the pitfalls could include:

(a) Lack of interest in the company-stipulated project, leading to a loss of motivation

(b) The research topic being too wide or too narrow or in some other way not appropriate for the requirements of your qualification

(Saunders *et al*, 2003)

Where there is this conflict between your needs and interests, as the student, and those of the sponsoring organisation, you should try to achieve some form of compromise. If you can motivate yourself by the thought that you are doing something of value to your employer and thereby enhancing your career prospects, this might help to overcome the problem of a lack of great personal interest in the topic itself.

9 POTENTIAL PROBLEMS OF ACCESS

We have already touched upon access to data as one of the factors to be considered when deciding whether the topic is feasible.

9.1 Introduction

Just because you are carrying out research, you will not automatically be granted access to an organisation, and it may well be that you have to rely on the goodwill and generosity of participants if you are asking them to respond to surveys or questionnaires. You must be prepared to explain the amount of time that people will be expected to make available to you, and what you will be doing with any information that they provide (Bell, 1999).

You should apply for permission to have access to information or to research a particular topic, at as early a stage as possible. Write formally to the individual or organisation, and be honest in explaining what you are planning to do and for what purpose you will use the information. If you think that your research might produce information that would be of use to the other party, emphasise that point, but do not over-stress it so that you are making potentially false claims. (Bell, 1999).

9.2 Why access might be difficult

Saunders *et al* (2003) have identified a number of reasons why access might be a problem. They are summarised here.

1 Organisations or individuals may not want to be involved in activities over and above the usual workload due to the time and resources required.

2 The organisation (especially if large or with a high public profile) may receive countless requests for information or access to carry out research activities

3 The person receiving the request may not see what value the research would have

4 The research topic selected may be very sensitive or involve highly confidential material

5 The person to whom you have made the request may have doubts about your credibility and/or competence

6   The organisation might have difficulties allowing you access due to some external issue or circumstances beyond its control. For example in the aftermath of the terrorist attacks in the United States on 11 September 2001, airlines and companies involved in tourism have become particularly sensitive about issues of physical access and access to information, due to heightened concerns as to security.

Many writers perceive access as an **ongoing procedure**, rather than a single event (Gummesson, 1991; Marshall and Rossman, 1999; Robson, 1993, all cited by Saunders *et al*, 2003). If you gain access initially to research one particular area, you may then have to re-negotiate it with someone else to research a different area. Gaining initial access does not mean that it is a foregone conclusion that your rights of access will be extended as far as is necessary for you.

Additionally, a representative of the management of the organisation will probably have granted you access. When you start to collect the data, you will in all likelihood be dealing with different employees: those who actually handle the data you require. You will need to gain informal acceptance from them if access is to prove successful. (Saunders *et al* 2003).

This is another aspect of your research work where good personal skills will help to smooth your path within the organisation. Granting of access is a basic starting point. You will need to be sensitive as to whether you are treading on any awkward issues of an organisational or personal nature.

Easterby-Smith *et al* (1991) explain that 'getting on within an organisation is largely a function of the personality of the researcher, and whether he or she is genuinely curious to find out what is happening; it is also a function of the researcher's skills in dealing with what are sometimes very complex interpersonal relationships'.

The term access can mean not only physical access to data (discussed above), but also to your ability to select the appropriate data to answer your research question. If the organisation only allows you access to certain employees, who all perhaps hold the same view of the employer, your sample may not produce reliable, bias-free results. This is reflected in the way in which television news coverage is meant to be presented free from bias: when a political issue is discussed, a representative from each political party is given an opportunity to speak.

Saunders *et al* (2003) refer to this wider form of access as **cognitive access**. They say

> '*Where you achieve this you will have gained access to the data which you need your intended participants to share with you in order to understand their social reality and for you to be able to address your research questions and objectives. Simply obtaining physical access into an organisation will be inadequate unless you are also able to negotiate yourself into a position where you can reveal the reality of what is occurring in relation to your research question and objectives.*'

Johnson (1975) takes the concept further. He says that, in reality, undertaking a research project may involve considering where you are likely to be able to gain access and then developing a topic to fit that access. Hence it may be helpful to research a topic within your own organisation, where, on that basis, there will be much more scope for research. You will be an internal (or participant) researcher, as opposed to an external researcher, and you and your research are therefore likely to be more acceptable.

The two topics of access and ethics in research are closely linked. Research ethics were discussed in detail in Chapter 2.

9.3   Power relationships and organisational conflict

Power relationships are more commonly discussed in the context of research ethics, but they also deserve a brief consideration here.

FOR DISCUSSION

Imagine that you are engaged in research into management control procedures in a company engaged in medical research. After protracted and delicate negotiation with the directors, you have been granted access to the company's records and employees. What types of power relationship might you become involved in or witness in operation? Think in terms of how power may be exerted over you and how you may exert it over others.

Power relationships can arise whenever you are dealing with people. You are likely to encounter them in your research in two ways.

Management power

Whether you are researching within your own organisation or you are an external researcher in another organisation, you will have been granted access to information by the management of the company. This means that they have done you a favour (Bell, 1999) and you are therefore beholden to them, or even in their debt. In return for allowing you access, management of the company may expect a fairly rosy and uncritical picture to be painted, or they may expect unlimited access to the opinions of the company you glean from the staff. This inferred existence of power exercised by management of the company over you can present you with an ethical dilemma, as it may cause bias to be present in your work.

Saunders *et al.* (2003) summarise the issue thus:

> *'Managers will be in a very powerful position in relation to researchers who request organisational access. They will remain in a powerful position in terms of the nature and extent of the access that they allow in an organisational setting.'*

The implication here is that if you as the researcher don't accord with management's view as to what you should be doing, access could be summarily withdrawn, to the obvious detriment of your research. Of course, in practice this may be more subtle. Whilst you may technically hold a piece of paper granting you access, you find you no longer have cooperation from the organisation.

The researcher's power

The other side of the coin is the power relationship you may find yourself in with regard to the people actually providing you with the information. As we have already seen, the granters of access and the providers of data are likely to be different groups of people. You will need to be aware of the myriad of ethical issues involved, as outlined in Chapter 2.

In carrying out research, you will be able ask questions in whatever way is best suited to the needs of your research. You may be able to ask quite probing questions of senior members of management, which 'may cause levels of discomfort' (Saunders *et al*, 2003). You will thus be exerting power over the interviewees. You must handle this power carefully if you are not to be in breach of the research ethics already discussed in Chapter 2.

Employees of the company may also tend to give you the answers that they think you want if they think that you are likely to pass their comments back to management. This is especially true where you are, for example, asking for their views on company procedures or management effectiveness. There is a risk that the results you obtain in such a situation may be distorted or biased due to the nature of the power relationship between you and the interviewees. Again, you need to be aware of the political issues that exist in the organisation.

You must also bear in mind that you will only be carrying out research on a relatively short-term basis, and will then return either to your normal role within the company, or leave it all together if you are an external researcher. The people who you have been interviewing, or otherwise obtaining information from, will need to work together after you depart (Saunders *et al*, 2003). This puts you in a position of power, as failure to protect their anonymity or the confidentiality of their disclosures to you could effectively harm their work relationships. Organisational conflict could then be the result. As the old saying goes, try to avoid 'lighting the blue touch paper and retiring to a safe distance'!

If you are researching within your own company, you may find it difficult to maintain your previous relationships with colleagues after you have interviewed them for research purposes. Judith Bell (1999) cites a study of research conducted by a teacher of English in a comprehensive school into the operations of the English department. She makes the point that

> '*As an insider, he quickly came to realise that you have to live with your mistakes after completing the research. The close contact with the institution and colleagues made objectivity difficult to attain and, he felt, gaining confidential knowledge had the potential for affecting his relationship with colleagues.*'

In many areas of research, power relationships are not a problem, and the topic may well prove not to be a factor in your research. However, you need to be aware of the fact that it could potentially be an issue. As a general statement, there may be scope for reducing the impact of some of the 'power politic' through the use of excellent people handling skills.

9.4   Creeping expectations

Another problem sometimes arises in research projects as well as in business and management. You may well find that you start with a well-defined topic but as you progress, management's expectations of the outcomes begins to grow. For example, a research project which commences as a study of consumer behaviour, begins to look like an exercise to develop a marketing strategy. This may provide the researcher with a nice challenge, but might, however, prejudice the completion of the dissertation.

Under the circumstances, instead of seeking access to information, unwelcome amounts of in-house reports and other data may be thrust upon you, in the raised expectation that you incorporate them either as part of your literature review or as part of your data collection process.

Make sure you are aware of any changes in the scope of your research project. Naturally, the fact that the organisation wants you to do more is probably a show of confidence in you and is likely to represent a career advancing opportunity. Use your personal skills to persuade the relevant organisation managers to allow you to finish your project first and let you complete the rest of what they would like after it. Use the conduct of the project to develop your practical problem-solving skills in developing 'win-win' solutions.

9.5   Strategies to gain access

Gaining access to the organisation may be one of the most difficult aspects of your research for your project.

We cover it here, in the chapter on developing your project proposal, as it is an issue which you must start to consider at this stage, as in your proposal you must convince the assessor that access to data will not be a problem. We cover it in some depth at this stage, and you will find that many of the points made are of equal relevance later on in the book and your project work.

You may like to refer back to this section when you are reading Chapter 5 on methods of data collection, as the access issue is also relevant there.

Saunders *et al* (2003) summarise these.

(a)   Allow yourself sufficient time

(b)   Use existing contacts and develop new ones

(c)   Give a clear account of the purpose of your access and the type of access required

(d)   Overcome organisational concerns about the granting of access

(e)   Identify any possible benefits to the organisation of granting you access

(f)   Use suitable language

(g)   Accompany a request for access with an easy means of reply

(h)   Gradually build up the level of access

(i)   Establish your credibility with the intended participants

Allowing yourself sufficient time

Don't forget that it can take a long time to organise access, especially if your request has to be passed up through various stages of the organisation. It may even take you some weeks to find out to whom you should be addressing your request.

If you have to arrange access to several individuals simultaneously, for example to set up a focus group, the time needed will probably be longer, and there may be a limited choice of dates.

The key message here is to ensure you apply proper planning to the process of gaining access.

Use of existing contacts and development of new ones

Many writers maintain that it is easier, where at all possible, to use existing contacts (Easterby-Smith *et al*, 2002). A person who already has knowledge of you and your academic background, and who trusts you and your motives, is more likely to agree to your request. Even if you only know a relatively junior person in an organisation, it is a starting point, and the fact that they can then introduce your name and endorse your request will add credibility to your application.

When you are trying to develop new contacts, try to ascertain the name of the person in an organisation you should be contacting, rather than just a job title. Again, this is an opportunity to develop and practice your relationship-building skills.

Activity 6 (5 minutes)

Which of these two letters would you be most likely to respond favourably to?

'Dear Mrs. Shah,

I have had a brief chat with your secretary, Ashley Austin, who suggested that you may be able to help me with some information. I am conducting research into........

Yours sincerely, Lucy Lew'

or

'Dear Product Development Manager,

I hope that you are the appropriate person to whom I should address my correspondence. If not, perhaps you could forward this letter to someone who might be able to provide me with information I require for my research project. I am conducting research into...

Yours faithfully, Lucy Lew'

If you cannot glean the necessary information from inside the organisation, you may find that a professional association will be able to help with the names of key individuals within an organisation. Other organisations, such as chambers of commerce or trade unions, may also be able to help. Sometimes, organisations may well have reasonably informative websites which you might find helpful.

A clear description of the nature of the access required

Providing a clear account of your requirements will allow your intended participants to be aware of what will be required of them (Robson, 2002). They are less likely to refuse if they fully understand what you want, and do not think that you will gradually increase or change your requirements.

You should always follow up any telephone conversation discussing access with friendly but professional a letter confirming what has been agreed, or providing any further information that has been requested.

EXAMPLE

Mr J Jacques	88 Sandy Lane
Niceko Ltd	Woodgrove
Primrose Business Park	Littleton
Littleton	Uniland
Uniland	DATE

Dear Mr Jacques

Just a brief note to confirm the arrangements we talked about over the phone this morning.

I shall come to your offices on Tuesday, 12 August 2008 at 2.30pm to discuss ...

I will bring along with me the dossier of information on .... which you suggested might be useful.

I look forward to meeting you

Yours sincerely

Barry Baroque

Overcome organisational concerns

Saunders *et al* (2003) identify three main areas of concern for the organisation:

(a)   The extent of the resources and time required

(b)   The sensitivity of the topic and whether it will present the company in a negative light

(c)   The confidentiality of the data to be provided and maintaining the anonymity of the organisation and of individual participants

To counter these concerns, the best advice is to be as honest as possible with the company. Do not under-estimate the amount of time that will be needed for an interview, knowing full well that it will actually take you longer. Try to accentuate the positive side of things if you are trying to negotiate access to information about a sensitive area. Provide cast-iron assurances to the effect that you will preserve the confidentiality of the organisation and the individuals involved. Provide such guarantees in writing if you are asked to do so and you feel that it would help.

Possible benefits to the organisation

It may be of value to the organisation to have research carried out on an aspect of its operations. Offer to give the organisation a copy of the research report once finished, or a summary of the relevant findings.

Saunders *et al* (2003) suggest that where access is granted in return for supplying a report of your findings, it might help to devise a simple 'contract' to set out clearly both sides' understanding of what has been agreed. The 'contract' can take the form of a letter and would make important points clear.

(a) The form of the report (in broad terms)

(b) The nature and depth of the analysis that you have agreed to do as part of it

(c) Whether you will supply a copy of the full dissertation or just the sections that are relevant to the organisation.

Using suitable language

Plan any introductory letters or the 'script' for any telephone conversations carefully. It may be your only opportunity to establish your credibility and competence with the organisation. If you fail to do it on this first attempt, it will be much more difficult subsequently.

Give some thought to the terminology that you will use. It has been suggested that student researchers applying for access should use terminology which is not perceived as threatening. (Buchanan *et al*, 1988, Easterby-Smith *et al*, 1991, Jankowicz, 2000). In fact Buchanan *et al* (1988) suggest a range of alternative words.

Usual research term	Replace with
Research	Learn from your experience
Interview	Conversation
Publish	Write an account

You may also prefer to refer to yourself as a researcher rather than a student or learner, as it could add to your credibility and will contribute to the impression of academic value to be derived from your research work (Easterby-Smith *et al*, 1991). However, if you feel that in the context of your work, 'researcher' could be perceived as a threatening term, as in the table above, describe yourself purely as a student.

Generally, your approach is likely to be driven by your assessment of the corporate culture of the organisation and the attitudes of its managers to academic matters. You may well find it beneficial to couch any communications you engage in using that particular organisation's own 'corporate speak' instead of using academic language. Whatever adjustments you make to the formal academic terminology should be considered from an ethical perspective to ensure that you do not engage in a form of 'double speak' that is tantamount to deception.

Gradually build up the level of access

When you are negotiating access to an organisation which is not your own (or indeed within your own organisation), you must try to remember that your request may be perceived as an imposition by the recipient. There is no intrinsic reason for that person or organisation to do you any favours.

FOR DISCUSSION

Imagine that you are the production and operations director of a multi-national company. How would you feel about receiving a request for an interview from a student you've never heard of?

How do you think that you, the student, could 'influence' the organisation to grant you access?

Johnson (1975) suggests a three-stage approach:

1   Ask to conduct an interview.

2   Negotiate access to undertake observation (which could be agreed at the interview stage).

3   Gain permission to tape record the interactions being observed.

Negotiating increased levels of access at each stage using this piecemeal approach can enhance your chances of success. At each stage, you can add to your credibility and reputation with the organisation, so that it is willing to grant you further favours. This is a more effective approach than asking for every form of access at the outset: a multiple request is more likely to be turned down, especially if you are not already known at the company.

The drawback of adopting such a 'softly softly' approach is that it takes time to go through the various stages of Johnson's strategy and build up a relationship with your contacts within the organisation. You should remember the importance of personal skills in building up trust that will keep open the necessary doors to complete your research project efficiently and effectively.

Establishing your credibility with the intended participants

The concept of credibility is one that has recurred throughout this section. For example you will enjoy greater credibility from the outset if you already have contacts within an organisation that you can then use to generate new contacts.

It is important that you build up your credibility as you proceed through your project work. You will need to repeat much of the process that you have used to gain entry into the organisation with the people who are charged with actually supplying you with information (Saunders *et al*, 2003).

You will need to explain to them:

(a)   The purpose of your work
(b)   What you are trying to achieve
(c)   How they can help you
(d)   That you can guarantee confidentiality and anonymity if necessary

As indicated above, you will need to build up a degree of trust with the participants, which will in turn lead to heightened credibility.

10 WRITING RESEARCH QUESTIONS AND OBJECTIVES

10.1 Introduction

The two most challenging elements in developing your research proposal are:

(a) The initial generation of ideas and

(b) Turning the idea into a research project title

Most of the authorities listed in the bibliography devote some time to the procedure whereby a topic is transformed into a title. You will probably find that it is a separate exercise in its own right. However, the use of techniques such as the Delphi Technique and the writing of a preliminary study (both discussed in section 7 above) could effectively give you a title, or something very close to it, as the end result, so that you do not have to refine the title as a separate exercise in its own right.

This section aims to help you to make that quantum leap from 'interesting topic which I might research' to clearly defined hypothesis or research objective.

As an analogy, when choosing a holiday you may be looking for 'somewhere exciting to go'. That is a matter of personal preference. You will need to translate 'somewhere exciting to go' into something concrete for you. If your definition of 'somewhere exciting to go' involves partying the night away, you might set the objective of going to Ibiza. If, to you, 'somewhere exciting to go' means going to a part of the world you have never visited before, you might fulfil the objective by booking a trekking holiday in the foothills of the Himalayas.

Your job now is to turn the general nature of the research idea into something specific that you can focus upon and around which you can design a research programme.

EXAMPLE

Here is an extract from an unpublished undergraduate dissertation to illustrate the procedure in general terms. It is given in the introduction to a project report.

Paragraph
1   This project evolved from a year's work in the Statistics and Finance Department in Q Ltd. During the year I spent much of my time analysing sales and contribution figures for individual areas and for the whole company. The other half of my job was to calculate commission payments each month and to authorise bonuses. At the time, it was clear that Q Ltd was experiencing deteriorating sales and declining contribution.
2   I was particularly interested in how the accounting and control systems within Q Ltd influenced behaviour and in turn what result these changes in behaviour had on the firm.
3   Therefore I set myself the aim to explore how effective different reward systems (which require accounting and control systems to operate) have been and could be used to motivate sales staff and sales performance, contribution and ultimately the profit of Q Ltd.
Conclusions are hard to prove but theory, opinion and logic can lead to some recommendations.

This encapsulates turning the topic into an objective:

(a) Paragraph 1 describes the context

(b) Paragraph 2 describes the general area

(c) Paragraph 3 defines the aim of the research

(d) You can now define the project aim by taking examples from the general category

'To show the influence of accounting control systems on behaviour by describing how commission reward systems at Q Ltd contribute to profitability in the light of relevant motivation theory.'

10.2 Refining research topics

The consensus among the authorities is that the next step in developing your research depends on which of the two main research paradigms you have chosen to work under.

(a) If you subscribe to the phenomenological paradigm, you will develop research objectives and questions.

(b) If you subscribe to the positivistic paradigm, you will develop the hypotheses you are going to test.

Luck (1999) sees this stage of research as a process of refining the project's content and thinking about what is feasible, in terms of access to information and ease of research.

EXAMPLE

You work in the National Health Service or a related organisation.

You want to do your research project on some aspect of perceptions of the NHS and the management of the NHS.

Step 1. Think through the characteristics of the NHS, as generally portrayed by the media:

- Delays in providing treatment
- Need for patients to be sent abroad for operations
- Central role of waiting lists
- Problems of funding
- Increasing bureaucracy and management interference
- Staff quality and dedication
- Some success stories

Step 2. On the basis of some aspect that interests you, pose a question. For example:

Has the introduction of traditional management accounting budgetary disciplines been effective in terms of clinical efficiency within the NHS?

Step 3. Consider the sources of information:

- Published waiting lists
- Hospital league tables of success rates, mortality rates and so on

95

- Published financial information
- Discussions with NHS Trust personnel

Step 4. What about the drawbacks?

- Available information may only be in limited form
- Dealing with very sensitive areas
- 'Loss of efficiency' a damning phrase
- Requests for discussions with personnel likely to generate a negative response

Step 5. So how to improve it?

- Retain the elements of the original wording but emphasise the positive, for example:

  'Has the introduction of traditional management accounting budgeting techniques contributed to clinical efficiency within the NHS?'

- This can then be restated as an objective rather than a question, along the lines of:

  'A demonstration of the improvement of clinical efficiency within the NHS due to the introduction of traditional management accounting budgeting techniques.'

- This is far more likely to generate a positive response from personnel involved, making the research more likely to succeed.

10.3 Identifying research questions, research objectives or hypotheses

Verma and Beard (1981) define a hypothesis as

> *'a tentative proposition which is subject to verification through subsequent investigation. It may also be seen as the guide to the researcher in that it depicts and describes the method to be followed in studying the problem. In many cases hypotheses are hunches that the researcher has about the existence of relationship between variables.'*

Hypotheses, therefore, make statements about relations between variables and provide a guide to the researcher as to how the original hunch might be tested (Bell, 1999).

Robson (1993) also uses the word 'hunch' in this context:

> *'......there is a sense in which hypotheses form part of all forms of enquiry. This is the hypothesis as tentative guess, or intuitive hunch, as to what is going on in a situation.'*

Sharp and Howard (1996) suggest that you should avoid too detailed a specification, limiting yourself to a single hypothesis with considerable potential for testing. If your hypothesis is too broad, you may find that you cannot get to grips with it and it lacks sufficient focus.

Jankowicz (2000) says that the hypothesis is usually, but not always, expressed as a question. This is in contrast to Saunders *et al.* (2003), who maintain that a good approach is to frame a general research question to generate a set of research objectives. They prefer objectives to questions as they argue that objectives lead to a greater degree of precision.

As suggested earlier, hypothesis development is more suitable to a positivistic approach to research where measurement is the researcher's priority, and the research scenario lends itself to the use of quantitative techniques. For example, the question may be 'Does giving more shelf space to the supermarket's own label baked beans increase sales? This could lead to the development of a hypothesis along the lines of 'increased shelf space increases the sale of a supermarket's own label baked beans'. This approach is always subject to the *ceteris paribus* (all other things being equal) assumption, which in research terms means being able to control all other variables while the research variables are being measured.

On the other hand, the researcher may wish to research the impact of introducing 'people greeters' to a supermarket. (A people greeter's job is to greet people as they enter a supermarket so as to express the store's warm welcome to customers.) Here your research question might be 'Has the introduction of people greeters improved customer satisfaction?' and a research objective might be stated in terms of 'To determine the extent to which the introduction of people greeters has enhanced the quality of customers' shopping experience'.

Under these circumstances, your research is likely to take a phenomenological inductive route.

EXAMPLE

Research idea 1

The fact that after the 'dot com bubble' some ICT businesses collapsed spectacularly, while others survived and indeed became profitable.

Leads to general focus research question

......What is it that the successful companies have done which has caused them to be successful?

Leads to research objective

.........To identify the factors in the establishment of ICT companies in the retail industry which have led to their survival.

Research idea 2

The impact of globalisation on a certain industry.

Leads to general focus research question

What effect has a policy of globalisation had on companies in the financial services industry?

Leads to research objective

To demonstrate that the move towards globalisation by a sample of companies in the financial services industry has had the effect of increasing profitability.

10.4 Research symmetry

Gill and Johnson (1997) define **research symmetry** as a 'way of reducing the risk in any project' by trying to 'ensure that whatever the findings from the work, the results will be equally of value'. Sharp and Howard (1996) explain that the extent to which the outcomes are of similar value is an indicator of the symmetry of the research. This view is supported by Jankowicz (2000) who refers to symmetry as 'balance' and relates to projects where outcomes are equally valuable whether your expectations are confirmed, or negated; an unbalanced project is one in which evidence that agrees with your expectations will leave you helpless, or equally, one in which the evidence that disagrees with your expectations will have no value.

Various examples of symmetrical and unsymmetrical research projects are outlined in the literature.

Symmetrical projects

    (a) Study of the impacts on managers' careers of holding a postgraduate qualification in a management subject (Gill and Johnson, 1997; Sharp and Howard, 1996)

    (b) Research into the idea that companies that have diversified into new products and services (manufacture and retailing of domestic garden hoses and fittings) are more resistant to takeover than those which have not diversified (Jankowicz, 2000)

Non-symmetrical projects

    (a) Research into venture capital firms' preferences for investing in business start-ups where a market niche is likely to be created, rather than in start-ups which deal in a commodity product. Evidence which confirms your expectations would be banal, while evidence which negated your expectations would be unlikely for this topic (Jankowicz, 2000; Gorman and Sahlman, 1986)

    (b) Research designed to investigate a possible link between psychoanalytical factors, such as the mid-life crisis, and the personality of the individual. If no link were established, the research outcome would not be interesting (Gill and Johnson, 1997)

'Symmetry depends in large part on prior beliefs about a topic which are held within a field of study. If, for example, there is strong support for the view that the eating of sweets damages children's teeth or there is little belief that the phases of the moon affect work output, experiments which confirm strongly held opinion will not be rated highly even though the design and conduct of these experiments cannot be criticised. Obviously, if the research findings were to contradict current belief they would be of potential value but this is unlikely in both cases cited'

(Sharp and Howard, 1996).

Jankowicz (2000) adds that balance is a matter of what is known already, of the potential value of positive and negative findings, and the likelihood of either kind of finding. A topic in which your expectations and hunches are unbalanced is a risky one in which to engage.

Sharp and Howard (1996) provide some examples of approaches that are unlikely to provide high symmetry.

(a) Experiments undertaken in laboratories by scientists and engineers

(b) Validation of an econometric model which has been developed, perhaps mainly from theory. You might wish to develop your own model of a part of your economy but you must be aware of the likely outcomes. For example, when interest rates used to fluctuate widely in the UK it might have been possible to establish a fit between, say, consumption of consumer durables and various market interest rates. But with interest rates now fairly stable and set by a Bank of England committee, the researcher is unlikely to find a strong link between spending on consumer durables and interest rates.

Saunders *et al.* (2003) concludes that without symmetry 'you may spend a considerable amount of time researching your topic only to find an answer of little importance. Whatever the outcome, you need to ensure you have the scope to write an interesting project report'.

10.5 Key words

Jankowicz (2000) has a helpful table incorporating some key words, or issues, which underlie performance. He suggests that you just ask yourself which one applies to your topic, and you will find your research objective, because you will be able to identify what your topic is really about.

Is my topic about	In other words
Efficiency	how accurately, quickly, resource-intensively can something be done?
Effectiveness	how well, in comparison to other alternatives, can something be done?
Appropriateness	how closely matched is something to a set of values, or to some preferred strategy?
Beliefs	are attitudes, beliefs, opinions and values primarily involved?
Constraints	what sort of resourcing, optimisation, minimisation of costs or maximisation of outcomes, best value factors are involved?
Choice	what options exist, what decisions need to be made?
Description	what's happening that's important to know about?
Causes	does the heart of the issue require a search for one or more causes, mitigating circumstances, contingency factors?
Comparison	how do other departments, organisations, other circumstances, do something?
Preferences	are matters resolvable against a single legitimate standard with clear rights and wrongs, or is some balance required between equally legitimate stakeholder positions?

© A.D. Jankowicz, 2000

10.6 The importance of theory in developing hypotheses and writing research questions and objectives

There are two approaches to theory development.

(a) **Deductive research**: formulate a theory, identify supporting hypothesis and test hypothesis. Confirm or reject theory.

(b) **Inductive research**: make observations, pose research questions, identify research objectives, gather data, interpret data and then formulate theory.

EXAMPLE

British Airways has been encountering severe falls in passenger numbers and revenue in recent years. Its managers may theorise that if they cut fares to compete with the budget airlines, passenger numbers will increase, although revenue itself may not. An increase in passenger numbers, however, will increase the confidence of investors and the public in the airline.

Saunders *et al* (2003) maintain that theory is something rooted in our everyday lives, and that every purposive decision that we take is based on theory. For example, if you leave the house at 7.30 am, in theory you should catch the 8.00 train. Therefore theory is also important in research, as research also involves examining the relationship between two variables and explaining and predicting those relationships. As Gill and Johnson (1997) state, 'explanation enables prediction which in turn enables control'. The work you do for your research project will test and possibly develop and amend theory.

Saunders *et al.* (2003) summarise it very neatly:

> '*Although intelligence gathering will play a part in your research, it is unlikely to be enough. You should be seeking to explain phenomena, to analyse relationships, to compare what is going on in different research settings, to predict outcomes and to generalise; then you will be working at the theoretical level.*'

11 WRITING YOUR RESEARCH PROPOSAL

11.1 Introduction

The research proposal is 'a document for decision' (Sharp and Howard, 1996). It should not be regarded as a routine document or as a bureaucratic hoop to be got through before starting the 'real work' of your research.

The proposal forms a critical part of your research project as a whole, and you cannot proceed with the main body of the work until your proposal has been approved, or you have carried out whatever modifications are required by your tutor.

11.2 Contents of the proposal

Remember that the proposal should be about 1,500 words in length.

Once produced and approved, you should regard it as a 'working document' (Luck, 1999) and use it regularly as a yardstick against which you can measure progress. Use it to compare where you expected to go in your research with the point you have actually reached.

11.3   What you are going to do

You should state the research objective and the working title of your project. The title may change as the work progresses (Saunders *et al*, 2003) but you should not perceive this as a problem.

You should give a brief introduction to the organisation within which you intend to do the work. You should also introduce the literature. At this stage you do not need to refer to all the literature you have looked at: half a dozen or so of the leading authorities would suffice. The purpose of referring to the literature here is to indicate to the assessor that you are familiar with some of the literature and have considered how your work will fit in with some of the existing sources.

11.4   Why you are going to do it (the background)

Here the main thrust should be towards justifying what you are going to do. Are you doing it:

(a)   Because it truly fascinates you?
(b)   Because you have researched this area for a project before?
(c)   Because it is directly relevant to your working environment?
(d)   Because you have identified a problem and a means of trying to solve it?

You will be expected to demonstrate a clear link between the previous work that has been done in the field and the content of your proposal (Saunders *et al*, 2003). Remember the key objective of your project is to advance existing knowledge and your proposal will need to show how your project is grounded in the academic literature.

11.5   How you are going to do it

'State the main research method and techniques which you intend to use, your research design and an indication of the sample or samples of people who will be providing you with your data.'   (Jankowicz, 2000)

Saunders *et al* (2003) suggest that, since this will be one of the two longest sections of the proposal (the other being the background discussed above), you could divide this section into two: research design and data collection.

The research design section will say where you will carry out the research. If it is in one organisation, this will be quite straightforward, but if you are looking at a specific industry or sector of the economy, you need explain what you will be looking at and why. You should also outline what combination of primary and secondary data you will be using.

The data collection section will outline how the data will be collected, for example by survey, questionnaires, and interviews or by use of secondary data, and how populations and sample sizes will be established, likely response rates and so on.

11.6   The resources you expect to utilise

Saunders *et al* (2003) summarise the three main resources as:

(a)   Finance
(b)   Data access and
(c)   Equipment

This part of the proposal will not be very long, but you must use it to convince the assessor of the practical feasibility of your research project. If your proposal indicates that your project will cost thousands of pounds, or will hinge on your gaining access to classified government documents, your tutor may well suggest that you to think again.

Think carefully what costs will be involved in collecting your data including items as mundane as travel costs. Can you afford it?

We have discussed data access at length earlier in this chapter, in Section 9.

One of the main things to consider under the heading of equipment is your ability to process and analyse the data you collect. Your proposal must indicate to your tutor that you have access to the appropriate computer hardware and software (which you must be able to use) to be able to analyse and present your data.

11.7   Your proposed timescale

You will find that it is helpful to you as much as to anyone else to establish a timescale. This will give you a target to work towards, and you will soon see, once you start the work, whether you have been realistic in your assessment.

Your tutor will also be able to form an opinion in the light of their own experience as to whether your deadline is manageable. Proper project management has been highlighted before. As discussed, you might like to use a project management tool such as network analysis. Alternatively, you might be more comfortable with something simpler like a Gantt chart. You may also have access to some project management software which might be helpful.

Chapter roundup

- You have seen in this chapter the vital importance of the project research proposal. It will provide the foundation for your entire research project, and is critical to your success.

- The main contents of the project proposal should be:
    ◦ the working title
    ◦ the background and academic context
    ◦ a statement of the research question and objectives
    ◦ some reference to the academic literature and authorities
    ◦ the methods you will use
    ◦ any potential problems of access
    ◦ your proposed timescale

- The main purpose of the research proposal is to organise your thoughts for the project, and establish the structure of how you plan to do the work.

- You should use a combination of rational and creative thinking techniques.

- In drawing together all the ideas you have had, you should consider critical factors such as:
    ◦ how interested you are in the topic
    ◦ how much you know about it already
    ◦ how difficult it is likely to be
    ◦ how easy it will be to access the data
    ◦ the expected time and costs involved

- There is a range of techniques for refining research ideas, such as the Delphi technique and the production of a preliminary study.

- If planning a project topic which has been generated by the organisation you work for, there are additional factors that you must take into account, such as whether the work ultimately produced will be suitable for both the organisation and the project itself.

- Access to data is sometimes one of the principal problems that a student may meet. It may take a fairly protracted 'softly softly' approach to negotiate adequate access for your purposes.

Answers to activities

1   According to Boulden (2002), 'creativity is the process of challenging accepted ideas and ways of doing things in order to find new solutions or concepts'. You may have come up with all sorts of different definitions of creativity.

2   You are likely to have written down:

    (a) Denmark
    (b) Elephant

3   The solution to the nine dot problem epitomises the 'thinking outside the box' approach advocated by creative thinking.

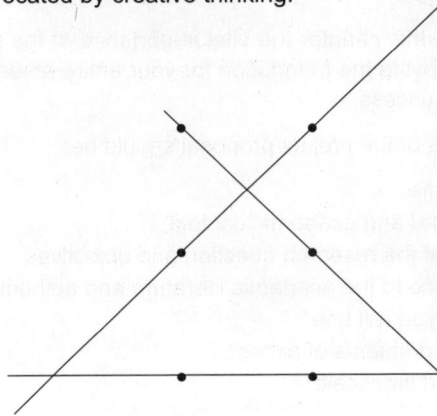

4   You are likely to have thought through a whole list of alternatives.

COUNTRIES	ANIMALS
India	Camel
Italy	Cat
Iran	Cheetah
Iraq	Cow
Indonesia	Chicken
Ireland	Calf
Iceland	Cobra
Israel	Caterpillar
	Chimpanzee
	Crocodile

5   Here are a few ideas. You may well have many more different ones.

(a) Install video cameras
(b) Employ more security guards
(c) Severely punish the miscreants
(d) Coat walls with something that cannot be written or drawn on
(e) Pass law abolishing paint spray tins
(f) Lock up all children or potential suspects
(g) Put curtains over offending graffiti
(h) Install fencing to prevent graffitists from getting close enough to walls
(i) Close down the shopping mall
(j) Turn the shopping centre into … a youth club, policy station, art gallery
(k) Demolish the shopping centre
(l) Open a graffiti college
(m) Hold graffiti competitions

6   The first letter is far more personal. The sender has obviously taken the trouble to find out the names of the relevant people within the organisation. It is much more likely to elicit a favourable response.

Chapter 4 :

THE LITERATURE SEARCH

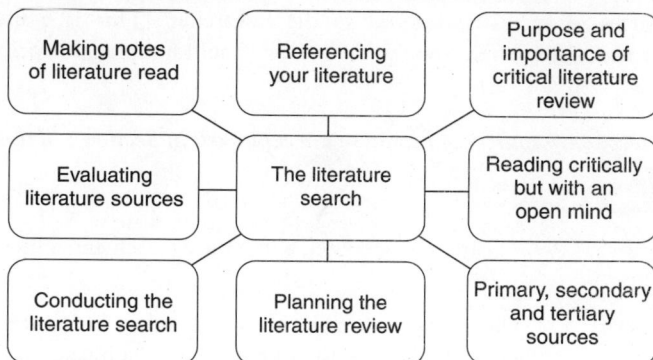

```
┌─────────────────┐   ┌─────────────────┐   ┌─────────────────┐
│  Making notes   │   │   Referencing   │   │  Purpose and    │
│ of literature   │   │  your literature│   │  importance of  │
│     read        │   │                 │   │ critical        │
│                 │   │                 │   │ literature      │
│                 │   │                 │   │ review          │
└─────────────────┘   └─────────────────┘   └─────────────────┘

┌─────────────────┐   ┌─────────────────┐   ┌─────────────────┐
│   Evaluating    │   │  The literature │   │Reading critically│
│literature sources│──│     search      │   │  but with an    │
│                 │   │                 │   │   open mind     │
└─────────────────┘   └─────────────────┘   └─────────────────┘

┌─────────────────┐   ┌─────────────────┐   ┌─────────────────┐
│  Conducting the │   │   Planning the  │   │Primary, secondary│
│literature search│   │ literature review│   │ and tertiary    │
│                 │   │                 │   │   sources       │
└─────────────────┘   └─────────────────┘   └─────────────────┘
```

In Chapter 2, we looked at an overview of the research process. In Chapter 3 we looked at the research proposal, choosing the topic for your research project and other planning issues. In this chapter, we shall look at how you will carry out the literature search of your Research Project in more detail.

Look back at the summary diagram of the research process in Section 3 of Chapter 1, to see where the literature search fits in.

Your objectives

In this chapter you will learn about the following:

(a)   The importance of conducting a literature review

(b)   Primary, secondary and tertiary sources of literature

(c)   How to carry out a literature search and evaluate your sources

(d)   How to reference the sources that you use

1 PURPOSE AND IMPORTANCE OF A CRITICAL LITERATURE REVIEW

1.1 Definition

Sekaran (2000) suggests that a 'literature survey is the documentation of a comprehensive review of the published and unpublished work from secondary sources of data in the areas of specialist interest to the researcher'. This is a useful general definition of a literature review, though the review should not preclude primary sources of literature.

Primary and secondary sources of literature are explained in Section 3 of this chapter.

Hussey and Hussey (1997) distinguish between a literature search and a literature review as follows.

Literature search: The process of exploring the existing **literature** to ascertain what has been written or otherwise published on a particular subject.

Literature review: A written summary of the finding of a **literature search** which demonstrates that the literature has been located, read and evaluated.

Jankowicz (2000) explains that the purpose of a literature search is to help you select, or develop, a framework that will enable you to address your research question. This involves a 'conceptual analysis of the material you encounter, a critical review of other people's ideas, concepts, research findings, models and theories'.

1.2 Scope of search

Brown, McDowell and Race (1995) suggest that 'academic research must show that it is based on a knowledge of previous relevant work and awareness of the relevant theories, debates and controversies'. Gill and Johnson (1997) suggest that a literature survey should provide the reader with 'a statement of the state of the art and the major questions and issues in the field under consideration'.

1.3 Learning approach

According to Bell (1999) 'methods used by other researchers may be unsuitable for your purposes, but they may give you ideas about how you might categorise your own data, the ways in which you may be able to draw on the work of other researchers to support or refute your arguments and conclusions'.

Thus, the process of doing a literature survey should help you to develop the academic writing approach and style you will need when you are writing up your project.

1.4   Benefits of literature searching

At the most basic and practical level you are unlikely to want to waste your valuable time researching something that has already been done. So, it is very important to develop a thorough feel for what is contained in the literature. According to Sekaran (2000)

> *'Sometimes an investigator might spend considerable time and effort to 'discover' something that has already been thoroughly researched. A literature review would prevent such wastage of resources and reinventing the wheel.'*

Saunders *et al* (2003) articulate the case for conducting a literature survey most powerfully by stating that 'your critical literature review will form the foundation on which your research is built'. They explain that the main purpose is to help you develop a good understanding and insight into relevant previous research and the trends that have emerged.

Activity 1   **(15 minutes)**

The various incentive and rationales for carrying out a critical review of literature are well documented in the many books published on research methodology. In the light of what has been covered above, have a go at trying to identify, say, ten key reasons for performing a critical review of literature.

---

2   READING CRITICALLY, BUT WITH AN OPEN MIND

2.1   Survey approach

Hussey and Hussey (1997) explain that 'it is not sufficient merely to describe other research studies which have taken place; you need to appraise critically the contributions of others, and identify trends in research activity and define any areas of weakness'. They suggest that 'this should enable you to argue that your own research is needed'.

Sekaran (2000) points out that a 'literature survey should bring together all relevant information in a cogent and logical manner instead of presenting all the studies in chronological order with bits and pieces of uncoordinated information'

Other authors reinforce the above theme:

> 'A common mistake with critical literature reviews is that they become uncritical listings of previous research.' (Saunders *et al*, 2003)

> 'Often they seem to be uncritical catalogues of all that has been found and vaguely relates to the topic regardless of the merits of the work.' (Gill and Johnson, 1997)

2.2   Handling what you find

Saunders *et al* (2003) advise that within your critical review 'you will need to juxtapose different authors' ideas and form your own opinions and conclusions based on these'. They reveal that 'the key to writing a critical literature review is therefore to link together different ideas you find in the literature to form a coherent and conclusive argument, which set in context and justify your research.'

Luck (1999) suggests that sources which go against the consensus should set your academic 'warning bells' going. He suggests you should consider the circumstances under which the material was assembled and to ask searching questions. There are of course messages for you as well, regarding the care and professionalism you should bring to your own research.

(a) The reasons for the observations made or particular facts recorded

(b) Level of access of the authors to recent evidence

(c) Use of a representative sample

(d) Application of the right controls

(e) Likelihood of the information being collected for one purpose but used for another

(f) Use of the information used to test a hypothesis (answer a research question) or to reinforce a prejudice

(g) Purpose of the work: for academic reasons or commercially sponsored

(h) The extent to which the facts have been summarised

2.3   Analysis, synthesis and accurate communication

Reading, analysis and criticism are all important as highlighted above. However an equally important part of your work is the synthesis and writing-up of all the hard work you would have done. You will need to demonstrate your academic writing skills and be able to write up your critical review of literature in a scholarly way, with precision and clarity. As you work through your literature review, you will no doubt pick up clues on how it is done, how various researchers write up their work.

Jankowicz (2000) emphasises the importance of being able to 'express yourself in a clear, logical and self-consistent manner'. He argues that words such as theories, models, concepts and ideas are often used 'interchangeably and inaccurately'. Jancowicz provides a useful summary of forms of argument and presentation you are likely to encounter in your reading of academic literature, and are yourself likely to use in your project.

Assertion	An utterance written down by yourself: a simple statement
Description	An account of whatever you see to be the case: a series of assertions which define something or some state of affairs. These assertions may or may not be accurate, detailed, or exact. Descriptions are always made from some point of view, or to some purpose; so alternative descriptions are always possible. The case studies which you are given in your lectures (especially at HND level) are neither explanations, models, nor theories: they are descriptions.

Assertion	An utterance written down by yourself: a simple statement
Explanation	A description which provides reasons and thereby removes uncertainty or increases understanding, by means of assertions which say something about the relationships between two or more variables, issues or events, and which draw on previously established principles. You can't claim to have explained something if all you've done is describe it. A very detailed description is almost an explanation, except for one characteristic: an explanation provides sufficient understanding of principles for you to envisage an alternative, or improved state of affairs; a description need not. Explanations are expressed by means of theories, and a theory is more than description.
Theory	A set of statements incorporating principles, using which it is possible to explain a particular occurrence as an instance of a wider set of affairs.
Principle	A statement about the relationships between variables, issues or events, which has been previously researched and found to be accurate in general as well as in specific instances.
Model	Sometimes used loosely to stand for a relatively inaccurate or underspecified theory, the word is properly used to stand for a systematic description which maps or represents some state of affairs. Another way of saying this is that it is a statement of what the state of affairs would look like if your description mapped them accurately or exactly. You design models as a starting point, to enable yourself to experiment with, and understand, the state of affairs.
Analysis	A critical account of the component parts or factors involved in some state of affairs: the variables, issues or events making up the state of affairs. However carefully the parts are described, an analysis doesn't explain the state of affairs, just as a description doesn't explain: you require some reference to principles in order to explain.

Figure 4.1 Forms of argument and presentation
(Jancowicz, 2000, adapted)

So, for example: a description of the lighting system in your room can be provided by a series of assertions about switches, light bulbs, wiring and power sources, enough for your reader to be able to put on the light. A model of the lighting system would be provided by an electrical circuit diagram, and an analysis provided by means of a list of electrical components involved. An explanation of the lighting system would be sufficiently detailed, and refer to just those principles, for your reader to be able to envisage a better system. The principles would be taken from a theory of electricity and, conceivably, materials (Jancowicz, 2000).

3 PRIMARY, SECONDARY AND TERTIARY SOURCES OF LITERATURE

The various publications on research methodology provide detailed lists of their understanding of what comprises primary, secondary and tertiary literature sources. We attempt to summarise these here.

3.1 Primary sources of literature

Primary sources of literature are the first occurrence of a piece of work and could include many sources. These are comprehensively listed below but some of the sources are likely to be more relevant to your research project than others.

(a) Other research reports and dissertations are the obvious source.

(b) Published sources such as some central and local government publications such as white papers and planning documents

(c) Unpublished manuscript sources such as letters, memos and committee minutes

(d) Other literature and pamphlets issued by central or local government. For example, if your research is the field of local government economic development policies, you are likely to be able to gain access to various documentation on economic development schemes.

(e) In-house company reports and documents such as mission statements, core values statements, procedure manuals, auditors' letters of recommendation, market research projects and management accounts.

(Saunders *et al*, 2003; author's own experience)

Luck (1999) warns that 'getting in to any piece of primary literature can be tough. The style may be unfamiliar and the author may have assumed a lot of background on the part of the reader. It can be especially difficult to overcome the feeling that the paper or article was intended for a small group of 'experts' of which you are not (yet) one, all of whom understand the jargon and can instantly recognise the significance of the work.'

Much research will involve looking predominantly at tertiary and secondary sources. However, where you are performing research within your employer or sponsor organisation, you may well obtain much primary data in-house.

Primary data sources

(a) Dissertations, theses and research projects
(b) Project reports
(c) Company annual reports
(d) Market reports and surveys
(e) Conference reports/papers
(f) Law reports
(g) Unpublished research reports
(h) Original articles in academic journals
(i) Research monographs
(j) Maps and charts
(k) Government reports and statistics (some)

(l)   Letters, memos and committee minutes

(m) Corporate brochures and booklets

(n)   In-house market research

(o)   In-house management consulting reports

(p)   Auditors' letters of recommendation

(q)   Original material on the Internet

(r)   Mission statements, core value statements and customer service standards

(s)   Business plans

(t)   Procedures manuals and systems specifications

(u)   Management accounts

3.2   Secondary sources of literature

Introduction

Secondary sources of literature utilise information already published in primary sources (Saunders *et al*, 2003). See below for a list of secondary sources. What follows is a summary of what Saunders *et al* have to say about secondary sources.

(a)   They include sources such as books and journals and subsequent publications of primary literature.

(b)   These publications are aimed at a wider audience.

(c)   They are (usually) easier to locate than primary literature as they are better covered by the tertiary literature (which we will be looking at after this section).

(d)   Many are in electronic form and can be accessed via the Internet or CD ROM.

Refereed academic journals

Saunders *et al* (2003) explain that journals, especially refereed academic journals, are the most important literature source for any research. Articles in **refereed academic journals** (such as the *Journal of Management Studies*) are evaluated by academic peers prior to publication to assess their originality and suitability. These are usually most useful for research projects as they will contain detailed reports of relevant earlier research.

Traditionally these were printed but nowadays you are also likely to find them on the Internet, CD ROM and microfiche. If necessary you can get hold of them via the inter-library loans system.

Practitioner sources of literature

You may also come across professional journals which often contain excellent articles written by distinguished practitioners. However, as Saunders *et al*, (*op. cit.*) caution, they 'are often of a more practical nature and more related to professional needs than those in professional journals'.

They will often reflect the author's views and comments on issues such as legislation or accounting standards and practices, and are not usually based on systematically conducted research. This does not mean that you must not include them in your literature review, but if you do you need to spell out the academic limitations and be able to distinguish between what are either assumptions, assertions, arguments, best practice and researched evidence. They of course may well reveal a wealth of research questions!

EXAMPLE

You might see an article promoting the use of the imprest system of managing petty cash. There are many strong arguments in making an intellectual case for what is essentially a best practice. However, there may be no empirical evidence, gained under properly controlled research conditions, that imprest systems are more effective in controlling petty cash than any other particular system.

Perhaps the above exemplifies the paradigm shift that students have to make from the way business students think to the way a business researcher thinks.

Literature in book format is widely available and well covered by abstracts and indexes. (Abstracts and indexes are described more fully in Section 5.2) Searches can be done on remote university OPACS via the Internet. If these are not available locally, once again, try the inter-library loan system.

Secondary data sources

    (a) Books
    (b) Journals
    (c) Newspapers
    (d) Literature reviews in dissertations and other Research Projects
    (e) Review articles in research journals
    (f) Government reports and statistics (some)
    (g) Radio and TV surveys and broadcasts
    (h) Training videos and disks
    (i) Product reviews
    (j) In-house records and systems
    (k) Electronic databases
    (l) Material on internet

3.3   Tertiary literature sources

Tertiary literature sources are discussed in Section 5 in the context of carrying out the literature review, as they are search tools.

4   PLANNING THE LITERATURE REVIEW

4.1   Introduction

Saunders *et al* (2003) advise that it is important that you plan your literature search carefully 'to ensure that you locate relevant and up-to-date literature'. They add that all their students found their literature search a time consuming process which took far longer than expected and suggest that time spent planning will be repaid in time saved while searching the literature.

Luck (1999) warns that 'reading literature for your project will probably demand higher rates of coverage and assimilation than you are used to. It would therefore be wise to make sure you can do it efficiently'.

4.2 Defining search parameters

Bell (1999) encourages you to identify some search parameters at an early stage, even though they may need to be refined as you go along and actually see the material resulting from your search. Here are some of the key parameters identified in the literature on research methodology:

(a) **The period to be covered by your research**. Your literature search should continue until you complete your research project, so that you remain up to date with developments that might be relevant to your work. You will have to decide how far back to look before the material begins to look out of date. This cut off date can of course be flexible and may be redefined as you do your reading (Bell, 1999; Saunders *et al*, 2003; Hussey and Hussey, 1997).

(b) **The geographic boundaries of your material.** If you live, say in Montevideo, you might want to restrict your search to Montevideo city, or the country of Uruguay itself, or perhaps the whole of South America. Alternatively, you might be brave enough to spread your search over material published in the entire Spanish speaking world.

(c) **The type of literature you would like to include in your search**. Books, journals, theses, government reports, in-house resources, Internet resources (Bell, 1999; Saunders *et al*, 2003).

(d) **Language**. There may be a tendency to restrict the search to material written in English. You may wish to consider material published in other languages, depending on your ability to deal with it.

(e) **Single or multidisciplinary approach**. You might wish to search publications outside your primary area of interest in case they contain important references. For example, if you were studying training, you might screen the corporate strategy literature for work on the role of training in implementing corporate strategy (Hussey and Hussey, 1997).

(f) **Single discipline, but multi-concept approach**. For example, the role of internal controls in improving shareholder value (Hussey and Hussey, 1997).

(g) **Business sector**. You need to decide how focussed you wish your search to be. For example, will you look at the entire retail sector or will you focus on a single sector, such as supermarkets or clothing retailers (Saunders *et al*, 2003)?

Setting research parameters will inevitably need a modicum of common sense. You may well find that the parameters you started with give you either too much literature or too little literature. You may therefore need to play around with your parameters till you achieve a body of literature which is appropriate to your Research Project.

4.3 Using key words

Saunders *et al* (2003) define key words as 'the basic terms' that describe your research question(s) and objectives and will be used to describe the tertiary literature'.

Bell (1999) advises that you should avoid making the focus of your search too narrow, and restricting the number of references you retrieve. To achieve this 'you should organise your topic into subject groups or *sets*, and analyse the keywords in each to try to find as many relevant search terms (key words) as possible'. She suggests that this task might be helped by using a thesaurus.

Brown *et al* (1996) suggests that you should 'play with combinations of key words'. They give the example that keyword 'X' might yield 104 references in a search and keyword 'Y' a further 73 references. Keywords 'X' and 'Y' together may yield only 9 references, which may well be the most important ones for your research.

Brown *et al* (1996) also suggest that it may not be easy to find the right keywords straight away and some trial and error may be involved. You need to be flexible: consider other ways in which the topic might be expressed and try alternatives.

5 CONDUCTING THE LITERATURE SEARCH

5.1 Available approaches

There are probably as many approaches to conducting a literature search as there are published books on research methodology. This is quite understandable as it essentially a practical endeavour and depends a lot on where you are living when you start.

EXAMPLE

(a) Student A lives and works in Birmingham in Britain, may well begin by regularly visiting the library of one of the several Universities in Birmingham, speaking to the librarians, looking through their catalogues, reviewing past research dissertations, searching databases and browsing books and journals on the library shelves.

(b) Student B works on a remote oil installation in Alaska, has access to a computer and is most likely to conduct his or her search on line.

(c) Student C lives and works in a small town fifty miles outside of Shanghai and has been able to negotiate access to the library of one of Shanghai's universities. He or she is likely to use a mixed approach and make use of the library facility by travelling into Shanghai occasionally as well as relying on on-line searching.

Saunders *et al* (2003) suggest various approaches.

(a) Scanning and browsing secondary literature in your library

(b) Obtaining relevant literature referenced in books and journal articles you have already read

(c) Searching using tertiary literature sources

(d) Searching using the Internet

114

5.2   Tertiary literature sources

These are also referred to as **search tools** and are designed either to help to locate primary and secondary literature or to introduce a topic. They therefore include indexes and abstracts as well as encyclopaedias and bibliographies (Saunders *et al*, 2003). A comprehensive list of tertiary sources is provided below.

Tertiary data sources

(a)   Indexes
(b)   Citation indexes
(c)   Abstracts
(d)   Bibliographies
(e)   Catalogues
(f)   Encyclopaedias
(g)   Dictionaries
(h)   Company search services
(i)   Corporate text search services
(j)   Librarians

Indexes

Indexes give details of articles from a range of journals and sometimes books, chapters from books, reports, theses, conferences and research.

Citation indexes

Citation indexes list, by author, the names of other authors who have cited that author's publication in their own subsequent publications. This may provide you with leads to other works that relate to the topic at which you are looking.

Abstracts

The abstract of a paper is a brief summary of its leading elements. Compilations of abstracts (sometimes also known simply, and confusingly, as abstracts) provide clues to the content of an article you are considering obtaining and reading.

You should not to rely on abstracts alone for your literature review as they might not include sufficient detail for your needs.

Indexes and compilations of abstracts are produced in printed and electronic (computerised) formats, the latter often being referred to as databases.

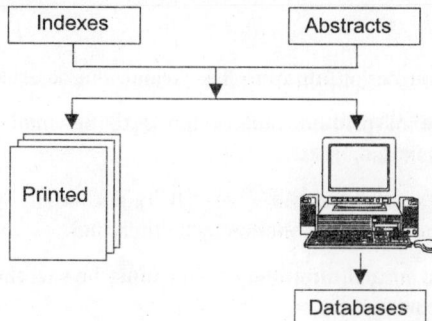

Databases may be in on-line form or off-line, eg in CD ROM form.

We referred to using university libraries' catalogues as one of the starting points for your literature search. In most cases, these are now available on the Internet, and it is possible to make use of other universities' libraries during vacations. Try contacting universities local to you for details.

Databases

When using databases, your key words must match the database's **controlled index language** of pre-selected terms and phrases or descriptors. Your first stage should be to check your key words with the **index** or **browse** option. Some databases will also have a **thesaurus** which links words in the controlled index language to other terms.

Some databases now allow **free text searching** of the entire database. This may seem to make life easier, but might lead to an overload of articles and many irrelevant articles.

In searching databases, you can use what are called 'Boolean operators' (ie the words 'and', 'or' and 'not') to combine, limit or widen the variety of items found.

EXAMPLE

We use an example provided in Hussey and Hussey (1997) to illustrate the use of 'Boolean operators'. Imagine your Research Project topic deals with the marketing of beer and cider in the UK. You decide that your key words are 'marketing', 'beer', 'cider' and 'UK'.

The following table reflects the results of a typical on-line search using 'Boolean operators'.

Search number	Search words	Number of items
1	Beer	712
2	Cider	45
3	Beer or cider	693
4	Marketing and UK	37,872
5	3 and 4	283

In all searches, you need to be aware of your tactics. A widely defined search will yield a lot of references which may be time-consuming to sort through and some of which may be irrelevant. A narrowly defined search may yield too few references.

Printed articles

The search for printed sources of literature has various characteristics.

(a) The coverage of printed indices tends to be smaller and possibly more specialised than databases.

(b) It is normally only possible to search by author or by one subject heading, although some cross-references may be included.

(c) Each issue or annual omnibus edition must be searched individually, which can be time-consuming.

(Saunders *et al*, 2003)

Books

Luck (1999) suggests that you should look at graduate/postgraduate level textbooks as they often have short bibliographies at the end of each chapter listing key references. However, you should check how recent the publication is. He also suggests you should look along the library shelves for related material as you may find something really useful.

Bell (1999) reinforces this message in explaining that a search for printed sources is 'linear in its execution, but you have the opportunity to browse, to see adjacent subject terms, and perhaps discover something relevant by chance. Serendipity is rarer in a computer search because it is more difficult to browse.'

Remenyi *et al* (1998) provide a formal definition of serendipity as 'the happy or pleasant occurrence of discoveries in the course of investigations designed for another purpose'.

However, Jancowicz (2000) suggests that 'simple surfing' of the web might not only be fun, but could lead to the discovery of sources that would otherwise not have occurred to you. He however cautions that this can be enormously time consuming!

Sharp and Howard (1999) advocate unplanned, intermittent and informal search activities.

(a) Browsing sections of the library where books related to your Research Project are kept.

(b) Regular inspections of the new titles shelves.

(c) Casual observation of books and journals.

All the books in your university library will be included in a catalogue, which may be in printed form (usually cards), microfiche or computerised database. Books are catalogued and shelved in accordance with a classification system, such as the well-known Dewey decimal system. This means that a book can only have one position on the library shelf. Books must be returned to their proper places when not in use, but some libraries prefer that you do not do this yourself, instead providing a drop-off point of some kind.

The use of computerised catalogues has been discussed in Section 5.2 above.

To help you access more books we have provided a table of selected publishers' and bookshops' Internet addresses. See below.

Name	Internet address	Contents
Publishers		
BPP Learning Media	www.bpp.com/learningmedia	Professional qualification text books and study materials for students
Blackwell Publishers	http://bookshop.blackwell.co.uk	Books and journals
Cambridge University Press	www.cup.cam.ac.uk	Books and journals, links to other university presses and publishing related services
Pearson Education Limited	http://vig.pearsoned.co.uk/	Business and management books for practitioners and students

Name	Internet address	Contents
Publishers		
The Stationery Office	http://www.tsoshop.co.uk/	TSO publications including full text of Statutory Instruments and Public Acts
Open University Press	http://mcgraw-hill.co.uk/openup/	Books and journals
Oxford University Press	www.oup.co.uk	Books and journals including full text online journals, a database of abstracts
Routledge	www.routledge.com	Books
Sage	www.sagepub.co.uk	Books, journals, software, CD ROMs
Bookshops		
Amazon	www.amazon.co.uk	Searchable database principally of books (UK site)
	www.amazon.com	Searchable database principally of books (USA site)
Blackwell	www.blackwell.co.uk/bookshops	Searchable database principally of books
Abebooks	http://www.abebooks.co.uk/	Global database of second hand book shops' stock

Bibliographies

We see bibliographies most frequently in the form of the lists of cited works that appear at the end of scholarly textbooks; sometimes, they are provided for each chapter rather than for the book as a whole. However, complete books and even series of books are produced on similar principles. These wider ranging bibliographies are books devoted to listing citations, usually in a particular subject area. They may be annotated with brief details of each work listed, so that they become similar to the compilation of abstracts discussed earlier. It is usually possible to use the subject search facility on the library's catalogue to locate bibliographies.

Previous research reports and dissertations

As previously suggested, past dissertations and reports can be very useful to a literature search, both in terms of content as well as providing leads to other literature to look at. Your college library may have a wide selection for various different qualifications.

5.3 Using the Internet

The Internet

The Internet is 'a huge network of networks that connects computers around the world to enable those using them to communicate' (Bell, 1999). It is the means by which email is sent and specific data addresses are accessed

The Internet may provide some useful material. However, as you probably already know, or will soon find out, it is not necessarily the answer to all prayers on research. It has drawbacks, and will almost always need to be supplemented by proper books!

Luck (1999) suggests that

> *'you may be lucky (!) and find a web site or discussion group devoted chiefly to your topic. It would be rare for this to tell you much of great research value, but it may help to inform you about where the main developments in your field are taking place. More likely is that you will pick up references to personal research pages put up by students, academics, research groups or libraries in other universities or research centres around the world. Many academics put up their lecture notes on the web and produce interactive computer aided learning (CAL) packages. These sources can give you references to methods, summaries of recent findings and researchers' names to look for. They will also give you a useful feel for the topicality of your subject. You might find some surprising contextual uses of your otherwise narrowly defined research area.'*

Saunders *et al* (2003) caution on the variability of the quality of materials found on the web. They cite an interesting passage by Clausen (1996) who compares the web to:

> *'... a huge vandalised library where someone has destroyed the catalogue and removed the front matter and indexes from most of the books. In addition thousands of unorganised fragments are added daily by a myriad of cranks, sages and persons with time on their hands to launch their unfiltered messages into cyberspace.'*

Often the terms 'Internet' and 'World Wide Web', though different, are used interchangeably in practice.

The World Wide Web

The World Wide Web, commonly referred to as 'the web' is an advanced aspect of the Internet. It consists of a huge volume of documents that you access and navigate *via* visually highlighted **hypertext links**. These are listed by **search engines** such as **Google** and embedded in the web pages themselves, so that you can move from one document to another.

Websites

Websites are collections of web pages prepared to facilitate access to linked information.

Search engines

A search engine is the most effective way of locating a wide variety of sites on a topic area. You enter the relevant key word(s) and the search engine will find all websites in which the key word(s) feature.

Saunders *et al* (2003) outline four categories of search engines:

(a) General search engines
(b) Meta search engines
(c) Specialised search engines and information gateways
(d) Subject directories

General search engines

(a) Normally searches parts of the Internet using key words and Boolean logic or a phrase

(b) Often find a very large number of sites

(c) The sites are not subject to evaluation and may therefore be inappropriate or unreliable

(d) It is advisable to try out several search engines until you find one or two that you know how to use well, and which bring you good results

(Saunders *et al*, 2003; Bell, 1999)

Meta search engines

(a) Allow you to search using a selection of search engines at the same time, using the same interface.

(b) The search may be easier and faster, but the downside is that it is less easy to control the sites that are retrieved.

(c) You may therefore get more inappropriate and unreliable hits than with using a general search engine.

(Saunders *et al*, 2003)

Specialised search engines

(a) Cater for specific subject areas
(b) It is important to define the general subject area in advance of the search

(Saunders *et al*, 2003)

Information gateways

(a) These guide you to collections of **evaluated** web resources which are organised in a systematic way.

(b) These are often compiled by staff from departments in academic institutions.

(c) The number of web sites obtained is fewer, but can be far more relevant , as each site is evaluated before being added to the gateway.

(d) It is necessary to define your general subject area prior to the search.

(Bell, 1999; Saunders *et al*, 2003)

Subject directories

(a) These are hierarchically organised indexes categorised into subject areas and are useful for searching for broad topics.

(b) These are partially evaluated and hence the number of sites retrieved is fewer and usually provide material that is more appropriate.

(c)   Most now offer some form of keyword search and links to other search tools

(Saunders *et al*, 2003)

E-mail mailing lists

This is a way of communicating with others who might be carrying out research in a similar or the same field as you and is recommended by Jancowicz (2000).

The characteristics of an e-mail mailing list are as follows:

(a)   It provides you with a single e-mail address to which you can send a message.

(b)   Messages sent to this central address are then in turn forwarded onto the other members of the mailing list.

(c)   The help is usually quite meaningful and freely given.

(d)   Some mailing lists are private and restrict access, whilst others are public.

Jankowicz (2000) suggests you should join one or two mailing lists. He suggests that 'a good one to try is the mailbase.ac.uk system, a collection of over 1,700 different mailing lists, including 79 in the business and administrative sciences'.

Research can be a lonely and solitary experience and joining an email mailing list can be a way, to help you to share your ideas and experiences with others and provide a modicum of social fulfilment from your research. As Jankowicz suggests:

> *'Membership of one or two research mailing lists provides you with an excellent opportunity to share your experiences, your troubles and triumphs!'*

Bookmarking

When you have found a useful Internet site, do remember to bookmark it or add it to favourites, depending on your Internet software.

5.4   Inter-library loans

If any book is not available from a library, it might be obtainable through the inter-library loan system. Before you make use of it, do check how much it will cost and how long it will take to arrive.

6   EVALUATING LITERATURE SOURCES

6.1   Relevance

Bell (1999) argues that 'the aim of your research is to retrieve information of direct relevance to your research and to avoid being side tracked or overloaded with material of a peripheral nature'. She suggests you should look at the following criteria:

(a)   Respectability of sources
(b)   Citing of the author's name by others
(c)   Appearance of author's name in other bibliographical sources
(d)   Referencing of vital points to facilitate checking
(e)   References are up-to-date with current developments

Saunders *et al* (2003) provide a useful checklist for evaluating the relevance of literature, which we have reproduced for you here.

    (a) How recent is the item?

    (b) Is the item likely to have been superseded?

    (c) Is the context sufficiently different to make it marginal to your research question(s) and objectives?

    (d) Have you seen references to this item (or its author) in other items that were useful?

    (e) Does the item support or contradict your arguments? In either case, it will probably be worth reading.

    (f) Does the item appear to be biased? Even if it is, it may still be relevant to your critical review.

    (g) What are the methodological omissions within the work? Even if there are many, it still may be useful.

    (h) Is the precision sufficient? Even if it is imprecise it may be the only item you can find and so still be of relevance.

(Sources: Saunders *et al*, 2003; Bell, 1999; Jancowicz, 1995; McNeill, 1990)

Luck (1999) provides a light hearted comment, and perhaps some encouragement, in relation to identifying relevant literature:

> 'You are likely to chase several shoals of red herring and many flocks of wild geese before the first part of the hunt is over, but don't dismay. Very often, knowing what you are not looking for is as valuable as finding the correct material straight away.'

6.2   Sufficiency

Whatever your topic and field of research, there is likely to be a lot of literature available for you to review.

According to Luck (1999) questions that researchers frequently ask can be summarised as follows.

    (a) How long does my literature survey need to be?
    (b) How many references do I need?
    (c) How much is expected?
    (d) When should I stop searching?

It will be impossible for you to read absolutely everything on the subject you are researching. Your tutor may be able to help you judge how much reading you need to do.

Luck (1999) offers the following pieces of wisdom:

> 'One thing to be very sure about is that covering the literature is not a competition – your examiners are looking for an appropriate amount of carefully selected and critically assessed reading and will not at all be impressed by a long list of unstructured material. Remember, the most interesting stamp collections are small, focussed and thematically organised rarities of great value; vast assemblies of random acquisitions are just so many squares of sticking paper.'

7   MAKING NOTES OF LITERATURE READ

7.1   Key message

It is important that you keep notes and think about the relevance of everything that you read. This means that you will be able to decide effectively whether to use given material in your research project.

Luck (1999) postulates three golden rules for what you have read:

(a) Do it properly

(b) Do it once and only once

(c) Do it for every paper you read

'Sooner or later some or all of the references will have to be compiled into a list for a dissertation or thesis or an article on an academic journal. They must, therefore, be recorded in sufficient detail to facilitate this process and preferably in such a way that the multiplicity of different referencing standards – for example, numbered in order of appearance, listed in alphabetical order – are readily accommodated.'

(Sharp and Howard, 1996)

7.2   Ways to record

There are essentially four ways you can record what you have read:

(a) Paper based methods, eg index cards

(b) Proprietary computer word processing software text files

(c) Proprietary computer database software such as Access

(d) Specialist bibliographical software such as Reference Manager for Windows, EndNote and Pro-Cite

Luck (1999) cautions that when using database or spreadsheet software, you must 'give sufficient thought to design the table right at the outset. Make sure you can enter and retrieve data easily, and avoid setting any constraints, such as filed data types or character limits, which might require you to compromise any information which is in an unusual format.'

7.3   Benefits of bibliographical software

Specialist bibliographical software may be expensive but has many benefits. They

(a) Prompt you for the appropriate information

(b) Produce output in any required style

(c) Have good searching facilities (you can create a keyword list)

(d) Have ways of preventing errors such as duplications and missing page numbers

(e) Can be set up to import data directly from on-line search engines, saving any typing completely

(f) Can be integrated with your personal computer allowing you to include references from your bibliography directly into your text at writing up time and also generating a complete, ready-made bibliography at the end of your Research Project   (Luck, 1999)

7.4 Backing-up your work

Luck (1999) issues the usual warning about making up back ups of computer files. They suggest making not one but two copies. The message is to be prepared for something disastrous to happen to your computer.

7.5 What to record

You should make notes on each item you read. Here is a list of possible entries drawn from various sources.

(a) Useful quotations (in full) with page number

(b) Where it was found: own library, inter-library loan, borrowed from supervisor etc

(c) The tertiary source used to help identify resources for follow up searches

(d) Date of items found on the Internet, as these may disappear

(e) Strengths and weaknesses of the work

(f) How the source relates to others ('follows from Smith, 2003', 'Repeats Jones, 1999', 'Disagrees with Frazer *et al*, 2001')

(g) Your current opinion of how useful the source is ('Useful', 'Informative', 'Speculative', 'Critical', 'Peripheral', 'Detailed', 'Rubbish' etc.)

(h) Methodological details

(i) Extracts from tables and graphs

(j) Any contradictions or paradoxes that might suggest research opportunities

(Saunders *et al*, 2000; Luck, 1999; Remenyi *et al*, 1998)

We have also made up illustrative examples of the essential bibliographical information you should record for a journal or research paper, a book or a book chapter.

Journal references

Author(s) – family name, initials	Knowles, I
Year of publication (in brackets)	(2003)
Title of article/paper	The Impact of Information Management in the Accountancy Profession
Title of journal (underlined)	Financial accounting research
Volume (bold)	3
Part/issue	2
Page number (preceded by 'p' for page and 'pp' for pages)	pp. 1-84

Figure 4.2 Journal/Research paper bibliographical details

Book references

Author(s) – family name, initials	Smart, A, Brave B and Wise, C
Year of publication (in brackets)	(2003)
Title and subtitle of book	*Management styles in the Accounting Profession*
Edition	4th
Place of publication (first listed place)	Oxford
Publisher	Edukatia

Figure 4.3 Book bibliographical details

Edited compilation references

Author(s) – family name, initials	Babeoke, U
Year of publication (in brackets)	(2003)
Title of chapter	Comparison of performance of firms with organic and mechanistic structures
Editor(s) of book – surname, first name initials	Wachem, I
Title and subtitle of book	Competition in the Accountancy Profession – Strategy and Structure of Practitioner Firms
Edition	3rd
Place of publication (first listed place)	Glasgow
Publisher	McArunie
Page numbers of chapter	267 – 321

Figure 4.4 Chapter in edited book bibliographical details

You might wish to begin by piloting your literature search records using a paper based pro-forma for two or three sources before you commit to developing a computerised version.

8   REFERENCING YOUR LITERATURE

8.1   Introduction

According to Bell (1999), 'as you write up your research you will use a **citation** to indicate in your text the source of a piece of information, a paraphrase or a quotation from another work'.

Hussey and Hussey (1997) formally define **citation** as

> *'An acknowledgement within the text of a document of the sources from which you have obtained the information.'*

You will then provide a formal reference list of the sources of your citations.

Bell (1999) explains that '**references**, then, give details of books, articles and any other types of material that you have cited in the text'.

Hussey and Hussey (1997) defines a reference as

> '*A detailed, alphabetical (Harvard System) or numerical (Vancouver System) list of sources from which information has been obtained and which have been cited in the text of the document.*'

Hussey and Hussey (1997) give three reasons for accurate citations and full references.

(a) They help the reader distinguish between your own ideas and findings, and those gleaned from the literature.

(b) They help your arguments by showing the extent to which independent theoretical and empirical sources support them, although this depends on the quality and appropriateness of those sources.

(c) They enable readers to refer to the original sources for themselves.

There are two main systems of referencing, the Harvard System and the Vancouver System. The Vancouver System is used primarily for physical sciences such as physics and chemistry whereas the Harvard System is used in social sciences and business studies fields. The Harvard method of citing and referencing is probably more suitable for the form of the HND Research Project. It is the system used throughout this book.

8.2 Harvard method of citation

The Harvard System of citation requires you to acknowledge certain information.

(a) The family name of the author(s)
(b) The year of publication
(c) The page number(s) where you have quoted material directly

In succeeding sentences or paragraphs, you need not repeat the year, provided it is clear you are citing the same work.

EXAMPLE

In a study on the financial structures of quoted food retailers companies, Chan (1998) reported that their current ratios were in the range 0.8:1.0 to 0.9:1.0, well below the 1.5:1.0 usually recommended in financial accounting textbooks.

In a study on the financial structures of quoted food retailers, it was reported that their current ratios fell into the range 0.8:1.0 to 0.9:1.0, well below the 1.5:1.0 usually recommended in financial accounting textbooks. (Chan, 1998)

In a study on the financial structures of quoted food retailers, it was reported that 'calculation of current ratios for all ten of supermarket chains listed on the Anyland Stock Exchange revealed that they operated with current ratios in the range 0.8 to 0.9, well below the 1.5 to 1.0 recommended in accounting textbooks'. (Chan, 1998, p. 88)

There will be circumstances where there is more than one authority that needs to be cited.

EXAMPLE

A number of research studies have been conducted into the level of implementation by clients of auditors' recommendations on internal control weaknesses (Sobers, 1997; Lara, 1998; Richards, 2001).

In other instances, you may need to cite multiple authors.

EXAMPLE

First citation

A study by Armstrong, Bean and Collins (2002) on the measures taken by UK companies to prepare for the implementation of International Financial Reporting Standards revealed that ...

or

A study on the measures taken by UK companies to prepare for the implementation of International Financial Reporting Standards (Armstrong, Bean and Collins, 2002) revealed that ...

Subsequent citation

A study by Armstrong *et al* (2002) revealed that ...

or

A study on the measures taken by UK companies to prepare for the implementation of International Financial Reporting Standards (Armstrong *et al*, 2002) revealed that ...

8.3   Listing references within the Harvard System

This is an example of how you might reference a book within the Harvard System.

EXAMPLE

Knott, Shirley Y. (2002) *Entrepreneurial risk taking in family businesses* (4th ed.), London: Publikatia

Deare, Ivan I. (2001) *Innovation in the Management Training* (3rd ed.), Melbourne: Platapus

There may be circumstances where you wish to refer to a chapter in a book which consists of contributions from many different authors. In such instances, you should acknowledge the editor of the book. You should reference both the chapter and the book, with the more specific reference coming first.

EXAMPLE

Cord, Annette (2002), 'The role of service charges in the motivation of catering staff' in Bowe, Dennis L. (ed.) *Rewards, Motivation and Performance in the Hotel and Catering Industry*, Grimsby: Lithoforia

Given the general presence of electronic sources of literature, you may need to include such in your list of references. We provide the following examples which are drawn from Hussey and Hussey (1997) who in turn have drawn on the work of Li and Crane (1995).

Full-text or bibliographic databases

Reference for a book

Author (date) *Title of book*, (edition) [Type of medium]. Available: Give sufficient information to allow retrieval of a book or abstract

Reference for an article

Author (date) 'Title', *Name of journal* [Type of medium] volume number (issue number) page numbers. Available: Give sufficient information to allow retrieval of article or abstract

Electronic Conferences (Interest Groups) or Bulletin Board Services

Author of message (date) subject of message, *Electronic Conference/Bulletin Board Services* [On-line]. Available e-mail: LISTSERV@e-mail address

Personal email

Author (date) *Subject of message* [e-mail to recipient's name], [On-line]. Available e-mail: Recipient's e-mail address.

Source: Hussey and Hussey (1997, p. 105)

Figure 4.5 General form for referencing main electronic sources

Activity 2 (20 minutes)

(a) George Franklin published a book in 1999, with a new edition in January 2006. The book was called 'Analysing the Retail Industry' and was published in Manchester by Business Publishers Ltd.

Show how you would acknowledge the most recent edition in the text of your report and in the bibliography.

(b) In the July 2003 issue of *Marketing Monthly* magazine there is an article by Sam Keller entitled 'Grasping the nettle: marketing the organic drinks phenomenon'.

Show how you would acknowledge the article in the text of your report and in the bibliography.

(c) The *Sunday Times* Business section contained a comment on the state of the British scheduled airline industry on page 3 of the issue of June 15th 2003. The comment had no attributable author name.

Show how you would acknowledge the comment in the text of your report and in the bibliography.

(d) On June 24th 2003, it was possible to read a comment by Anthea Rose on the ACCA's website (www.acca.co.uk) to the effect that the government is imposing too much red tape on small businesses. The comment was included in an article entitled 'Raising the audit threshold – raising the risk of fraud' which was originally posted on May 15th 2003.

Show how you would acknowledge this in the text of your Report and in the bibliography.

Chapter roundup

- The literature review is a review of published and unpublished work from secondary sources of data.

- Your literature review will probably include primary, secondary and tertiary sources of literature.

- It is important to plan your literature review adequately, to make the best use of your time.

- the Internet will form an important element in your literature review, but should be used with care and not used exclusively.

- Literature sources should be evaluated for relevance and sufficiency.

- It is essential that you adequately record your sources of literature, to enable you to reference them.

- References should be done following the Harvard system of citation.

Answers to activities

1   1   Provides background to and justification for your Research Project. It is an activity that should also help to 'guide and inform' your research (Hussey and Hussey, 1997).

    2   Helps to refine research question(s) and objectives; ensures these are stated with precision and clarity (Sekaran, 2000; Gall *et al*, 1996).

    3   Helps avoid repeating research already done (Luck, 1999; Sekaran, 2000).

    4   Prevents the likelihood of going down 'blind alleys' which others have already encountered. (Luck, 1999)

    5   Identifies the gaps in current knowledge (Hussey and Hussey, 1997; Luck 1999).

    6   Highlights research opportunities that have been overlooked implicitly in research to date (Gall *et al*, 1996).

    7   Discovers explicit recommendations for further research (Gall *et al*, 1996).

    8   Adds value to or provides informed criticism of what has gone before (Luck, 1999).

    9   Discovers and provides insights into research strategies and methodologies (Cresswell, 1994; Sharp and Hough, 1996).

    10 Acknowledges and makes proper reference to previous work. This will help to avoid the risks of plagiarism (Luck, 1999; Saunders *et al*, 2003)

2   (a) In the text:
         (Franklin, 2006)
         In the bibliography:
         Franklin, G. (2006) Analysing the Retail Industry 2nd edition, Manchester, Business Publishers.

    (b) In the text:
         (Keller, 2003)
         In the bibliography:
         Keller, S. (2003) Grasping the nettle: marketing the organic drinks phenomenon, Marketing Monthly, July

    (c) In the text:
         (The Sunday Times, 2003)
         In the bibliography:
         The Sunday Times (2003) Business section, June 15th, p.3

    (d) In the text:
         (Rose, 2003)
         In the bibliography:
         Rose, A. Raising the audit threshold – raising the risk of fraud. www.acca.co.uk 15th May 2003. Accessed on 23rd June 2003

Chapter 5 :

METHODS OF DATA COLLECTION: PRIMARY AND SECONDARY SOURCES

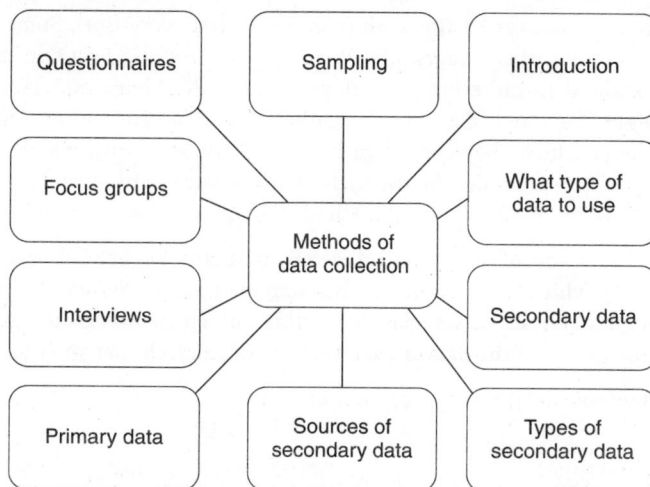

```
┌─────────────────┐   ┌─────────────────┐   ┌─────────────────┐
│ Questionnaires  │   │    Sampling     │   │  Introduction   │
└─────────────────┘   └─────────────────┘   └─────────────────┘

┌─────────────────┐                         ┌─────────────────┐
│  Focus groups   │                         │  What type of   │
└─────────────────┘      ┌──────────┐       │   data to use   │
                         │ Methods of │      └─────────────────┘
                         │    data    │
┌─────────────────┐      │ collection │      ┌─────────────────┐
│   Interviews    │      └──────────┘        │ Secondary data  │
└─────────────────┘                          └─────────────────┘

┌─────────────────┐   ┌─────────────────┐   ┌─────────────────┐
│  Primary data   │   │   Sources of    │   │    Types of     │
│                 │   │ secondary data  │   │ secondary data  │
└─────────────────┘   └─────────────────┘   └─────────────────┘
```

Your objectives

In this chapter you will learn about the following:

(a) The difference between primary and secondary data and when they should be used

(b) Types of secondary data

(c) Sources of secondary data

(d) The main types of primary data: interviews, focus groups and questionnaires

(e) The uses of sampling in data collection

1 INTRODUCTION

The word data is very wide-ranging. Hussey and Hussey (1997) define it as 'known facts or things used as a basis for inference or researching'. The key distinction is that between primary and secondary data, and your research will probably involve a combination of both. There is a lot of disparity in the means of gathering data. As Sharp and Howard (1996) point out:

> 'On occasions it may be necessary to await rather infrequent events, as in a study of volcanic eruptions, or the actual process of obtaining the measurements may be long drawn out, as in certain biomedical tests.'

You should therefore not expect the earth to move for you every time. Some data are far more difficult to obtain than others, and this might be usefully borne in mind as you approach the main data-gathering part of your work. As Sharp and Howard (1996) remark, the *process* by which data may be gathered and recorded often sets a definite limit on the *rate* at which they can be gathered and the ease with which they can be analysed. In some very complex fields, such as radio astronomy, virtually all data are gathered and recorded by computerised methods (Sharp and Howard, 1996).

Before we explore some of the practical detail, it might be helpful to consider the assumptions upon which your choice of research methods is based. As discussed in Chapter 3, individual researchers may have different epistemological outlooks. This might affect your review of the data or even the type of research that you do.

Here we illustrate some contrasting approaches.

Activity 1 (30 minutes)

What would you say are the key differences between the research methods below?

Situation 1

You have just been into a lecture on financial reporting. After the lecture a member of the training staff approaches you and says 'I am carrying out a survey into how students view the quality and service we provide. By collecting a representative view of our students' needs, we will be able to improve our training service. The results will be fed into a database and anonymity is guaranteed'. You are then asked a series of pre-scripted questions, to which you must choose an option for an answer. (For example, 'would you rate our trainers as poor, fair, good or excellent?') After answering the questions, the interviewer takes some of your personal details, thanks you and then proceeds to another student asking the same questions.

Situation 2

A pharmaceutical company is researching a new type of vaccine for influenza. Its scientists believe there could be a relationship between certain aspects of the virus's chemistry and the immune system.

It has given small doses of the vaccine to ten paid volunteers, who for the duration of the test are living in a special research facility. These volunteers are being monitored to see how the vaccine affects them when they are exposed to flu. At another research facility, the same number of volunteers is being given a 'placebo' and are also exposed to the virus.

Blood tests will be taken, so that scientists can see how the vaccine affects the body's response to the flu virus.

Situation 3

You have been asked to join a small group of five people for an evening to do some 'focus group research' on makes of car. The researcher introduces topics of conversation and asks people what they feel about motoring, what they feel about different brands of car, what their motoring habits are, and what frustrates them most about motoring and motor cars.

The researcher intervenes from time to time to steer the conversation to topics of interest or to clarify what people have said.

Situation 4

A researcher for an investment banking firm is reviewing companies engaged in e-commerce. She has obtained financial statements of twenty firms, and also details of movements in their respective share prices over the past four years. From this she compares data and compiles a report.

1.1 Types of data

As we have seen, the two main categories of data are primary and secondary. We look at these from your perspective as a researcher.

	Secondary data	Primary data
What they are	Data neither collected directly by the user nor specifically for the user, often under conditions unknown to the user – in other words, data collected by someone else for their own purposes or for general use	Data that are collected specifically by or for the user, at source – in other words by you in the course of your research.
Quantitative, 'factual' or 'objective' example	Government reports – in the UK a good example is Social Trends, which contains government statistics about British society, employment in different industries, attitudes and so on. Such a report might be relevant to a dissertation involving some aspect of human resources, personnel development or consumer marketing.	A survey you conduct with a questionnaire you have designed, with regard to a sample. You aim to be able to evaluate results statistically.

An experiment. |

	Secondary data	Primary data
	A company's published financial statements summarise and interpret company transactions data for the benefit of shareholders, not the needs of your dissertation.	
Qualitative example	An article in the Harvard Business Review or in a book about theories of motivation.	A focus group you have conducted (in the manner of Situation 3 above) to talk about motivation

Activity 2 (15 minutes)

Below are some scenarios from an unpublished undergraduate dissertation. Have a look at them and try to identify areas of primary and secondary research.

1   Initially the work I carried out on the project was extremely informal in that whenever I met a salesman or spoke to a manager I would ask about their feelings towards the present pay scheme or the method by which targets were allocated. When salesmen complained about errors in their commission payments due to faults in the payment scheme, I was in an ideal position to suggest changes and refinements in the pay scheme to managers.

2   Following this initial exploration, I decided to familiarise myself with the theory behind targeting specifically and, more generally, how information and control systems influence behaviour. At the same time, I spoke to people outside Q Ltd, both from academic backgrounds and in other selling companies, so as to develop wider ideas and to compare Q Ltd with other selling firms.

3   Once I felt well briefed about the problem, I sought permission from the Southern Sales Director (Mr X) to interview his sales managers. He requested a questionnaire which I forwarded to him. Mr X made minor adjustments to this in form rather than content. For example, one question I asked was, 'Why do you think Q Ltd has higher turnover of salesmen than other similar companies?', this was changed to: 'Do you think Q Ltd has a higher turnover of salesmen than other similar companies? If so, why? (see appendix 1).

4   I developed the questionnaire with the background knowledge I had acquired and discussed some of the questions with Mr A, the Statistics and Finance Manager, my immediate superior.

> 5   Over a period of about a month I interviewed five sales managers, each interview lasting about one hour. I felt the questionnaire was a little restrictive, therefore I chose to approach the interviews informally using the questionnaire as a check that I had covered most of the points. This was specifically important as I felt that the atmosphere of the interview would be at least as important as the mechanics of the interview. I realised that this would require me to be flexible, but I didn't realise just how flexible I would have to be. I organised one interview and found that this manager shared his room with another manager so I spent much of the interview making notes on discussion between the two of them, acting as a catalyst when discussion waned. This particular interview was especially useful since it uncovered issues such as the education and training of management that would otherwise have been overlooked. I decided to make written notes rather than a tape-recording because I though that might be off-putting to the managers.
>
> 6   During the interviewing and recording process I tried to avoid personal bias and judgement and when incorporating findings into this text I tried to avoid jumping to simplistic conclusions without considering their implications.

Duffy (1999) provides a useful further explanation of the difference between primary and secondary data.

(a) 'Primary sources are those which came into existence in the period under research' (for example the minutes of company board meetings) and

(b) 'Secondary sources are interpretations of events of that period based on primary sources' (for example a summary of the activities of the year derived from the board meeting minutes, among other sources)

Stewart and Kamins (1993) explain that:

*'the use of secondary information is often referred to as **secondary analysis** (or research). Secondary analysis is simply a further analysis of information that has already been obtained. Such analysis may be related to the original purpose for which the data was collected, or it may address an issue quite different from that which prompted the original data-gathering effort. It may involve the integration of information from several sources or a reanalysis of data from a single source'.*

2   WHAT TYPE OF DATA TO USE

2.1   The mixed methods approach

The **mixed methods approach** combines secondary data and primary data collected using a variety of methods.

This approach can overcome one of the main drawbacks of secondary data, which is that it is often **not of direct relevance** to your research objective. By using appropriate primary data to 'plug the gaps' you should be able to obtain the complete picture. This might be the case where you are researching an issue within an organisation.

Authors tend to agree that it is useful to use more than one method of data collection. Bell (1999) says that efforts should be made to cross-check findings by the use of different methods that lead you to a consistent conclusion. This is called **triangulation** and is defined by the Open University (1998) like this:

'......*cross checking the existence of certain phenomena and the veracity of individual accounts by gathering data from a number of informants and a number of sources and subsequently comparing and contrasting one account with another in order to produce as full and balanced a study as possible.*'

Activity 3   **(15 minutes)**

You are carrying out research into the effectiveness of different management structures. You would like to confirm a research hypothesis that an organic structure with a team-working and information-sharing culture is more effective for a publisher of financial and business books than a mechanistic structure based on classical management principles and with strong demarcations of responsibility and individual retention of information. What sort of areas would you research?

Bell (1999) suggests what she calls a **'problem-oriented approach'**. You would start with secondary sources: reading what has already been discovered about the subject would provide essential background and help to establish the focus of your work. You would then proceed to the relevant primary sources, which will help you to move your research a stage further on, possibly to the point of developing new theory.

Jankowicz (2000) provides a good summary of the role of secondary data.

'*The balance of primary and secondary data can make the difference between a good and a poor project. It would be very unusual to find a good project with no reference to other people's writings, whether the references are presented as a formal separate literature review, or are interpreted among your own material. Similarly, a project with no empirical content which you'd originated yourself would be unlikely to be successful.*'

3 SECONDARY DATA

3.1 Advantages of secondary data

Cost-effectiveness

Collecting primary data can be very expensive and this may mean that you are restricted to gathering a limited amount of data. The collecting of secondary data is more cost-effective, especially in the case of very wide-ranging or large-scale data, such as that included in official statistics.

Time

The collection of primary data can be very time-consuming. Even the distribution, chasing up and subsequent analysis of the results of a questionnaire can take a period of months, and that amount of time may be a luxury that you don't have. You may take the view that it is more efficient (and economic) to utilise data from other sources. This would enable you to use a wider range of data and spend more time analysing and interpreting it (Saunders *et al*, 2003).

Quality

Secondary data (for example government department statistics) will often be of much higher quality than that you could expect to gather yourself (Stewart and Kamins, 1993). This is because the collector of the information will have been able to allocate far more time and resource (especially financial resource) to the exercise than you. This is especially true of data that has been gathered over a long period of time, as you are not in a position to gather data for a period of years.

Similarly, you would never be in a position to gather as much demographic information as can be found in a document such as the UK government's ten-yearly census.

Discretion

The use of secondary data within an organisational context can be more discreet than the use of primary data. It will not be immediately obvious what you are researching and your research will be far less obtrusive; this may be of help if you are researching a sensitive topic, such as employee motivation.

Use as a benchmark

Secondary data can be useful as a benchmark to compare with your own primary data. This can put your primary research into context and highlight any unexpected discrepancies. If the results of your research are not compatible with the results of more far-reaching and detailed work, you should be alerted initially to potential problems within your own results.

Unexpected discoveries

It is sometimes the case that an important discovery is made as a result of research into something completely different. An illustration is the inadvertent discovery of penicillin by Fleming, who was actually investigating the properties of staphylococci at the time.

A permanent source of information

It is commonly acknowledged that secondary data is permanent (as it has been published) and is available in a form that can be accessed and checked reasonably easily by others (Denscombe, 1998). The data and your research findings are more open to public scrutiny (Saunders *et al*, 2003) meaning that they inspire greater confidence in those relying on the data.

3.2   Disadvantages of secondary data

You should be aware of the potential disadvantages of secondary data. Some of them will be of particular relevance when you are evaluating the secondary data you have collected.

Access

Much data is protected by intellectual property law and is only available for a fee, if at all. Where the original collectors of data have incurred a lot of expense in gathering them, it is less likely that they will provide them to you free of charge. Large-scale market research reports, for example, may cost hundreds of pounds. You may be able to access documents such as these in a library, but according to Saunders *et al* (2003) such material is often barred from the inter-library loan service, meaning that you would have to travel a long way to visit a library copy.

Relevance

By definition, secondary data have not been initially collected by or for you. Someone else has collected them for his or her specific purpose, under conditions unknown to you. This means that they may not exactly match your research objective, and you will have to engage in additional, possibly primary, research to complete the picture. The example cited by Saunders *et al* (2003) concerns the age of the secondary data concerned and the fact that the information is not sufficiently current. You might have to engage in primary research to bring data up to date.

There may also be an impact on the means of presentation of the data, depending on the purpose of the original report. This is especially the case for internal organisational documents and external documents, such as company published accounts and newspaper reports (Saunders *et al*, 2003). The document you are seeking to rely on may have been prepared for a specific and limited purpose, and there may therefore be insufficient supporting data for your purposes.

Reliability

It may not be apparent who collected the secondary data and for what purpose. If you do not know whose research it is, it may be unwise to rely on it without carrying out some corroborative research to verify it. The authority of the source of the secondary data and the procedures used to produce the original data will need to be evaluated in order to establish its credibility as a source of information for you (Denscombe, 1998).

The preparer of the secondary data may have been biased or have had some personal or corporate axe to grind. Trade associations, for example, may not include data that run counter to the interests of their members.

In particular, where sampling techniques are used, their correctness may be unclear, and you may not therefore be confident that the conclusions are valid.

Activity 4   **(5 minutes)**

The French producer of the natural spring water, Vittel, published the results of a survey in late 2001. It indicated that a majority of people who participated in tests felt healthier after drinking a glass of Vittel than they did after drinking a cup of coffee.

What reservations might you have about using this survey as a source of evidence in your own research?

---

4   TYPES OF SECONDARY DATA

'Secondary data include both quantitative and qualitative data and can be used in both descriptive and explanatory research.' (Saunders *et al*, 2003). Additionally the data may be described as **raw** in that it has not been processed to any degree, or it may be described as **compiled** in that it has undergone some form of selection or summarising. (Kervin, 1999).

Saunders *et al* (2003) have drawn on various works on the classification of secondary data, and distilled these into three main sub-groups of secondary data:

(a)   Documentary data
(b)   Survey-based data
(c)   Multiple source data

They are summarised in Figure 5.1.

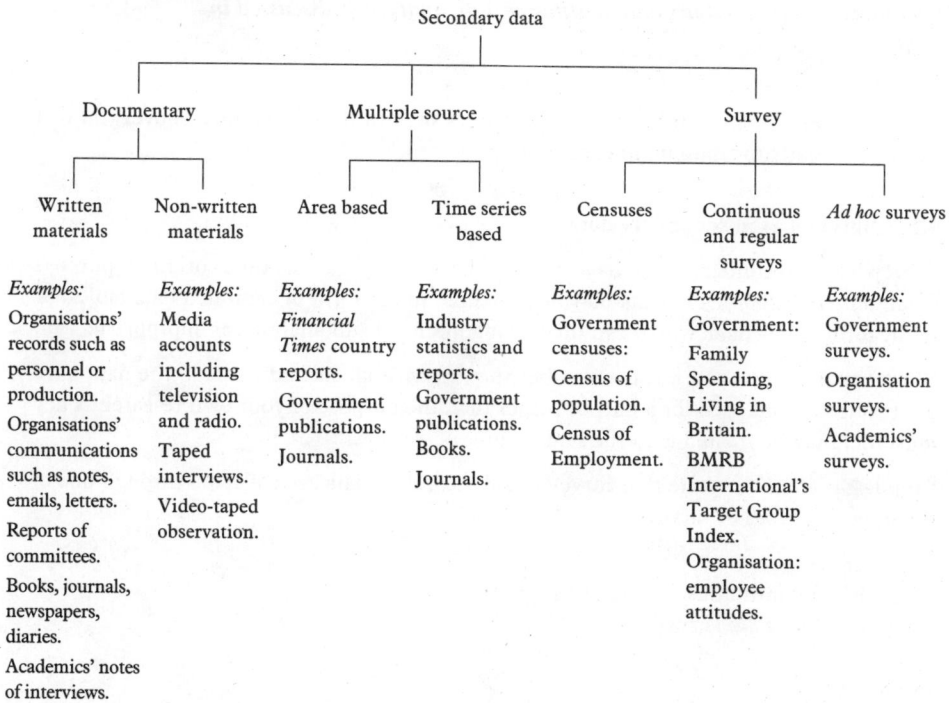

Secondary data						
Documentary		**Multiple source**		**Survey**		
Written materials	Non-written materials	Area based	Time series based	Censuses	Continuous and regular surveys	*Ad hoc* surveys
Examples: Organisations' records such as personnel or production. Organisations' communications such as notes, emails, letters. Reports of committees. Books, journals, newspapers, diaries. Academics' notes of interviews.	*Examples:* Media accounts including television and radio. Taped interviews. Video-taped observation.	*Examples:* *Financial Times* country reports. Government publications. Journals.	*Examples:* Industry statistics and reports. Government publications. Books. Journals.	*Examples:* Government censuses: Census of population. Census of Employment.	*Examples:* Government: Family Spending, Living in Britain. BMRB International's Target Group Index. Organisation: employee attitudes.	*Examples:* Government surveys. Organisation surveys. Academics' surveys.

Figure 5.1 Sub-groups of secondary data

Source: Saunders *et al* (2003)

4.1   Documentary secondary data

This sub-classification contains both **written** and **non-written** documents (Saunders *et al*, 2003).

The written documentary data includes, for example:

(a)   Books

(b)   Journal and magazine articles

(c)   Newspapers

(d)   Transcripts of speeches

    (e) Diaries

    (f) Public records

    (g) Company records, such as notices, correspondence, minutes of meetings, press releases and reports to shareholders

The non-written sources of documentary data include:

    (a) Tape and video recordings
    (b) Pictures and drawings
    (c) Films and television programmes

Saunders *et al* (2003) maintain that the non-written documentary data can be analysed both quantitatively and qualitatively.

Quantitative data analysis and qualitative data analysis is discussed in Chapter 6.

If you use both written and non-written sources such as those described above, you will also find it easier to **triangulate** your findings.

4.2   Survey-based secondary data

Survey-based secondary data have already been analysed for their original purpose (Saunders *et al*, 2003). The data may be presented in the form of compiled data tables or in the form of raw data, which can then be manipulated and analysed as appropriate.

Whatever the form, you must remember that, as with all secondary data, the data have been collected and used for a purpose other than the purpose of your own research. They must therefore be treated with the same degree of wariness.

Saunders *et al*, (2003) state that survey-based secondary data are collected through one of three specific types of survey:

    (a) A census
    (b) A continuous or regular survey, or
    (c) An *ad hoc* survey

Census

A national government usually carries out a census, and participation is invariably compulsory. In the UK, for example, a census is held once every 10 years, the most recent having been in 2001. Each census provides very comprehensive and complete demographic information, and it is its completeness that makes it of particular value to the student researcher, although its main purpose is to provide information for government departments and local government.

Continuous and regular surveys

These are surveys that are repeated over time. This could mean that they are regularly repeated or they are continuously ongoing.

EXAMPLE

Saunders *et al* (2003) list some examples of continuous and regular surveys.

Continuous	Regular
The UK General Household Survey	Labour Force Survey (within the European Union)
Family Spending	BMRB International's Target Group Index

Again we would also point you to surveys done at your local level by local government and local non-government organisations (NGOs). These may well be easily accessible from the offices of the organisation itself or from your local library.

One of the values of survey-based secondary data lies in the fact that they can be used as a **benchmark** against which to evaluate your own data, whether primary or from other sources. You are likely to have greater faith in your own data if they are corroborated by evidence from government or other official surveys.

Ad hoc surveys

Saunders *et al* (2003) discuss unique 'one-off' surveys that generally address a specific issue. They may include data from surveys undertaken by government or individual companies or organisations. They will be more difficult to track down, but they may be a useful source of raw data which you can then use for your own research purposes.

Other

You may well find UK local government organisations to be a rich source of survey information. Under the Best Value regime, such organisations are obliged to consult their customers, the rate payers. You may well be able to gain access to a lot of useful information from such sources.

Another source of surveys is think tanks. You can find these *via* the Internet.

4.3 Multiple source secondary data

Multiple source secondary data are likely to be either documentary or survey data, or a combination of the two; 'the key factor is that different data sets have been combined to form another data set prior to you accessing the data.' (Saunders *et al*, 2003). Examples include The Times newspaper's listing of the top 1000 companies and share price listings for different stock markets

Most of this type of information is readily available in university libraries.

Multiple source secondary data can be useful to carry out time series data analysis, analysing data over a long period in order to identify a trend.

5 SOURCES OF SECONDARY DATA

The gathering of secondary data can have much in common with the search of the literature (Sharp and Howard, 1996).

The literature search is covered in detail in Chapter 4, and many of the techniques described there will also apply to this chapter. In some fields, it is possible that the literature search is one of the main sources of data.

5.1   Introduction

Most of the recommended textbooks suggest a wide range of sources of data, some in general terms and some in more specific terms, for example providing lists of addresses of potentially helpful websites.

Most authorities split the sources of secondary data into these categories:

(a)   Books and journals
(b)   Technical publications
(c)   Official publications
(d)   Trade association data
(e)   Computer databases

We shall consider each of these in more detail in the next section.

5.2   Finding secondary data

Books and journals

You should make books and journals your first port of call (Denscombe, 1998). As Denscombe suggests:

> '...they contain the accumulated wisdom on which the research project should build, and also the latest cutting-edge ideas which can shape the direction of the research.'

There will almost certainly be some core text on the area that you are researching, which will provide you with a starting point and refer you to other sources of information. A university library or local government central library will be able to locate specific books for you if they do not themselves hold them. You can also key subject areas into a website like Amazon (www.amazon.co.uk) and see what texts are generated. You don't have to buy them: it will just give you ideas.

Denscombe (1998) provides some guidelines for evaluating books and their publishers. Their relevance and reliability must be evaluated in the same way as for any other form of secondary data.

Denscombe (1998) suggests that you ask yourself these key questions:

1   Have you heard of the publisher before? If you have, it might be reassuring.

2   Is the publisher a university press, such as Oxford University Press? If it is, this could offer some confidence about the academic quality of the work.

3   Is the book in a second or subsequent edition, or has it been reprinted a number of times? If it is, it means that the first edition was sufficiently in demand for the book to warrant new editions or reprints. You will be able to find these details right at the front of the book, usually on the second or third page.

4   If it is a library book, has it been borrowed a lot? If it has, it probably means that the book has been recommended by lecturers or other researchers, and may therefore be good.

Denscombe (1998) offers some similar rules of thumb when evaluating journals as a source of secondary data. The key questions here are:

1   How long has the journal been in existence? If it has been published for some time, you can probably have a reasonable degree of confidence in it.

2   Does the title of the journal include some national element, such as the *British Medical Journal* or the *American Journal of Sociology*? If it does, it may indicate that the journal carries some authority.

3   Does a professional association publish the journal? For example the journal *Accountancy* in the UK is published by the Institute of Chartered Accountants in England and Wales.

4   Does the journal contain a list of its editorial board and editorial advisers, and are these people well-known in the field?

5   Are articles in the journal refereed, which means do experts review them prior to publication? The referral process is also known as peer-review.

Technical publications

There are handbooks and manuals to cater for every area of research interest. Anyone already working in the field of your research would probably be able to tell you what technical publications are available. Equipment manufacturers publish detailed performance specifications (for example, those published by motor manufacturers) as do trade associations and bodies such as the British Standards Institution (Sharp and Howard, 1996).

Refer back to the chapter on searching the literature (Chapter 4) for suggestions on techniques that will enable you to locate the technical publications available in an academic library.

Official publications

The amount of material published on behalf of governments is enormous and forms an important reference source for many types of research (Sharp and Howard, 1996). Government publications are often classified separately in libraries, due to their sheer volume.

In the UK, HMSO (Her Majesty's Stationery Office) lists out all government publications, on an annual, monthly and sometimes daily basis, and there is also the bi-monthly *Catalogue of British Official Publications not published by the Stationery Office.*

Government departments compile and publish statistics, as do many other public bodies, such as the Chartered Institute of Public Finance (Sharp and Howard, 1996). Overseas and international organisations such as the OECD and UNESCO publish information of international relevance that can be useful for comparison purposes. Many are published in the United Nations Statistical Yearbook.

Denscombe (1998) says that you should be careful in your use of government statistics. They are an attractive source of information for the researcher, as they are:

(a)   Authoritative, having been produced by the state, with access to huge resources and expert and professional staff

    (b)   Objective, since they have been produced by officials; and

    (c)   Factual, as they tend to be the product of unambiguous figures

However, Denscombe (1998) points out that since government and other official statistics are often produced for the benefit of the government in office, it is possible even for these to be manipulated so that they become a less reliable source of evidence.

Denscombe(1998) suggests the consideration of three factors in evaluating government statistics.

    (a)   The extent to which the event or thing being measured is **clear-cut** and **straightforward**. If the data cover something that can only be measured in one way, such as the rate of company liquidations, you can rely on it with some certainty. The data present an incontrovertible fact that it is difficult to dispute. If on the other hand the data could be measured in a multitude of ways, such as unemployment statistics, which can be interpreted and presented in many ways, you may want to investigate the means of gathering the data quite carefully.

    (b)   Whether there are **vested interests** in the statistics that are produced. This is quite closely linked to the point in paragraph 1 above. Sometimes parties, including governments, have a vested interest in presenting information in a particular light. Such information could include educational standards, waiting lists for medical treatment and sales and trade figures. You should regard such statistics with caution until you are completely confident as to their accuracy.

    (c)   The extent to which the statistics are the **outcome of a series of decisions and judgements** made by people. If data has relied on the exercise of judgement by individuals, for example on the extraction of a sample of people interviewed, the data itself could be more open to challenge. Denscombe (1998) describes this as a situation where

    'official statistics can be regarded as 'social constructs' rather than a detached, impartial picture of the real world.'

Trade association data

Trade and industry associations can provide valuable data about the technical and economic operation of their members (Sharp and Howard, 1996). The economic data are more detailed than those found in government statistics. You can find information about UK trade associations in the *Directory of British Associations*, and then contact the relevant association direct to see what information can be made available.

Computer databases

Many universities and other institutions have developed databases for research purposes, and they are often made available to researchers from outside the organisation.

It is possible to transfer details of a database onto your own computer system, by means of a computer network such as JANET in the UK, or via the Internet. However you may need technical help in order to be able to do this, and you could also incur a significant cost, as if the data are supplied on a commercial basis the cost could be several hundred pounds. In that case you would need to budget for updating the database at regular intervals.

Summary of sources

Saunders *et al* (2003) set out two useful tables of possible secondary data sources. We have updated these tables where necessary for the 2010 edition of this text.

Guides to secondary data sources

Guide	Coverage
Office for National Statistics (2000) *Guide to Official Statistics*, London, HMSO	Official statistics produced by UK government
Croner (no date) *A-Z of Business Information Sources*, Kingston, Croner Publications	Loose-leaf regularly updated. Alphabetical list of subjects showing relevant sources including trade associations and institutional; UK focus
Smith, G. (ed.) (annual) *Business Information Yearbook*, Headland, Headland Press	Annual survey. Covers company and market information, on-line business information and a who's who in business information
Mort, D. (2006) *Sources of non-official UK statistics*, Aldershot, Gower Publishing Limited	Statistics compiled by major organisations such as trade associations, professional bodies and banks
Mort, D. (1992) *European Market Information: a Handbook for Managers*, London, Pitman	General unofficial and official statistical publications on a country-by-country basis; lists of who produces these data
Library Association (2002) *Libraries in the United Kingdom and Republic of Ireland*, London, Library Association	Lists of 2,500 libraries in the UK and EIRE
Dale, P. (1992) *Guide to Libraries and Information Units in Government Departments and other Organisations* (30th ed.) London, British Library	List libraries and information services in UK Government departments and related agencies
Dale, P. (1993) *Guide to Libraries in Key UK Companies*, London, British Library	Lists libraries in UK companies which are prepared to accept serious enquiries from outside
Patzer, G.L. (1995) *Using Secondary Data in Marketing Research: United States and World-wide*, Westport, CT, Quorum Books	Includes lists of sources specific to marketing, global information sources, US Census data, and more general business-related sources
McGuiness, K. and Short, T. (1998) *Research on the Net*, London, Old Bailey Press	Lists over 4,000 Internet sites that offer information of research value. Chapters include accounting and finance, business, industry and labour as well as country-by-country information

Figure 5.2 Published guides to possible secondary data sources (Saunders et al, 2003) amended

Secondary data web sites

Name	Internet address	Comment
Business Zone	www.businesszone.co.uk	Up-to-date resource. Browsable library of research findings in condensed format
Data Archive	http://www.data-archive.ac.uk/	UK digital archive of research data
FT Info	www.info.ft.com/companies	Company information on 11,000 companies including financial performance
Hoover's Online	www.hoovers.com	Company information on 12,000 US and international companies with links to CNN and Washington Post
Statbase	http://www.statistics.gov.uk/statbase/mainmenu.asp	UK national statistics
Organisations	www.adassoc.org.uk	Advertising Association
	www.asa.org.uk	Advertising Standards Authority
	www.acas.org.uk	Advisory Conciliation and Arbitration Service
	www.ama.org	American Marketing Association
	www.acca.co.uk	Association of Chartered Certified Accountants
	www.businesslink.co.uk	Business Link
	www.cbi.org.uk	Confederation of British Industry (CBI)
	www.cib.org.uk	Chartered Institute of Bankers
	www.cimaglobal.com	Chartered Institute of Management Accountants
	www.cim.co.uk	Chartered Institute of Marketing (CIM)
	http://www.theworkfoundation.com	The Work Foundation, successor to The Industrial Society
	www.iod.com	Institute of Directors
	http://www.managers.org.uk/	Institute of Management
	www.cipd.co.uk	Institute of Personnel and Development
	www.ipa.co.uk	Institute of Practitioners in Advertising (IPA)
	www.kpmg.co.uk	KPMG UK
	www.londonstockexchange.com	London Stock Exchange
	www.tuc.org.uk	Trade Union Congress (TUC)

Figure 5.3 Selected secondary data sites on the Internet (Saunders et al, 2003) amended

6   PRIMARY DATA

We now turn our attention to the collection of primary data. Remember this is data collected by you for the specific purpose of your research.

The main sources of primary data for business projects are interviews, focus groups and questionnaires.

7   INTERVIEWS

7.1   Definition

According to Robson (1993) an 'interview is a kind of conversation: a conversation with a purpose. Interviews are a very commonly used approach to research, possibly in part because the interview appears to be a quite straightforward and non-problematic way of finding things out.'

Denscombe (1993) however, cautions that interviews involve a set of assumptions and understandings about the situation which are not normally associated with a casual conversation (Denscombe, 1983; Silverman, 1985).

Saunders *et al* (2003) explain that 'in reality, the research interview is a general term for several types of interview. This fact is significant since the nature of any interview should be consistent with your research question(s) and objective(s), the purpose of your research and the research strategy you have adopted.'

7.2   Types of interview

Bell (1999) draws on Grebank and Moser (1962) in suggesting that the various types of interview can be described in terms of 'a continuum of formality'. Bell explains that

> *'at one extreme is the completely formalised interview where the interviewer behaves as much like a machine as possible. At the other is the completely informal interview in which the shape is determined by individual respondents. The more standardised the interview, the easier it is to aggregate and quantify the results.'*

We have prepared the following summary of the key types of interview, drawn from various sources.

Type of interview	Characteristics
Fully structured	• A pre-determined or standard set of questions is asked.
	• The wording of the questions and their order are set.
	• The respondent is invited to choose from a list of limited-option responses: these provide pre-coded data output.
	• Responses are recorded on a standardised schedule.
	• The same tone of voice is used for all questions so as achieve 'stimulus equivalence' and thus avoid bias.
	• The data collected can be statistically interpreted but large samples are required to provide adequate confidence levels.

Type of interview	Characteristics

Semi-structured	• Questions are worked out in advance, but depending on the context of the 'conversation', the interviewer may adopt the schedule from one interviewee to the next as follows:
	
	  – Change the wording of the questions
	
	  – Provide explanations
	
	  – Omit particular questions which seem inappropriate with particular interviewees
	
	  – Add further questions
	
	• The responses are open-ended and there is more emphasis on the interviewee elaborating points of interest.
	
	• Responses are recorded by taking notes, or where the interviewee agrees, by tape recording.

Unstructured	• There is no list of questions
	
	• The interviewer has a general area of interest and concern
	
	  – allows the conversation to develop within this area, ie is non-directive
	
	  – should be as unintrusive as possible
	
	• Also referred to as 'in depth' interviews. The aim is 'discovery', rather than 'checking'

(Robson, 1993; Denscombe, 1998; Saunders *et al* 2003)

Hussey and Hussey (1997) suggest that structured interviews are associated with a **positivistic** methodology, whereas unstructured interviews are more in keeping with a **phenomenological** approach.

Where an unstructured format is used within a phenomenological paradigm, the researcher will need sufficient interpersonal skill to gain the confidence of the interviewee so that relevant issues may be discussed and explored in-depth and in an open manner.

Easterby-Smith *et al* (1991) caution that 'although interviewing is often claimed to be 'the best' method of gathering information, its complexity can sometimes be underestimated. It is time consuming to undertake interviews properly, and they are sometimes used when other methods may be more appropriate.'

7.3 Role of interviews in data collection

Robson (2002) expresses the role of interviews accurately in stating that

'interviews can be used as the primary or only approach in a study, as in a survey or many grounded theory studies. However, they lend themselves well to use in combination with other methods, in a multi-method approach. A case study might employ some kind of relatively formal interview to complement participant observation. An experiment could often usefully incorporate a post-intervention interview to help incorporate the participant's perspective into the findings.'

Denscombe (1998) suggests that as 'an information gathering tool, the interview lends itself to being used alongside other methods as a way of supplementing their data, adding detail and depth'.

Use	Details
Preparation for a questionnaire	• Fine-tune the questions and concepts that will appear in a questionnaire. • Gain the detail and depth required to ensure that the questionnaire asks valid questions.
Follow-up to a questionnaire	• Pursue in greater detail and depth any interesting lines of enquiry thrown up by a questionnaire administered. • To complement the data gathered from a questionnaire.
Triangulation with other methods	Can be used as a means of corroborating data gathered by other approaches.

(Denscombe, 1998)

Saunders *et al* (2003) relate the various types of interview to exploratory, descriptive and explanatory studies.

Type of study	Type of interview
Exploratory study	• Unstructured interviews can be very helpful to 'find out what is happening [and] to seek new insights (Robson, 1993, p. 42) • Semi-structured interviews also lend themselves to exploratory studies
Descriptive study	• Structured interviews can be used as a means to identify general patterns
Explanatory study	• Semi-structured interviews may be used in order to understand the relationship between variables • Structured interviews can be used in a statistical sense

(Saunders *et al*, 2003)

The various types of interview may also be used to complement each other.

(a) **Unstructured interviews** may be used initially to identify variables. Data gathered is then used to design **questionnaires** or a further **interview schedule.**

(b) **Semi-structured interviews** may be used to explore and explain themes that have emerged from the use of your questionnaire.

(c) **Semi-structured** and **in-depth interviews** may be used as a means of validating findings from questionnaires already administered.

7.4 Validity

According to Denscombe (1998) the validity of using interviews is high because 'direct contact at the point of the interview means that data can be checked for accuracy and relevance as they are collected'.

7.5　Interviewer bias

Saunders *et al* (2003) describe **interviewer bias** as arising 'where the comments, tone or non-verbal behaviour of the interviewer creates bias in the way that interviewees respond to the questions being asked'.

Freedom from interviewer bias is essential. As discussed above, in a structured interview this includes ensuring that questions are communicated in a consistent manner from one interviewer to another. Bell (1999) warns that 'the same question put by two people, but with different emphasis and in a different tone of voice can produce very different responses'. The perceptions and standpoint of the interviewer should not impact on the interviewee's response, nor the way it is recorded.

With qualitative research, such as the conduct of unstructured interviews, the approach is usually to explore the world of the interviewee. The interviewee has space to express his or her views and hence there should inherently be less scope for the interviewer to influence the interviewee's response (Easterby-Smith *et al*, 1991).

Bell (1999) cautions that 'where a team of interviewers is employed, serious bias may show up in the data analysis, but if (only) one researcher conducts a set of interviews, the bias may be consistent and therefore go unnoticed.' Bell cites the advice offered by Garron (1966) that 'it is difficult to see how (bias) can be avoided completely, but awareness of the problem plus constant self-control can help'.

Bell (1999) warns that an interviewer can lapse into in leading the interviewee. Hussey and Hussey (1997) suggest that 'it is difficult to predict or measure potential bias, but you should be alert to the fact that it can distort your data and hence your findings'.

7.6　Interviewer effect

The appearance as well as the behaviour of the interviewer is likely to impact on the response of the interviewee. These include:

(a) Gender, age and ethnic origins of the interviewer
(b) The personality of the interviewer
(c) The occupational status of the interviewer
(d) The appearance and manners of the interviewer
(e) The neutrality of the interviewer

(Denscombe, 1990)

Easterby-Smith *et al* (1991) refer to the work of Jones (1985), who points out that 'interviewees will 'suss out' what researchers are like, and make judgments from their first impressions about whether the interviewer can be trusted or whether they might be 'damaged' in some way by data that could be so used. Such suspicions do not necessarily mean that interviewees will refuse to be interviewed, but it might mean, as Jones indicates, that they just '...seek to get the interview over as quickly as possible, with enough detail and enough feigned interest to satisfy the researcher that he or she is getting something of value but without saying anything that touches the core of what is actually believed and cared about in the research'.'

It is common sense that you should dress in an appropriate way which is in keeping with the interview setting as well as the expectations of the interviewee. Thus, if you are interviewing a CEO of a public listed company, you are likely to wear smart business wear. If you are interviewing workers on a building site, you are likely to don a helmet, boots and informal clothes. You should however avoid being too blatant in mirroring the appearance of your interviewees.

The issue of gender bias is highlighted by the work of Rosenthal (1966), as cited in Hussey and Hussey (1997), which suggests different data collection results depending on whether the interviewer and interviewee are either male or female.

(a) Female subjects tend to be treated more attentively and considerately than male subjects.

(b) Female researchers tend to smile more often than male researchers.

(c) Male researchers tend to place themselves closer to male subjects than do female researchers.

(d) Male researchers tend to show higher levels of body activity than do female researchers; when the subject is male, both male and female researchers tend to show higher levels of body activity than they do when the subject is a female.

(e) Female subjects rate male researchers as more friendly and as having more pleasant and expressive voices than female researchers.

(f) Both male and female researchers behave more warmly towards female subjects than they do towards male subjects, with male researchers the warmer of the two.

7.7   Interview skills

We have looked at the risk of interviewer bias. One of the factors that might minimise the incidence of interviewer bias is the application of good interviewing skills by the researcher.

Denscombe (1998) has explored the key elements of interviewing skills, which we have summarised here.

Skill	Key points
Attentiveness	• The interviewer should maintain the thread of the discussion and continue to listen closely while writing notes, reading body language or checking the tape recorder is working.
Sensitivity to feelings of interviewees	• Courtesy is required. • Sensitivity helps to get the best out of an interview by encouraging the interviewee to be helpful and open about providing data.
Ability to tolerate silences	• Courteous silence gives interviewees the chance to develop their responses. • Silence on the part of the interviewee does not necessarily presage the failure of the interview.
Ability to use prompts effectively	• Prompts can encourage the interviewee to speak, but they must not amount to leading.

Skill	Key points
Ability to use probing questions	• Applied where the interviewer would like to delve more deeply into a topic because the interviewee's response appears incomplete or inconsistent.
	• Should be subtle and avoid an aggressive stance.
Ability to use checks	• Involves summarising what has been said at strategic points during the interview.
	• Allows the interviewee to confirm or correct the details of the discussion.
Ensuring the interviewees have their say	• Timid or nervous interviewees may need encouragement to speak fully.
Non-judgmental approach	• The interviewer should avoid allowing his personal values to intrude or to show emotions like disgust, surprise or pleasure through facial gestures.

Based on Denscombe (1998)

Easterby-Smith *et al* (1991) have developed a useful description of the various ways probing questions can be used.

1 The **basic probe** simply involves repeating the initial question and is useful when the interviewee seems to be wandering off the point.

2 **Explanatory probes** involve building onto incomplete or vague statements made by the respondent. Ask questions such as 'What did you mean by that?', 'What makes you say that?'

3 **Focused probes** are used to obtain specific information. Typically one would ask the respondent 'What sort of...?'

4 **The silent probe** is one of the most effective techniques to use when the respondent is either reluctant or very slow to answer the question posed. Simply pause and let him or her break the silence.

5 The technique of **drawing out** can be used when the interviewee has halted, or dried up. Repeat the last few words she said, and then look expectant or say, 'Tell me more about that', 'What happened then?'

6 **Giving ideas or suggestions** involves offering the interviewee an idea to think about – 'Have you thought about...?' 'Have you tried...?' 'Did you know that....?' 'Perhaps you should ask Y...'

7 **Mirroring or reflecting** involves expressing in your own words what the respondent has just said. This is very effective because it may force the respondent to rethink his or her answer and construct another reply which will amplify the previous answer – 'What you seem to be saying/feeling is...'

To avoid bias, probes should never lead. An example of a leading probe might be 'So you would say that you were really satisfied?' Instead the interviewer should say, 'Can you explain a little more?' or 'How do you mean?'

Robson (1993) provides a useful description of an interview process.

Step 1.   Introduction includes

- Personal introduction
- Explanation of purpose
- Give assurance on confidentiality
- Discuss procedures for making a record of the interview

Step 2.   **Warm up**. Use of easy, non-threatening questions to settle interviewer and interviewee.

Step 3.   **Interview**. Conduct main body of the interview.

Step 4.   **Cool off**. Use straightforward questions to defuse any tensions that may have arisen.

Step 5.   **Closure**. Say thank you and goodbye. Accompany interviewee to door with courtesy.

8   FOCUS GROUPS

8.1   Introduction

According to Hussey and Hussey (1997) '**focus groups** are normally associated with a phenomenological methodology. They are used to gather data relating to the feelings and opinions of a group of people who are involved in a common situation.

Focus groups draw on the effects of group dynamics to provide useful research data. 'The explicit use of the group interaction to produce data and insights that would be less accessible without the interaction found in a group.' (Morgan, 1988)

8.2   The focus group process

Hussey and Hussey (1997) provide a process for forming a focus group which we have summarised in Figure 5.4.

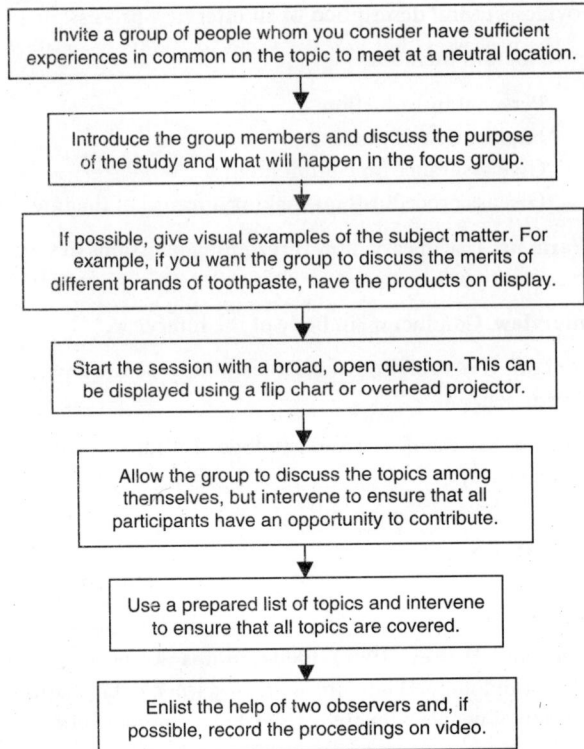

```
┌─────────────────────────────────────────────────────┐
│   Invite a group of people whom you consider have     │
│   sufficient experiences in common on the topic to    │
│            meet at a neutral location.                │
└─────────────────────────────────────────────────────┘
                          │
                          ▼
┌─────────────────────────────────────────────────────┐
│   Introduce the group members and discuss the purpose │
│    of the study and what will happen in the focus     │
│                       group.                          │
└─────────────────────────────────────────────────────┘
                          │
                          ▼
┌─────────────────────────────────────────────────────┐
│  If possible, give visual examples of the subject     │
│  matter. For example, if you want the group to        │
│  discuss the merits of different brands of            │
│  toothpaste, have the products on display.            │
└─────────────────────────────────────────────────────┘
                          │
                          ▼
┌─────────────────────────────────────────────────────┐
│   Start the session with a broad, open question. This │
│   can be displayed using a flip chart or overhead     │
│                     projector.                        │
└─────────────────────────────────────────────────────┘
                          │
                          ▼
┌─────────────────────────────────────────────────────┐
│   Allow the group to discuss the topics among         │
│   themselves, but intervene to ensure that all        │
│   participants have an opportunity to contribute.     │
└─────────────────────────────────────────────────────┘
                          │
                          ▼
┌─────────────────────────────────────────────────────┐
│   Use a prepared list of topics and intervene         │
│   to ensure that all topics are covered.              │
└─────────────────────────────────────────────────────┘
                          │
                          ▼
┌─────────────────────────────────────────────────────┐
│   Enlist the help of two observers and, if            │
│   possible, record the proceedings on video.          │
└─────────────────────────────────────────────────────┘
```

Figure 5.4 Process for forming a focus group
(Adapted from Hussey and Hussey, 1997)

Focus groups usually involve between six and eight participants and the process is usually facilitated by a moderator (Denscombe, 1998); or, possibly, moderated by a facilitator, no doubt.

According to Hussey and Hussey (1997), 'focus groups combine both **interviewing** and **observation**. They are often used in pilot studies to develop a **questionnaire** or **interview schedule** for quantitative study.' However, as Hussey and Hussey explain, 'the data generated from a focus group (are) qualitative'.

8.3 Reliability

Saunders *et al* (2003) argues that 'the assumption behind this type of research is that the circumstances to be explored are complex and dynamic. The value of the non-standardised approach is derived from the flexibility that you may use to explore the complexity of the topic. Therefore an attempt to ensure that qualitative, non-standardised research could be replicated by other researchers would not be realistic or feasible without undermining the strength of this type of research.'

Drawing on the work of Marshall and Rossman (1999), Saunders *et al* suggest that this weakness might be mitigated by making good notes about three things.

(a) The design of the research
(b) The reasons for underpinning the choice of strategy and methods
(c) The data gathered

Saunders *et al* (2003) suggest that 'these records can be referred to by other researchers in order to understand the processes that you used and to enable them to re-use the data that you collected'.

9   QUESTIONNAIRES

9.1   Definition

Hussey and Hussey (1997) define questionnaires as 'a method for collecting data in which a selected group of participants are asked to complete a written set of questions to find out what they do, think or feel'. They argue that questionnaires may be used within both positivistic and phenomenological paradigms.

9.2   Positivistic paradigm

Hussey and Hussey (1997) identify various characteristics relating to the use of questionnaires within a positivistic paradigm.

(a)   They lend themselves to large scale surveys.

(b)   Closed questions are used.

(c)   Each question can be coded at the design stage.

(d)   Completed forms can be easily analysed with the help of a computer.

(e)   Every respondent should be asked, and should understand, the questions in the same way.

However, Denscombe (1998) has also identified certain weaknesses relating to the use of closed questions.

(a)   *'There is less scope for respondents to supply answers which reflect the exact facts or true feelings on a topic if the facts or opinions happen to be complicated or not or do not fit into the range of options supplied by the questionnaire.'*

(b)   *'The respondents get frustrated by not being allowed to express their views fully in a way that accounts for any sophistication, intricacy or even inconsistencies in their views.'*

The positivistic paradigm is likely to be associated with explanatory or analytical research where the relationship between variables is examined, usually to try to confirm a cause-effect link.

9.3   Phenomenological paradigm

Questionnaires used within a phenomenological paradigm have different characteristics.

(a)   Open ended questions are used.
(b)   Coding is done only after the forms have been completed by the respondents.
(c)   They not lend themselves to large scale surveys.

(Hussey and Hussey, 1997)

According to Denscombe (1998) open questions have several advantages.

(a) The respondent is allowed to decide the wording, length and content of the answer.

(b) Long answers can be easily accommodated.

(c) Responses are more likely to reflect the richness and complexity of the views held by the respondents, who are allowed the space to express themselves in their own words.

And there are also potential disadvantages.

(a) More effort is required of the respondent which might discourage completion of the questionnaire.

(b) The data obtained is usually 'raw' and may need a lot of time-consuming analysis before they can be used.

(Denscombe, 1998)

A positivistic paradigm is likely to be associated with **descriptive** research, which attempts to describe variances in behaviour.

9.4 Role of questionnaires

Questionnaires will generally be used as part of a multi-method approach and will therefore be accompanied by some other method of gathering data.

EXAMPLE

A questionnaire is used to identify customer buying habits for groceries. This research might be supplemented with the use of in depth interviews to explore and understand the underlying reasons and background to the behaviour.

You might envisage a more sophisticated scenario than the above that combines observation with a structured questionnaire and a programme of unstructured interviews.

EXAMPLE

In a study on the effectiveness of a company's processes for rolling out change management initiatives, the researcher decides to use a multi-method approach.

(a) First, the researcher observes employee behaviour and attitudes in implementing the re-engineered processes.

(b) Subsequently, a self administered questionnaire is used to identify employees' views on the way the change has been implemented

(c) Thereafter, unstructured interviews are conducted with management to ascertain their side of the story

There is no 'holy grail' that will provide ‌ best method of gathering research data. In fact, there are important benefits to using different methods to collect data on the same subject.

(a) Each method can look from a different angle – from its own distinct perspective – and the researcher can use these perspectives as a means of comparison and contrast. This will help the researcher to understand the topic in a more rounded and complete fashion than would be the case had the data been drawn from just one method.

(b) The use of several methods allows the findings from one method to be checked against the findings from another. This can enhance the *validity* of the data and can help reassure that the findings are not too dependent on the method of data collection.

9.5 Types of questionnaire

Questionnaires are usually divided into two categories:

(a) Self administered
(b) Interviewer administered

You are likely to have some personal experience of both types. For example, you are likely to have received questionnaires of the self administered variety through the post. Also, you might occasionally have been stopped 'in the street' by an interviewer and asked if you would be willing to answer some questions.

The table below gives examples of the types of questionnaire that fall within each category.

Interviewer administered	Self administered
• Face to face questionnaire	• Postal questionnaires
• Telephone questionnaires	• On-line questionnaires

9.6 Criteria for using a questionnaire

Whether you decide to use a questionnaire to collect your research data will depend on several factors.

(a) The **nature of the information** you need to gather based on your research questions and objectives. The data sought should not be too complex or controversial. Questionnaires lend themselves to *factual* and *opinion* questions.

For example:

Factual: What did you eat for dinner last night?

Opinion: What is your favorite type of food?

(b) The **characteristics of the respondents** should be considered.

(i) They need to be amenable and capable of providing meaningful answers. For example, before you decide to use a self-administered questionnaire, you need to be aware of the extent of the potential respondent's literacy.

(ii) There must be an **open social climate** that encourages respondents to provide full and honest answers.

(iii) You need to avoid any loss of **reliability** of your data as result of **contamination** of responses; contamination in this sense arises where the respondent makes up, embellishes or guesses at the answers. You also need to be aware that respondents may give unreliable answers for a variety of reasons, such as to please the interviewer, to raise their own self-esteem and to help themselves pass the time of day because they are lonely.

(c) The **necessary sample size**. You need an adequate sample of respondents for the questionnaire method to provide meaningful results. You must have some idea of the likely response rate you are likely to achieve. Sample sizes are discussed later in this chapter.

(d) The **amount of data** required. If there is a lot of data to be collected, an interviewer-administered approach may be preferable. Potential respondents may well avoid filling in lengthy questionnaires on their own.

(e) **Costs**. You will need to prepare a forecast of the likely costs of administering a questionnaire. These will usually include items such as printing, paper and postage and sometimes travelling and payments to interviewers, if used.

(f) **Logistics**. You will also need to draw up a projected timetable of all the various steps that will be involved, including design of the questionnaire, pilot testing, word processing, printing, posting, awaiting replies and follow up of non-respondents.

(Saunders *et al*, 2003 and Denscombe, 1998)

Collection tool	Advantages	Disadvantages
Face to face questionnaire	• Flexibility in terms of mix of questions between open and closed • Can accommodate collection of relatively large amounts of data • Interviewer clarification of questions possible • Interviewer can establish rapport with respondent, read body-language and provide encouragement • Can deal with complex and sensitive questions • Visual aids can be used to help respondent interpret questions • In-depth or 'rich' answers can be obtained • In practice, reasonable response rates are usually obtained	• Contamination can creep in by respondents giving unreliable responses or the interviewer distorting the response recorded • Interviewers must be properly briefed and perhaps may need training • The processes may be time consuming and expensive, especially if a large geographical area is being covered

Collection tool	Advantages	Disadvantages
Telephone questionnaire	• Easy to select sample; especially in terms of geographical coverage • In practice, reasonable response rates usually obtained • Flexibility in terms of mix of questions between open and closed • Some personal rapport may be achieved • Cost efficient to administer • Respondent anonymity retained • Responses can be recorded in real time on a computer	• Not everyone has a telephone or is listed in the telephone directory • Complex questions do not work very well • Ethical considerations may be involved, eg catching respondents at inconvenient times • Body language of the respondent cannot be read • Contamination can creep in by respondents giving unreliable responses or the interviewer distorting the response recorded
Postal questionnaire	• Wide geographical reach • Sample selection is facilitated • Respondents can complete in their own time • Much respondent anonymity is retained • Token incentives to complete can be given, such as entry into prize draw, provision of free pen and so on. • Optical mark readers can be used to electronically capture responses	• In practice, low response rates usually obtained • There is an element of self-selection in the replies received and hence there may be an element of bias • Clarification of questions cannot be provided • Can be time consuming to administer • Can be expensive in terms of printing and postage costs • Non-respondents should be chased up, usually with a further copy of the questionnaire • Non-respondent bias on the results needs to be borne in mind

Collection tool	Advantages	Disadvantages
Delivery and collection questionnaire (self-administered but delivered to homes and collected by researcher,)	• Similar advantages as postal questionnaires • Response rate can be made higher by the collection process	• Clarification of question cannot be provided • Can be time consuming to administer • Can be expensive
On-line questionnaire	• Enables large geographically dispersed samples to be administered • Easy to administer, speedy delivery and cost efficient • Input may be automated	• Potential respondents must have a computer and be IT literate • Questions should not be too complex • Response rate is usually moderate to low

(Saunders *et al*, 2003; Hussey and Hussey, 1997; Sekaren, 2000)

9.7   Dealing with non-responses

You are unlikely to achieve a 100% response rate to your questionnaire. However, a high non-response rate may suggest that the data collected is not representative. This is because there may be material differences between those who respond and those who do not.

Non-responses to a questionnaire may happen for a variety of reasons.

(a) **Ineligibles.** These refer to people who have been selected, but then do not meet the criteria to participate in the research. This problem should be minimised by being more careful in ensuring that only eligible people are originally included in the population from which the sample is to be drawn.

(b) **Unavailables.** These may occur for a variety of reasons; the person has gone away, is slow in opening the post, is on holiday or gone away on business. The input of such people will not be represented in the data you collect.

(c) **Refusals.** These refer to people who have been approached or have received a questionnaire and do not wish to participate in your research, without giving a reason.

Other sources of non-response are:

(a) There may also be cases where the respondent has agreed to take the questionnaire but has not responded to or refused to respond to certain of the questions.

(b) Incorrect responses, like ticking more than the required number of boxes. This would also be regarded as a non-response.

Hussey and Hussey (1997) cite Wallace and Mellor (1988) regarding three methods for dealing with questionnaire non-response.

(a) Follow up respondents who do not reply to the first request and try to get responses from them. Compare the data collected from respondents to the first request with the data collected from people who replied to the subsequent follow-up procedures.

(b) Compare the characteristics of the respondents, with those of the overall population, as far as you know them.

(c) Compare the characteristics of the respondents, with those of the non-respondents, so far as you know them eg age, gender, occupation etc.

In practice, follow-up procedures are susceptible to the law of diminishing marginal returns. The practical advice is that there are benefits in sending three reminders. This could increase your response rate by as much as a third more respondents.

Bell (1999) suggests that a second request should be sent out a week after the first, but this does seem a little premature. Taking into account postal delivery times, a ten day wait before sending out the second request seems to be a reasonable interval. In practical terms, you should enclose a further copy of the questionnaire as well as a prepaid envelope for the return mailing.

Zikmund (1997) suggests a more proactive approach whereby you would try to make it more attractive for the prospective respondent to complete a postal questionnaire.

(a) Enclose a user-friendly covering letter

(b) Provide a token incentive

(c) Include strategically placed 'interesting questions'

(d) Apply a systematic follow-up process

(e) Use advanced notification of the questionnaire being administered, by telephone or letter

(f) Sponsorship by a credible body

9.8 Self-selection bias

You need to be aware of this problem when using self-administered questionnaires, as it may compromise the representativeness of the responses you collect. Often, the people who take the time to complete a self-administered questionnaire are likely to be those who have strong feelings about the matters covered, perhaps as a result of a particularly bad or good experience with the organization concerned.

EXAMPLE

A hotel provides a customer satisfaction form for guests to complete before they check out. It has 20,000 guests in 20X3 and it receives 2,000 customer satisfaction forms from them. 250 responses rated 'food quality' as 'poor' and 500 graded it as 'could be better.' 300 marked the food as 'excellent' and 600 scored it as 'good'

Would it be valid to conclude that 38% of guests were of the opinion that the hotel's food is poor or could be better, and 45% thought it was good or excellent, considering that only 10% of guests took the trouble to fill in a form? Is it likely that the forms returned were biased towards those who had an extreme experience with the hotel's food?

Given the low level of responses and the self-administered nature of the questionnaire, there must be some suspicion that the data collected is biased towards the views of those people who developed extreme opinions of the hotel's food.

Generally, with self-administered questionnaires, there is an over-representation of people with extreme views and an under-representation of people with views in the middle. Given the low level of responses, it would be important to perform some of the follow-up procedures outlined above.

9.9   Identifying the data to be collected

The data to be collected and hence the questions you will include in your questionnaire, will be driven by the objectives of your research.

The data you gather will also be influenced by whether you are working within a positivistic or a phenomenological paradigm.

(a)   Within a positivistic approach, your questionnaire is likely to be of an analytic or exploratory nature. Your approach will be deductive and attempt to test theory. Variables will be identified and work will be done to prove relationships between them. (Gill and Johnson, 1997; Saunders *et al* 2003)

(b)   Under a phenomenological paradigm, your questionnaire is likely to seek data of a descriptive nature. Your work is likely to be inductive, building theory from the data you collect. You will be looking at variability in phenomena. (Saunders *et al*, 2003; Gill and Johnson, 1997)

Within both paradigms, the data accumulated in your literature review will help to inform the nature of what primary data you will need to collect by means of your questionnaire. Saunders *et al* (2003) also suggest that you involve 'colleagues, your project tutor and other interested parties' in the process of identifying what data is required. They also emphasise that where you are conducting your research within an organisation, it is vital to develop a good understanding of the organisation, including a review of corporate publications and its website.

Saunders *et al* (2003) recommend that you use a **data requirements table** to summarise the data you want to collect. They define such a table like this:

A table designed to ensure that, when completed, the data collected will enable the research question(s) to be answered and the objectives achieved.

We have reproduced the table from Saunders *et al* (2003) to provide you with an example of what a data requirement table looks like. The table reflects a positivistic approach and would have to be adapted accordingly if you were going down a phenomenological research route.

Sarah was asked to discover staff attitudes to the possible introduction of a no smoking policy at her workplace. Discussion with senior management and colleagues and reading relevant literature helped her to firm up her objective and investigative questions. A selection of these is included in the extract from her table of data requirements:

Research question/objective: To establish employees' attitudes to the possible introduction of a no-smoking policy at their workplace

Type of research: Predominantly descriptive, although wish to examine differences between employees

Investigative questions	Variable(s) required	Detail in which data measured	Check included in questionnaire √
Do employees feel that they should be able to smoke in their office if they want to as a right? (attitude)	Attitude of employee to smoking in their office as a right	Feel ... should be allowed, should not be allowed, no strong feelings	
Do employees feel that the employer should provide a smoking room for smokers if smoking in offices is banned? (attitude)	Attitude of employee to the provision of a smoking room for smokers	Feel ... very strongly that it should, quite strongly that it should, no strong opinions, quite strongly that it should not, very strongly that it should not	
Would employees accept a smoking ban at work if the majority of people agreed to it (behaviour)	Likely behaviour of employee regarding the acceptance of a ban	Would ... accept with no preconditions, accept if a smoking room was provided, not accept without additional conditions (specify conditions), would not accept whatever the conditions	
Do employee attitudes differ depending on: Age? (attribute) Whether or not a smoker? (behaviour)	(Attitude of employee – outlined above) Age of employee Smoker	(Included above) To nearest 5-year band (youngest 16, oldest 65) Non-smoker, smokes but not in office, smokes in office	
How representative are the responses? (attributes)	Age of employee Gender of employee Job	(Included above) Male, female Senior management, management, supervisory, other	

When identifying the data you need to collect, you will also need to consider the detail with which they are to be measured. (Saunders *et al*, 2003)

In deciding on the questions to include, you will need to keep in mind how the data collected will be used.

(a) Plan ahead how the results will be analysed, presented and written up.

(b) Assess how the data collected might be triangulated with the points identified in your review of literature.

You should be aware of the available techniques that can be used to analyse your data. It would therefore be well worth while to become comfortable with the techniques set out in Chapter 6 before you embark on designing your questionnaire. Otherwise you might fall into one of two traps.

(a) The data collected is difficult to analyse or interpret.

(b) There are good data analysis techniques that go unused because you have not collected any relevant data.

There is generally given advice that with questionnaires, you only have one opportunity to put your questions to the respondent. Therefore you must make sure you take great care in properly identifying what data is important.

9.10 Designing the questionnaire

There is no 'golden formula' for ensuring that you design the perfect questionnaire. You will need to 'apply discretion, make trade-offs and exercise judgment when producing and implementing a questionnaire' (Denscombe, 1998).

The design of a questionnaire involves two key areas.

    (a) The questions included
    (b) The overall appearance of the questionnaire

The subject of questions included will cover aspects such as wording, form of question, number of questions and sequencing. Appearance will include aspects such as impression, length, introduction and instructions.

9.11 Types of questions

The key characteristics of the various types of questions that could be included in a questionnaire are set out in the following table.

Type of question	Characteristics
Open-ended	• Questions seek a response in the respondent's own words. For example, 'State the three most important attributes you consider when deciding an exam-training provider'. • Useful where there is likely to be a big range of potential responses. • Response is influenced by the amount of space allowed for writing in. • The responses need to analysed more carefully before a suitable coding structure can be applied.

Closed	• Provide a number of alternative responses from which the respondent is asked to choose. For example,
	
	  – Tick the appropriate box to indicate your sex; male or female?
	    Male ☐
	    Female ☐
	  – Are you working full time? Please tick the appropriate box.
	    Yes ☐
	    No ☐
	  – Would you agree or disagree with the following statement:
	  – In today's world, business people require the additional knowledge and skills that qualifications such as an HND can provide
	    Agree ☐
	    Disagree ☐

Type of question	Characteristics
	• Minimal writing is required.
	• Responses can be pre-coded to facilitate subsequent analysis.
	• The alternatives must be mutually exclusive and collectively exhaustive. If any alternatives overlap, there is likely to be respondent confusion. If the alternatives provided are perceived to be incomplete, respondents may become frustrated and add their own alternatives.
	• Sometimes supplemented at the end of the questionnaire with an open-ended question tyhat gives the respondent an opportunity to comment on anything that has not been adequately covered

	• Bell (1999) cites Youngman (1986) as identifying six types of closed questions
	  – List
	  – Category
	  – Ranking
	  – Scale
	  – Quantity
	  – Grid

List	A list of responses is provided from which any number may be selected. For example, Please tick the relevant boxes to indicate which of the following Learn-a-lot Limited's products you have used. Textbooks ☐ Revision kits ☐ Revise-a-lot cards ☐ Question cards ☐ Learnmore tapes ☐ Learnmore videos ☐ Learnmore CD ROM ☐ Virtual campus ☐
Category	The respondent is provided with a set of categories from which one should be selected. For example, How often do you visit the Learn-a-lot website? Tick the appropriate box to indicate your response. Daily ☐ Once a week ☐ Once a month ☐ Once every two months ☐ Quarterly ☑ Longer than quarterly ☐

Type of question	Characteristics
Ranking	• The respondent is asked to place things in rank order. This provides data on the respondent's priorities. For example, Please number the following factors in order of importance in selecting a professional exam-training provider. Quality of tutors ☐ Quality of materials ☐ Availability of face to face courses ☐ Catering arrangements ☐ Teaching methods ☐ Location of centres ☐ Historical pass rates achieved ☐ Leisure facilities ☐ • In practice, respondents can rank seven or eight items in a face to face questionnaire but no more than three to four items over the phone. For face to face questionnaires, it usually helps to show the respondent a prompt card listing the things to be ranked.
Scale	• This type of question is used to gauge the attitudes and beliefs of a respondent in respect of a specific attribute. • The most commonly used form of question is the *Likert scale*. For example,

	Strongly agree	Agree	Disagree	Strongly disagree
Learn-a lot's textbooks are well written				
The tutors are not supportive				

• The four point scale shown above forces the respondent to make a clear choice between agreement and disagreement. A five-point scale provides a "Neither agree not disagree " box in the middle, thereby allowing respondents to 'sit on the fence'.

Type of question	Characteristics
	• Another form of scaling question is the Osgood semantic differential. This type of question takes one attribute and seeks to measure the respondents views in terms of a series of opposing attributes, eg:

Learn-a-lot's courses are:

Technically accurate						Contain technical errors
Boring						Interesting
Exam focused						Subject focused
Too long						Too short
Student driven						Tutor driven
Provide an ideal learning environment						Provide a poor learning environment
Interactive						One way – tutor to student
Use few teaching techniques						Use many teaching techniques
Excellent illustrative examples						Poor illustrative examples
No visual-aids						Many visual-aids

Type of question	Characteristics
Quantity	• Quantity questions are designed to elicit a numerical response
	• They can be used to gather attribute or behaviour data. For example,

State your year of birth [   ]

How long does it take you to get from home to your Learn-a-lot centre, door to door?

[   ] minutes

Grid or matrix	These are usually used for large-scale research, such as national censuses. They are therefore not recommended for academic projects, dissertations, theses and the like.

9.12 Avoiding pitfalls in questionnaire wording

Great care needs to be exercised in the wording of your questions. You must ensure that they are effective in collecting the appropriate data to address your research question and research objectives. The various authorities on questionnaire design give a lot of advice on the wording of questionnaires and the language to use.

Pitfall	Advice
Ambiguity	• Be careful that some questions may be interpreted and answered in different ways. For example, When did you decide to study for a business qualification?
	• This could mean either 'State the date you first made the decision' or 'What event persuaded you to take up business studies?'.

Pitfall	Advice
Imprecision	• Beware of using imprecise and vague words like 'on average', 'in the near future', 'a lot', 'relevant' or 'as soon as possible,' eg: How often do you visit relevant websites? A lot ☐ Average frequency ☐ Not much ☐ • The interpretation of what is a relevant website is likely to differ between respondents, as is their interpretation of 'a lot', 'average' and 'not much'. This will reduce the meaningfulness of the data collected.
Assumption	• Be careful of making unwarranted assumptions. For example, What type of computer do you have for the purpose of studies? Desk top ☐ Laptop ☐ • You would need to precede this question with a filter question. For example, Q4 Tick the appropriate box to indicate whether you have the use of computer for the purposes of your studies. Yes ☐ No ☐ If your answer is no, skip question 5 and go straight to question 6.
Leading	• Leading questions suggest a particular answer or point of view to the respondent. Such questions will diminish the quality of you data because the responses will not reflect the respondents' actual opinions or experience. For example, 'Constant reworking of past examination papers is the best way of reinforcing learning. This approach therefore increases the chances of passing an examination.' Tick the appropriate box to indicate whether you agree with this statement. Agree ☐ Disagree ☐ • The above data would probably be better gathered using a multiple-choice question asking respondents to tick the box which they believe represents the most effective approach to preparing for an examination.

Pitfall	Advice
Double questions	• Double questions are actually two questions combined into one. Respondents may be confused by such a question if they wish to make different responses to each part but the questionnaire only allows for one answer. For example, Do you enjoy the challenge of attending college and sitting the exams for a qualification? Yes ☐ No ☐ Clearly, a student may have different views on attending college and on sitting exams.
Memory	• Beware of asking questions that rely on the respondent's memory. The older the memories, the less reliable they are likely to be. For example, List the three favourite activities you most enjoyed in primary school.
Negatives and double negatives	• The inclusion of the words 'not' and/or 'no' often confuses respondents and should therefore be avoided. For example, Do you believe it is not a good idea to do no revision before an examination? Yes ☐ No ☐
Hypothetical questions	• These tend to be of little use and any data gathered will be unreliable. For example, If you won the lottery, would you carry on working? There is no way of telling how people would react if they won a lot of money, relative to how much they already possessed.
Sensitive topics	• Care must be taken to avoid or suitably word questions on sensitive issues. • However, this depends on the current social environment and some consumer surveys include questions about some very personal products.
Social desirability/ prestige	• The reliability of responses to such questions needs to be considered. This may occur for example on questions of personal hygiene such as how many times the respondent baths or showers a week. Hence someone who perhaps baths or showers twice a week may feel it socially necessary to state that he or she does so on a daily basis. Similarly, questions regarding how often the respondent goes on holiday may solicit an inflated response. Hence a person who has occasionally taken a second holiday in any year may state that he or she regularly takes two holidays a year.
Jargon	• Use plain English as much as possible. Avoid technical jargon.

9.13   Questionnaire appearance

The presentation and appearance of your questionnaire is likely to make a positive contribution to its success, especially where it is to be self-administered by the respondent.

For postal questionnaires, you should include a covering letter, giving an introduction to the questionnaire and clear but polite instructions for completing it. The covering letter should ensure that the research objectives are transparent and provide proper reassurance regarding the context in which the data provided will be used.

Using proprietary questionnaire design and analysis software will enhance the appearance of your questionnaire and help increase your chances of persuading a potential respondent to complete it.

Tips and hints on questionnaire layout

The following advice relates mainly to self-administered questionnaires, but where applicable, the underlying principles apply as well to questionnaires administered face-to-face

Layout aspect	Advice
Easy and difficult questions	• Begin with the easier factual questions and move towards the more demanding or more sensitive questions
	• If possible, place interesting questions at strategic intervals to sustain respondent motivation in completing the questionnaire
	• A suitably interesting question at the very end of the questionnaire may encourage the respondent to send it back to you
Instructions	• Ensure that the respondent fully understands how to complete the response. Each question should carry a clear instruction in capitals.
	INDICATE YOUR SEX BY TICKING THE APPROPRIATE BOX BELOW.
	Male ☐
	Female ☐
Questionnaire length	Ideally a questionnaire should be no more than six to eight pages long. You may therefore need to edit your questionnaire to ensure it is not too long, but without sacrificing the collection of any crucial data.
Location of response boxes	Practical experience indicates that the response boxes should be positioned as far as possible, in line, towards the right hand edge of the page.
Non-leading sequence	There is a temptation to design the questionnaire to have a theme running through it whereby the preceding questions virtually lead respondent to 'inevitable' responses to subsequent questions. You should try as far as possible to avoid this effect, without making your questionnaire seem too disjointed.

Layout aspect	Advice
Classification questions	• There are differing views as to where questions relating to matters such as the respondents age, sex, education and so on should be best positioned in a questionnaire
	• Placing such questions toward the beginning of the questionnaire may be beneficial if they are brief and straightforward. However, they may be intimidating and off-putting if they are numerous or deal with sensitive topics. Placing them at the end is a more cautious approach.
Quintamensional approach	• This approach was first introduced by Gallup as far back as 1947 and is useful in identifying attitudes and opinions. It involves the following five steps.
	(i) Apply an open question to identify the respondent's level of knowledge of the topic concerned.
	(ii) Ask a further open-ended question to establish the respondent's general perceptions or feelings about the topic.
	(iii) Administer a closed question to focus on the respondent's attitude towards a specific aspect of the topic.
	(iv) Follow-up with another open-ended question to explore the respondent's justification for their attitudes regarding the specific topic.
	(v) Finally, ask a rating question to identify the strength of the respondent's attitudes towards the specific aspect of the topic being looked at.
Use of colour	• If you have the resources, consider using colour in the ink and paper used for the questionnaire .
	• Remember that soft warm pastel colours such as pink or cream are more likely to stimulate action than the colder colours such as green or blue. Bright colours like red, purple or orange should be avoided.
Use of tick boxes	• Asking respondents to tick a box is easier for the respondent to understand than asking them to circle choices.
	• A completed questionnaire using the tick box approach is also easier to analyse than one using the circle answers approach
Thank you	• The questionnaire should end with a final note of thanks to the respondent
	• You might also consider providing feedback on your findings. This may help to encourage the respondent to return the form.

9.14 Piloting the questionnaire

You may be tempted to administer your questionnaire as soon as possible after you have designed it. However, the risks of failure could be high. Practical experience indicates that a first draft is likely to contain flaws and problems. The general advice is therefore that you pilot test the questionnaire. This will enable you to spot any ambiguities or areas of potential misunderstanding. Hussey and Hussey (1997) suggest that 'it may take several drafts, with tests at every stage, before you are satisfied that you have got it right.'

In practice, a pilot will also provide you with an opportunity to make sure that your coding system works well and the data can be collated efficiently. Time spent on running a good pilot is likely save you time later in administering the questionnaire and analysing the responses.

From a technical standpoint, a pilot should also be used to provide reassurance on the **content validity** of your questionnaire; that is, the data collected are satisfy the requirements of your research question and research objectives.

Ideally, the pilot should involve 'a sub-sample of respondents who have characteristics similar to those identifiable in the main sample to be surveyed.' (Gill and Johnson, 1997). You should probably try to pilot the questionnaire on a minimum of about 10 respondents (Fink, 1995).

Bell (1997) suggests that if you cannot do a formal pilot, you should not be averse to having to 'press-gang members of your family or friends' to provide a modicum of assurance that your questionnaire at least appears to be sensible and that there appear to be no glaring anomalies.

Gill and Johnson (1997) suggest that 'where an interviewer-administered questionnaire is to be used, piloting provides the opportunity to refine and develop the interviewing and social skills of the researcher and helps to highlight any possible sources of interviewer bias.'

Bell (1997) sets out the key questions you should ask pilot respondents.

(a) How long did the questionnaire take to complete?

(b) Were the instructions clear?

(c) Were any of the questions unclear or ambiguous? If so, will you say which, and why?

(d) Did you object to answering any of the questions?

(e) Was the layout of the questionnaire clear/attractive?

(f) Any further comments?

9.15 Coding the responses

Zikmund (1997) defines coding as 'the process of identifying and classifying each answer with a numerical score or other character symbol.' This facilitates the transfer of responses from questionnaires to a computer.

So, where you are planning to process your data by computer you will have to code the questionnaire responses. With closed questions this would be done preferably before you administer the questionnaire. With open-ended questions, you would need to have a look at the responses you have received, classify these into suitable categories and then decide on a coding structure.

The following example is adapted from a UK Rail Traveller's Survey issued by the Strategic Rail Authority.

Q12a   **How much inconvenience, if any, have you experienced over the last 6 months due to the disruption of rail services in general?**

A lot of inconvenience	A little inconvenience	Not much inconvenience	No inconvenience	
1	2	3	4	(401)

Q12b   **Please write in the space provided below, in your own words, what your experiences have been of the services over the last six months. Please summarise any disruption that you have experienced personally.**

....   (402)

....

....

9.16   Testing for reliability

Easterby-Smith *et al* (1991) explain reliability as follows.

(a) Under a positivist approach, reliability is a measure of whether your questionnaire will yield the same results on different occasions, assuming that there has been no real change in what is to be measured

(b) Under a phenomenological approach, reliability is a measure of whether similar observations will be made by different researchers on different occasions

Bell (1999) explains the concept using the example of a watch. If every time you look at it, it is consistently 10 minutes fast, it could be useful because you can adjust for the ten minutes. However, it could be anywhere between say 5 to 15 minutes fast you would not be able to rely on it.

Hussey and Hussey (1997) explain that for positivistic research work, reliability has to be high and you must be able to **replicate** your results.

For a phenomenological study, reliability may not be given so much status, or it may be interpreted in a different way. Here we are concerned with whether similar observations and interpretations can be made on different occasions and/or by different observers. (Hussey and Hussey, 1997)

The data you collect might not be reliable for a variety of reasons relating to the questionnaire.

(a) The questions may contain errors such as ambiguous wording.
(b) The respondent may become bored.
(c) There may be antagonism between the researcher and respondent.

(Hussey and Hussey, 1997)

Sekaren (2000) divides reliability into **stability** and **consistency**.

Stability is the ability of a questionnaire to elicit the same data over time, whatever the testing conditions and the state of the respondents themselves. Two tests of stability are the **test-retest method** and the **parallel form test method**.

Consistency is a measure of the **homogeneity** of the questionnaire or sub sections of the questionnaire. It looks at whether the items and subsets of items in the questionnaire are highly correlated. Two ways of identifying consistency are the **interim consistency method** and the **split halves method**.

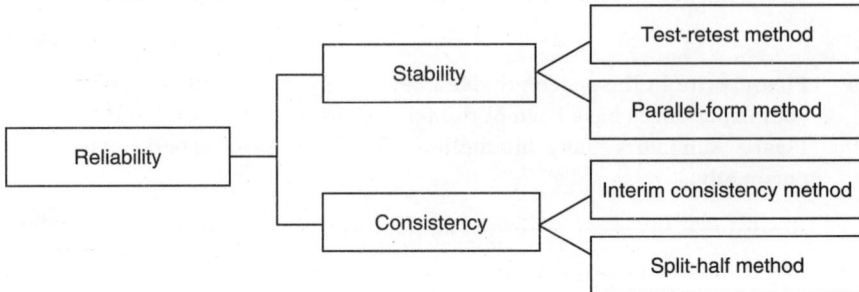

```
                                              ┌──────────────────────────┐
                                         ┌───▶│    Test-retest method    │
                              ┌───────────┐   └──────────────────────────┘
                         ┌───▶│ Stability │
                         │    └───────────┘   ┌──────────────────────────┐
┌─────────────┐         │                 └──▶│   Parallel-form method   │
│ Reliability │─────────┤                     └──────────────────────────┘
└─────────────┘         │
                         │                     ┌──────────────────────────┐
                         │    ┌─────────────┐ ┌▶│ Interim consistency method│
                         └───▶│ Consistency │─┤ └──────────────────────────┘
                              └─────────────┘ │ ┌──────────────────────────┐
                                              └▶│    Split-half method     │
                                                └──────────────────────────┘
```

Test-retest method

(a) The same questions are administered to the same group of respondents at two different dates

(b) The time interval must not be so long that it becomes a factor itself in any variation in responses

(c) The test-retest co-efficient is computed to provide an index of reliability

(d) The practical difficulty is being able to persuade people to complete the same questions twice and in a conscious way

Parallel form method

(a) This involves asking the same question in a different way eg:

Rice satisfies my hunger more than pasta? Yes/No

Pasta satisfies my hunger more than rice? Yes/No

The obvious problem here is making the questions look different without introducing material differences in their impact.

(b) The questions would also appear in different locations within the alternative questionnaires

(c) The results are correlated to determine the level of error arising from wording and ordering of questions

Interim consistency method

(a) Every response is correlated with every other response in the questionnaire and a correlation co-efficient derived, usually Chronbach's *alpa*.

(b) The downside of the method is that it involves substantial computing facilities and software.

Split-halves method

(a) The responses are split into two equal halves, for example into those relating to odd numbered questions and those relating to even numbered questions.

(b) A split-halves co-efficient is then computed.

Generally, these methods involve a lot of work and you should talk to your tutor regarding what you need to do to ensure the reliability of your questionnaire.

10   SAMPLING

10.1   Identifying a suitable approach

Your approach to sample selection will depend on whether you are working within a positivistic paradigm or a phenomenological paradigm.

(a)   For a positivistic study, sampling is a fundamental element

(b)   For a phenomenological study, sampling is less important. You may well only gather information from one person, such as the chairman of the company.

(Hussey and Hussey, 1997)

In practice, there are likely to be time and cost constraints that will make it difficult for you to gather information from every person in the population being researched. You will therefore need to rely on some form of sampling. (Denscombe, 1998)

In practice, you should ensure you keep in touch with your tutor to make sure that your ideas for defining the population and your sampling approach are suitable. You want to avoid a situation where having collected your data, you subsequently find that your tutor has reservations over your sampling approach.

10.2   Types of sample

There are essentially two types of sampling.

(a)   Probability or representative sampling
(b)   Non-probability or judgmental sampling

10.3   Probability sampling

Probability sampling is also commonly referred to as **representative** sampling because the results you obtain can be generalised to the population as a whole, with a specified degree of confidence. To ensure that there is no bias, each item in the population should have an equal chance of being selected.

Because of the facility to generalise results, probability sampling is more often associated with a positivistic research approach.

The following diagram is provided to help you understand the probability sampling process.

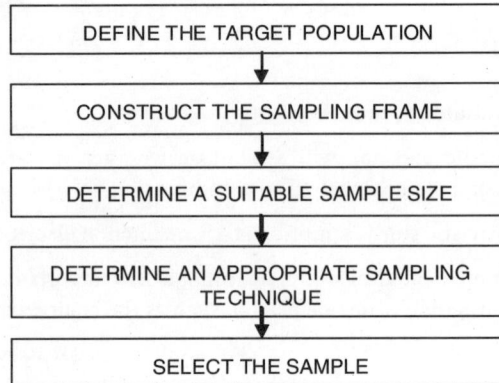

```
┌────────────────────────────────────────┐
│      DEFINE THE TARGET POPULATION        │
└────────────────────────────────────────┘
                    ↓
┌────────────────────────────────────────┐
│     CONSTRUCT THE SAMPLING FRAME         │
└────────────────────────────────────────┘
                    ↓
┌────────────────────────────────────────┐
│     DETERMINE A SUITABLE SAMPLE SIZE     │
└────────────────────────────────────────┘
                    ↓
┌────────────────────────────────────────┐
│    DETERMINE AN APPROPRIATE SAMPLING     │
│               TECHNIQUE                  │
└────────────────────────────────────────┘
                    ↓
┌────────────────────────────────────────┐
│          SELECT THE SAMPLE               │
└────────────────────────────────────────┘
```

Figure 5.5 Sample size factors

Defining the target population

The **target population** includes every individual item in the group about which information is required. For example, items may be people, animals, documents, events, production output items, vehicles and so on. The target population must be carefully defined. For example, if you were studying student attitudes at your college, you would have to decide whether to include full-time students, day-release students, students seeking different levels of qualification, students in different age groups, people who had registered as students but dropped out and so on.

Constructing the sampling frame

The **sampling frame** is the group of items from which the sample is to be drawn. This may be the same as the population, but not necessarily. For example, if you decided on a telephone sample of students, your sample frame would include only those students for whom you could obtain telephone numbers.

Avoiding bias in the sampling frame

Care should also be taken in recognising how up to date source of your sampling frame is. For student research purposes it is probably acceptable to use the latest telephone directory or electoral register, provided it is unlikely that there have been any material changes in its character and composition. There may of course be problems if you select people who have moved house or changed telephone number. Consideration should be given to the validity of using the new house occupant or new holder of the telephone number in your sample. The issue is whether you are substituting **like for like**. Again, you should discuss this with your supervisor.

Determining a suitable sample size

There are three key factors that influence sample size.

(a) Population size
(b) Confidence sought
(c) Precision of results

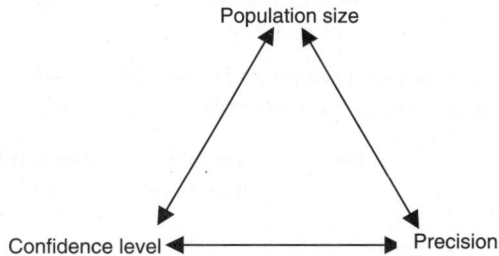

Population. Sample size is a function of population size. The larger the population, the bigger the sample you will require, although the relationship is not altogether directly proportional.

Confidence. This is the level of certainty that the data collected reflects the characteristics in the population. It is usually expressed as a percentage such as 95%. In practice, 95% and 99% are commonly specified levels of confidence sought.

Precision. This refers to how accurately you will be able to express your result. In market research parlance, this is referred to as **margin of error**.

The above principles can be seen from a review of the following table of sample sizes.

Population	Margin of error			
	5%	3%	2%	1%
50	44	48	49	50
100	79	91	96	99
150	108	132	141	148
200	132	168	185	196
250	151	203	226	244
300	168	234	267	291
400	196	291	434	384
500	217	340	414	475
750	254	440	571	696
1,000	278	516	706	906
2,000	322	696	1,091	1,655
5,000	357	879	1,622	3,288
10,000	370	964	1,936	4,899
100,000	383	1,056	2,345	8,762
1,000,000	384	1,066	2,395	9,513
10,000,000	384	1,067	2,400	9,595

EXAMPLE

Your college has 1,000 students, some of whom wear spectacles and some who do not. You wish to use sampling to establish the breakdown between spectacle wearers and non-spectacle wearers.

You want to be 95% confident that your research results are within plus or minus 3% of the real breakdown in the total population.

From the table you see that a sample of 516 will be required. You use random sampling to identify pupils and your sample shows the following results.

	Number	Sample percentage	You can be 95% confident that the situation in the population is in the range between
Spectacle wearers	148	29%	26% and 32%
Spectacle non-wearers	368	71%	68% and 74%
Total	516	100%	

If you wanted a more precise result of say a 1% margin of error you would, from the table, have to use a sample of 906.

Adjusting for response rates

In determining a sample size it is important to take into account potential non-responses. In accounting parlance, you should increase the initial sample up to ensure that the net responses actually received are sufficient. The practical problem however is estimating the rate of potential non-respondents.

Various books quote different non-response rates, so you should investigate the rate relevant to the type of research you are engaged in. The Internet can provide useful up-to-date figures and you should discuss any decision you come to with your tutor who should have the relevant experience.

EXAMPLE

Referring to the above example study on spectacle wearers, suppose that the estimated response rate was 66%. Hence, the actual sample size you would require to give you a net sample of 516 students is 516/66% = 782.

Determining an appropriate sampling technique

Selection techniques most commonly associated with probability sampling are as follows:

    (a) Simple random
    (b) Systematic
    (c) Stratified random
    (d) Cluster
    (e) Multi-stage

Simple random

    (a) Each item in the population should have an equal probability of selection. The method is sometimes compared with the process of drawing tickets in a raffle or selecting lottery balls for a lottery

    (b) In practice, there are various commonly recommended ways of doing this such as using random number tables or a computer

Systematic sampling

This technique involves taking your sample at regular intervals from the population e.g. you select five people from a bus queue of forty people, by picking every eighth person in the queue.

A small practical problem is selecting a random starting point. This can be done in a variety of ways, such as using random numbers or using the serial numbers on a currency note (but remember to cover yourself by keeping an 'audit trail' of anything that might be questioned at a later date).

If you have all the items in your sampling frame sequentially numbered on a spreadsheet you can set up a simple formula to identify your sample items, taking into consideration the initial random item.

A potential weakness may arise when using systematic sampling, where there is an element of systematic arrangement of the items in the sampling frame itself. For example, a list of customers' names is arranged by name, husband's name followed by wife's name. You may well find that there is an element of systematic arrangement with electoral registers because they tend to show the names by household; father, mother, sons and daughters. However, you will see small families and big families with single person households interspersed in between, effectively breaking up the pattern.

Stratified sampling

This technique involves organising a sampling frame into a number of strata, layers or bands based on specified attributes. Then items are drawn from each strata depending on the relative proportion each strata bears to the total population.

EXAMPLE

You want to select 100 people from a company employing a total 1500 people made up of 200 managers, 900 sales staff and 400 administration staff. Your stratified sample would look like:

	Population numbers	Population percentage	Stratified sample
Managers	60	4.0%	4
Sales staff	790	52.7%	53
Admin staff	650	43.3%	43
Total	1,500	100.0%	100

This technique provides some control over the representativness of the sample. In the above example, with only 60 managers, a random selection could have caused a bias in the number of managers selected if say 2 or 6 of them were selected causing under or over representation.

Having determined the number of items to be selected from each stratum, you can then apply random sampling or systematic sampling to pick the individual items.

Various attributes can be used to stratify your population. Examples include:

    (a) Salary bands
    (b) Age bands
    (c) Department
    (d) Geographic region
    (e) Profession or trade
    (f) Gender

You may also wish to use more than one attribute to drive your classification e.g. by salary band per department

Cluster sampling

This technique involves dividing the population up into a number of convenient clusters and randomly selecting a certain number of clusters for research. Hence your sampling frame would not comprise individual people or items but groups of people or items.

EXAMPLE

In a survey of petrol station staff training levels in the UK, instead of selecting a sample of staff randomly from petrol stations across the country, the county is broken down into local authority areas and a random selection taken of such areas e.g. Amber Valley, Hertsmere and Runnymede etc. Then all the petrol stations in the selected areas would be subjected to the specified research enquiries regarding their staff training levels.

This technique assumes that the compositions of individual clusters are similar to each other, though the contents of individual clusters may not be homogeneous.
Various approaches can be used to form the basis of clustering.

    (a) Geographic areas
    (b) Companies or businesses
    (c) Offices within an organisation

Beware of trying to cluster on the basis of departments within an organisation: professional background and role may materially influence opinion. For example, the attitude of sales people to granting credit to customers may be well be very different from those of people in the finance department.

Multi-stage sampling

This is a technique derived from cluster sampling. Instead of selecting the entire cluster, a sub sample is picked.

EXAMPLE

The clusters, as represented by local authority areas is selected as in the above example, but not all the garages in the area are included in the sample. Instead only a sample is selected from each area.

	Total number of garages	Sub sample
Amber Valley	123	31
Hertsmere	211	53
Runnymede	66	16

10.4 Non-probability sampling

Non-probability sampling uses selection techniques that result in samples that do not necessarily represent the population and hence the results cannot be generalised. Non-probability sampling might be used for several reasons.

(a) It is not feasible so select samples large enough
(b) The population itself is difficult to define
(c) There may be problems accessing all the people making up the sample.

The key characteristic of non-probability sampling is that in effect it is really about the reasons for the selection that is made. It usually involves selecting items or people based on some subjective criteria. The samples involved could therefore be biased.

Because of the impact of sample bias on your results, you should take care to explain your sampling technique in your report. It would also be sensible to discuss the matter with your tutor so that you do not go down the wrong road.

Non-probability techniques are usually associated with a phenomenological approach. For example, if your research is looking at the attitudes of employees to implementing various management change initiatives in a certain organisation, you might target specific departments that have been impacted by the changes as well the relevant project managers.

Non-probability samples may be useful in the exploratory stages of research projects.

There are various techniques of non-probability sampling.

(a) Quota
(b) Purposive
(c) Snowball
(d) Self-selection
(e) Convenience

181

Quota selection

This is a technique commonly used in market research.

It is similar to stratified sampling in that you will divide your population into groups with specified attributes. However, unlike stratified samples you do not pick a random sample from each group. Instead, you work out a quota for each group and allow the researcher to determine which person or item to pick. Usually this is on a 'first to hand' basis.

EXAMPLE

Refer back to the example given for stratified sampling above. Instead of using random techniques or a systematic basis to pick the actual sample, you might say simply take the first 4 managers on your list of managers, the first 53 sales staff, provided the lists are not listed in any hierarchical order but say alphabetic order.

EXAMPLE

You would like 100 mothers to provide data on their views about baby pushchair buying criteria. Your sampling approach is to stop the first 100 mothers with pushchairs you come across in the street.

Quota sampling is considered to avoid 'waste' where a pre-selected person or item does not provide data for whatever reason.

Quota sampling is relatively easy to set up, but a weakness is that if you have too many groups, the quota for each category will be small.

Purposive sampling

As the alternative name, judgmental sampling suggests, the people or items selected are driven by a specific purpose which the researcher has in mind, i.e. they are 'hand picked'. It therefore does not claim to be representative. In practice there may be various judgmental criteria that would influence the cases selected.

    (a)   Extreme cases
    (b)   Homogeneous subgroups
    (c)   Heterogeneous subgroups
    (d)   Critical cases
    (e)   Typical cases

The technique is useful for exploratory research and can help to ensure that you develop a well-designed questionnaire.

The technique is more suited to situations where you have a small population, such as kitchen staff in a hotel.

Snowball sampling

With snowball sampling, you would use a respondent to help you identify your next respondent. The technique is usually associated with phenomenological research and the samples obtained might not be representative.

You can of course begin with more than one respondent and each respondent can be asked to steer you to more than one other respondent.

The advantage is that the inherent multiplier effect can give you a reasonable sized sample.

The technique is compatible with purposive sampling, e.g. a respondent can be asked to identify the next person with certain attributes in terms of sex, age, organisational status and so on.

Self-selection sampling

As its name implies, the members of a self-selected sample select themselves. The samples achieved will obviously be biased to an over-representation of people who have strong feelings about the research topic. This is, to some extent, the nature of all postal samples.

EXAMPLE

A local authority sends out self-administered questionnaires to every council-tax payer to discover their opinions on the refuse collection service. Data analysis will be based on only those residents who took the trouble to complete and send in the questionnaire. Here, there is likely to be a strong bias towards respondents who have in the past had problems with their rubbish collections.

Convenience sampling

Convenience sampling involves constructing samples consisting of people or items that you can access most easily.

EXAMPLE

Debbie has been given a school assignment to study people's attitudes to fast food. She decides to administer a face to face interview to the first 25 customers she encounters coming out of her local burger-bar on the next Friday and then on the Saturday to interview the first 25 customers she encounters coming out of her local fried chicken outlet.

This is obviously quite a convenient way of finding respondents but the sampling approach is not academically rigorous and is would not be able to carry a claim of being representative. The views would be based on only two fast food outlets and there is no profiling of the respondents' characteristics.

Chapter roundup

- You will almost certainly use a mixture of secondary and primary data in your research project (the mixed methods approach). You will create primary data yourself, for your research purposes; secondary data will have been created in the past by other people for their own purposes. You should check the applicability of secondary data to your research by means of triangulation.

- Secondary data is cost effective to use, can be of very high quality and can act as a benchmark for your own research. Its use can also be more discreet than the collection of primary data. However, it may be subject to intellectual property protection and of questionable relevance and reliability.

- The main sources of primary data that you are likely to use in the course of your research are interviews, focus groups and questionnaires.

- Interviewing requires specific skills and interviewers must take care to avoid interviewer bias and interviewer effect. Interviews can have high validity.

- Focus groups are used to gather data and develop understanding of feelings and opinions. They exhibit low reliability but can provide valuable qualitative data.

- Questionnaires are useful under both the positivistic and phenomenological paradigms. They can be administered by the researcher or self-administered by the subject of the research. Non-response to self-administered questionnaires must be managed.

- Questionnaire design must satisfy the research objectives, include appropriate types of question and encourage response. Questionnaires should normally be piloted.

- Sampling is an important research technique. Sample selection is preceded by definition of the target population, construction of the sampling frame, determination of the sample size and determination of the sampling technique to be used.

- Probability or representative sampling produces results that cab ne generalised to the population as a whole. The three key factors that influence sample size are population size, the level of confidence sought and the desired precision of the results (margin of error).

- Non-probability sampling might be used if a sample large enough to allow probability sampling cannot be obtained or if the population is difficult to define. Samples are selected according to the researcher's subjective criteria. It is very easy for such samples to be subject to bias.

Answers to activities

1   **Situation 1**

Seeks to find out objective facts that have some statistical relevance, from which inferences can be drawn. This sort of research is quantitative in that it aims to obtain a sample of data and generalise responses from it. It is descriptive in that is describes the current state of affairs. It might also seek to examine the relationships between two variables: rating of quality of the lecture and the business sector in which the trainee works. Does a student's work background correlate with their appreciation of the lectures?

Situation 2

Seeks to draw out objective facts, and is testing a hypothesis against empirical data. Of course, a small sample of ten may not be enough to get a general view, but it is strong evidence that further research could be useful.

Situation 3

Features quite often in the early stage of market research and, indeed, in other areas of research. It is called qualitative research.

Clearly the researcher is not trying to prove anything, nor is the researcher trying to find out objective facts from which statistical inferences can be made – the sample is obviously not meaningful and the questioning is not controlled. The researcher is trying to tease out ideas from what people say they feel about the situation.

What the researcher is probably doing is trying to come up with ideas for further research, no more. If, say, one of the people in the group was to say that 'car designers have no appreciation of the needs of parents carrying heavy shopping and looking after children', this would give them a lot to think about.

Situation 4

The data is easily obtained, and it is not new knowledge. The main purpose of the research is, however, to analyse and draw relationships between different areas of the data, to see if there might be common features which all the sample of companies share.

To summarise, here are some key words describing the type of research encountered in the situations.

Situation	Key words	Summary
1 Market research	Statistical Objective Descriptive Quantitative	Describing facts and relationships
2 Research into a vaccine	Objective Experimental Testing hypotheses Scientific	Testing hypotheses

3	Focus group	Qualitative Non-statistical Relationships Generate ideas	Exploring ideas
4	Investment banker	Relationships Analysis Factual	Analysis

2   You probably won't be surprised that the vast majority of the scenarios are primary research both quantitative and exploratory. Secondary research is only referred to in paragraph 2.

3   As well as researching and analysing pure profitability, you could consider researching other areas. These could include:

(a) Employee motivation
(b) Staff development
(c) Staff turnover
(d) Customer focus
(e) Marketing message
(f) Customer satisfaction
(g) Market image
(h) Core values
(i) Corporate culture

You could adopt a range of data collection methods including interviewing key personnel, review of market research carried out and an investigation into the management structures of other similar companies within the industry.

The results of the triangulation in which you will have engaged will enable you to gain a wider perception of the company as a whole, adding to the level of confidence you have in your research into profitability. If all the results 'stack up' they are more likely to be trustworthy.

4   The risk of bias. A water producer is unlikely to publish results in favour of drinking coffee! The data could have been manipulated in some way, or the people who participated in the survey may not have been a truly representative sample.

Chapter 6 :

DATA ANALYSIS

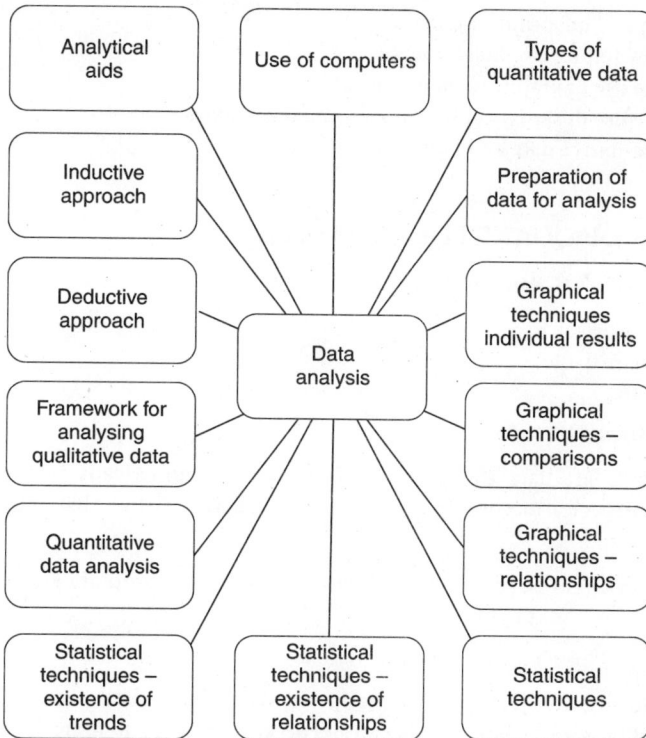

```
┌─────────────┐      ┌──────────────┐      ┌──────────────┐
│  Analytical │      │Use of computers│    │   Types of   │
│    aids     │      │              │      │quantitative data│
└─────────────┘      └──────────────┘      └──────────────┘

┌─────────────┐                            ┌──────────────┐
│  Inductive  │                            │Preparation of│
│   approach  │                            │data for analysis│
└─────────────┘                            └──────────────┘

┌─────────────┐                            ┌──────────────┐
│  Deductive  │                            │  Graphical   │
│   approach  │        ┌──────────┐        │  techniques  │
└─────────────┘        │   Data   │        │individual results│
                       │ analysis │        └──────────────┘
┌─────────────┐        └──────────┘        ┌──────────────┐
│Framework for│                            │  Graphical   │
│  analysing  │                            │ techniques – │
│qualitative data│                         │ comparisons  │
└─────────────┘                            └──────────────┘

┌─────────────┐                            ┌──────────────┐
│ Quantitative│                            │  Graphical   │
│data analysis│                            │ techniques – │
└─────────────┘                            │relationships │
                                           └──────────────┘
┌─────────────┐    ┌──────────────┐        ┌──────────────┐
│ Statistical │    │  Statistical │        │              │
│techniques – │    │ techniques – │        │ Statistical  │
│ existence of│    │ existence of │        │  techniques  │
│   trends    │    │relationships │        │              │
└─────────────┘    └──────────────┘        └──────────────┘
```

Introduction

These days it is commonplace for students to have their own personal computers (PCs) and hence most data analysis is now performed by computers. In days gone by, when most people did not have their own PCs, data were analysed by hand or by large mainframe computers. It goes without saying that performing data analysis by hand is a very time-consuming process and one which is unlikely to generate error-free results.

The main aim of this chapter is to introduce you to the ways in which you can analyse the data that you have collected using computerised analysis software, such as Excel or Lotus 123.

You are probably relieved to hear that there are computer programs available that will analyse the data that you have collected, draw high-quality graphs and perform complex statistical techniques for you. However, the quality of the results obtained will only be as good as the raw data that was input into the software in the beginning. There is one thing that most computers will not do, and that is to put your data into the format required by the computer program; this is something that you will probably have to do yourself. Most analysis software will only accept data that has been entered into a table that is known as a **data matrix**. We will be looking at data matrices in more detail later on in this chapter, but before that, we will consider the different types of data that you need to know about.

Your objectives

In this chapter you will learn about the following:

    (a) Type of quantitative data
    (b) How to prepare data for analysis
    (c) The use of graphs in data analysis
    (d) The use of statistical techniques in data analysis
    (e) Qualitative data and how to analyse it

1 TYPES OF QUANTITATIVE DATA

At the most basic level, data can be classified as follows.

    (a) Categorical
    (b) Quantifiable

1.1 Categorical data

Categorical data are data which cannot be measured numerically but which can be placed into categories (according to the specific characteristics that they possess) or placed in rank order.

Categorical data might be subdivided into **nominal data** and **ordinal data**.

Nominal data

Nominal data are also known as **descriptive data**. Such data cannot be measured numerically but once the data have been categorised according to their descriptions, it is possible to establish which category occurs the most often and how spread out the data are. For example, a record of how many of the children in a class have brown eyes, how many have blue eyes and how many have eyes of some other colour would provide nominal data.

Ordinal data

Ordinal data are also known as **ranked data**. Whilst the actual results of these data are not measured, the overall position of the individual data items is recorded. For example, the results of a class mathematics test might not reveal individual scores, but might simply place the students in rank order with the student who scored the highest mark in first place.

1.2 Quantifiable data

Quantifiable data on the other hand, are those data that, while variable, can be measured numerically. The main subdivisions of this data type are **discrete** variables and **continuous** variables.

Discrete variables

Discrete variables are only capable of taking whole number values. An example would be the number of goals scored by First Division football clubs in February 2009. A football team can only score a whole number of goals, it cannot score half or a quarter of a goal.

Continuous variables

Continuous variables can take on any value on a continuous scale. A good example is temperature, which can be recorded to a degree of precision limited only by the technology in use.

Discrete and continuous data can also be further subdivided into **interval** and **ratio data.**

Interval data

Interval data state the differences between two data values. For example, the differences between the exam marks achieved by two different students in two exams are interval data.

    (a)   Difference between 68% and 88% = 20%
    (b)   Difference between 59% and 79% = 20%

The results shown above are the same when comparing the intervals, but the individual data items are different.

Ratio data

Ratio data state the relative difference between any two data values. For example, if Student A scored 25% in his history exam and Student B scored 50% in the same exam, we could say that Student B scored twice as many marks as Student A in the history exam. We could also say that the ratio of Student A's marks to Student B's marks was 1:2.

It is important to realise that the different data types provide different levels of **numerical measurement**. The way in which data is measured will have an effect on the way in which you will need to prepare your data for analysis and the subsequent coding of your data.

Figure 6.1 below shows a summary of how data may be classified in the way that we have described in this chapter.

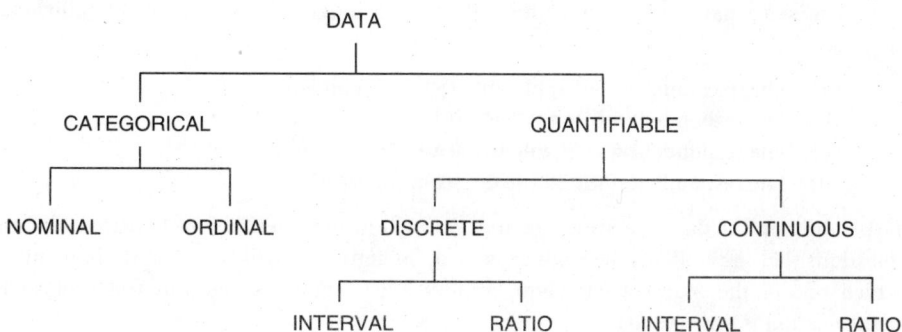

Figure 6.1 Classification of data

2   PREPARATION OF DATA FOR ANALYSIS

Once you have collected your data by one of the methods described in Chapter 5, you will need to prepare your data for analysis. The preparation of data for analysis involves the following.

(a) Data cleaning and editing
(b) Insertion of data into a data matrix
(c) Data coding
(d) Weighting of cases: differential response rates

2.1   Data cleaning

The main objective of **data cleaning** is to 'identify omissions, ambiguities, and errors in the responses' (Aaker, Kumer & Day, 1995 cited in Diamantopoulos & Schlegelmilch, 2000).

The process of data cleaning is often referred to as **data editing**. Data editing can take place either when the data is being collected or immediately after it has been collected. Data editing during data collection is known as the **'field edit'**.

Once the data have been collected, the **'central office edit'** deals with identifying any ambiguous, inconsistent or missing data. It is important to identify any problems with the data before attempting to analyse them: failing to do so will result in unnecessary delay.

'Central office edit'

The main drawback with a **'central office edit'** is that you will be unlikely to clarify any ambiguous, missing or inconsistent data with the original respondent. However, there are ways that you can minimise the occurrence of these problems. For example, you are less likely to obtain ambiguous answers if you don't ask ambiguous questions. Therefore, if you are asking respondents when they last went on holiday, make sure that you state whether you would like them to give their answer in terms of:

(a) Weeks
(b) Months
(c) Years
(d) Actual dates (ie 24/09/2004)

Missing data

One of the most common problems that you will come across when editing your data is that of **missing data**. Respondents may not answer a question for one of the following reasons.

(a) The question was not applicable to the respondent
(b) The respondent refused to answer the question
(c) The respondent was unable to answer the question
(d) The respondent omitted the question (in error)

Depending on the data you are collecting, you will need to decide how best to deal with questions that respondents have not answered. Sometimes it will be necessary to identify which one of the four reasons above applies and sometimes you will feel that such identification is unnecessary.

2.2 Insertion of data into a data matrix

The best way of presenting raw data (after it has been cleaned and edited) is in the form of a table that is known as a **data matrix**. Most analysis software will only accept data that has been entered into a **data matrix**.

It is also worth noting that **secondary data** that are collected from the **internet** or from **CD-ROMs** may not need to be re-entered into a data matrix if they are saved in an appropriate format.

Data matrix

The data matrix is the **starting point for analysis** and its structure defines the extent to which data can be analysed. A simple data matrix has a number of **rows** which are **horizontal** (say, N) and a number of **columns** which are **vertical** (say, M). You have probably come across data matrices when using spreadsheets (for example, Excel).

EXAMPLE

In order to demonstrate many of the aspects of quantitative data analysis, we are going to refer to the results of a survey that was conducted in order to determine information about the following variables for 1,000 respondents.

   (a) Age
   (b) Sex
   (c) Nationality
   (d) Annual income
   (e) Number of holidays last year
   (f) Preferred holiday type
   (g) Whether they ever holiday in Britain
   (h) If they holiday in Britain, their preferred accommodation

When we wish to refer to this survey in this chapter, it will be called the '**holiday survey**'. Information relating to three of these respondents is shown in the extract of a simple data matrix, Figure 6.2 below.

<table>
<tr><td colspan="9" align="center">COLUMNS = M</td></tr>
<tr><td></td><td>M1</td><td>M2</td><td>M3</td><td>M4</td><td>M5</td><td>M6</td><td>M7</td><td>M8</td></tr>
<tr><td></td><td>Age</td><td>Sex</td><td>Nationality</td><td>Annual Income</td><td>Number of holidays last year</td><td>Preferred holiday type*</td><td>Holiday in Britain?</td><td>If M7 = yes Preferred accommodation? **</td></tr>
<tr><td rowspan="3">ROWS = N</td></tr>
<tr><td>N1</td><td>37</td><td>Female</td><td>British</td><td>£46,000</td><td>3</td><td>Beach</td><td>Yes</td><td>B&B</td></tr>
<tr><td>N2</td><td>39</td><td>Male</td><td>American</td><td>£98,000</td><td>1</td><td>Skiing</td><td>Yes</td><td>Hotels</td></tr>
<tr><td>N3</td><td>45</td><td>Male</td><td>British</td><td>£42,000</td><td>0</td><td>Skiing</td><td>No</td><td>N/A</td></tr>
</table>

  * Respondent to choose from one of four options (beach, skiing, sailing, other)
 ** Respondent to choose from one of four options (B&B, hotels, self-catering cottages, other)

Figure 6.2 Extract from a simple data matrix

You will see in the extract above that the number of rows indicates the **number of items that are being studied,** that is, the size of the sample (or population) under review. The columns (M1 to M8) indicate the **number of variables** that are being investigated. In this case, the extract from the data matrix contains variable information about three individuals (N1, N2 and N3). You can see that this data is summarised very neatly in the data matrix. We will return to this example when we look at **data coding** in the next section of this chapter.

2.3   Data coding

Code books

A **code** is a system of numbers or letters which are used to represent others. In quantitative data analysis you are most likely to use a system of **numerical codes** which can be read by a computer. A list of codes that gives a detailed explanation of responses is known as a **code book**.

The code book relating to the **'holiday survey'** is shown below.

Code	Description	Variable
1	18–25 years	Variable M1 = AGE
2	26–35 years	
3	36–45 years	
4	46–55 years	
5	56–65 years	
6	More than 65 years	
10	Male	Variable M2 = SEX (see note 1)
11	Female	
20	British	Variable M3 = NATIONALITY (see note 2)
21	American	
22	European (excluding British)	
23	African	
24	Asian	
25	Australian/New Zealand	
30	Up to £10,000	Variable M4 = ANNUAL INCOME (see note 3)
31	£10,001 – £20,000	
32	£20,001 – £30,000	
33	£30,001 – £40,000	
34	£40,001 – £50,000	
35	£50,001 – £60,000	
36	More than £60,000	
40	Beach	Variable M6 = PREFERRED HOLIDAY TYPE
41	Skiing	
42	Sailing	

Code	Description	Variable
43	Other	
50	YES	Variable M7 = HOLIDAY IN BRITAIN?
51	NO	
60	B&B	Variable M8 = PREFERRED HOLIDAY TYPE
61	Hotels	
62	Self catering cottages	
63	Other	
64	N/A – don't holiday in Britain	

Figure 6.3 'Holiday survey' codebook

Notes

1.   This is descriptive data – for the purposes of this survey, respondents are either male or female, and each sex is coded 10 or 11.

2.   This is descriptive data – in most cases respondents will be described as having one main nationality.

3.   When entering this information into the data matrix, initially the salary is coded as the actual value. For example, £46,000 would be coded as 46000 as shown in Figure 6.4 below. Once this basic coding has been entered into the matrix, you can use analysis software to re-code the data into one of the categories coded 30 to 36. This is discussed below.

4.   Note that there is no code for the number of holidays taken last year. The number of holidays must be stated to the nearest whole number (discrete data).

We can use the 'holiday survey' codebook in order to code the data in Figure 6.2 and produce the table below.

		M1	M2	M3	M4	M5	M6	M7	M8
									COLUMNS = M
		Age	*Sex*	*Nationality*	*Annual Income*	*Number of holidays last year*	*Preferred holiday type★*	*Holiday in Britain?*	*If M7 = yes Preferred accommodation? ★★*
ROWS = N	N1	3	2	1	46000	3	1	1	1
	N2	3	1	5	98000	1	2	1	2
	N3	3	1	1	42000	0	2	2	5

Figure 6.4 Extract of a coded data matrix

Re-coding

Sometimes actual values may be used as codes for quantifiable data. For example, Column M4 in Figure 6.4 above includes salaries in the data matrix as actual values: £98,000 is originally coded as 98000. Analysis software can be used to re-code data into categories which contain similar values. Figure 6.5 below shows how annual incomes (for respondents N1, N2 and N3) can be re-coded using the 'holiday survey' codebook.

Original Annual Income	Coded Annual income	Re-coded Annual Income
£46,000	46000	5
£98,000	98000	7
£42,000	42000	5

Figure 6.5 Re-coding of annual incomes using 'holiday survey' codebook

Existing code books

If you are using secondary data, you may find that a coding scheme is already in existence. Such a scheme is known as an **existing code book** and would have been created when the data were first collected. However, there will be circumstances when you will need to create your own code book, as will be the case when you are collecting primary data. (You may also need to create your own code book in certain situations where you are using secondary data. You will need to look at each case individually and consider the level of precision that will be required).

Existing code books can be used for many variables. The examples below were identified by Saunders *et al* (2003).

    (a) **Industrial Classification** (Source: *Central Statistical Office 1997*)
    (b) **Occupation** (Source: Office of Population Censuses and Surveys, 1990a, b)
    (c) **Social Class** (Source: Office of Population Censuses and Surveys, 1991)

It is recommended that you use existing code books whenever you can because they have the following advantages.

    (a) They save time

    (b) They have usually been extensively tested

    (c) You can make comparisons with other survey results because you will be comparing like with like.

The codes contained within the existing code book are known as **pre-set codes** and should be included on your survey forms so that they can be referred to by the person filling in the form.

When should you code your data?

You can either code your data at the **time of collection** or **after collection** – it is up to you, but you should bear the following points in mind.

    (a) If you are confident that there will be **limited number of responses** to your questions, then you will probably have a list of **pre-set codes** and can code your forms as you collect the data.

    (b) If you are unsure of the number of likely responses to your questions or if there are a large number of possible responses, then it is best to create your code book once you have reviewed a sample of responses. In such a situation, it will be best to code your responses **after** data collection.

Piloting your questionnaire will help you to make this decision.

Creating a code book

If you are not in a position to use an existing code book, you will need to bear the following points in mind when you create a code book.

(a) Examine the preliminary results from the first batch of questionnaires completed.

(b) Draw up a list of possible groups.

(c) Consider the level of precision required and then create further sub-groups using this information.

(d) Allocate codes to the groups and sub-groups that you have identified. Make sure that groups which may be combined into larger groups (made up of several similar groups) are given adjacent codes so that the data may be re-coded easily.

If you refer to the 'holiday survey' codebook in Figure 6.3 you will see that the codes for variable M1 start at 1 and end at 6. Codes for variable M2, however, do not start until 10. This allows additional codes (7, 8 and 9) to be inserted if the age categories need to be amended at some point in the future.

Missing data codes

We have already mentioned that there are four main reasons why respondents may not respond to a question and hence data will be missing from the data matrix. Missing data are usually indicated by a **missing data code** and are excluded from analysis if necessary. Sometimes, however, it might be necessary to indicate the reason why the data were missing by assigning different **missing data codes**.

Multiple response and multiple dichotomy methods of coding

You may come across situations where there are many possible answers to a question asked in a survey. For example, suppose the 'holiday survey' asked one further question, such as:

'List the things you like about going on holiday.'

Some of the possible answers are as follows.

(a) Not going to work
(b) Change of scene
(c) Sunbathing
(d) Eating out

The **multiple dichotomy method** of coding would involve identifying whether each respondent either 'listed' or 'did not list' each of the variables (responses) shown above. A separate code would then be allocated to 'listed' and 'did not list'. This would then enable you to identify how many respondents listed 'not going to work' or 'eating out', for example, things they like about going on holiday.

An alternative to this coding method is the **multiple response method**. Whilst conducting your survey, you might wish to enquire (once again) as to the reasons why people like going on holiday. The multiple response method of coding would ask the following question:

'Which of the following reasons for enjoying holidays would you consider applies to you?'

(a) Not going to work
(b) Change of scene
(c) Sunbathing
(d) Eating out

Possible codes would be:

1 = applies
2 = does not apply

Therefore each reason would be coded 1 or 2 as in the example below.

Variable	Response
Not going to work	1
Change of scene	2
Sunbathing	1
Eating out	1

The main difference between these coding methods is that the **multiple dichotomy method** asks an open question, and the number of respondents listing the same variables (reasons) can then be determined. On the other hand, however, the **multiple response method** asks a closed question, and each respondent must then select which variables (reasons) apply to him and which do not.

Coding errors

Errors are likely to occur no matter how carefully you code and enter your data! While checking your data for errors is very time-consuming, it is an essential part of the data analysis process. If data is not checked, the final results may be incorrect and you will be in danger of drawing incorrect conclusions from your results. Bear the following points in mind when you check your data for errors.

(a) Make sure that there are no **illegitimate codes**. For example, with numerical codes, make sure that the number 0 (zero) is not replaced by the letters o or O. Similarly, the letter I may be incorrectly used instead of the number 1.

(b) Investigate any **illogical relationships**. For example, if a respondent has an annual income of £5,500 and took seven holidays last year, this might require further investigation to ensure that the details have been entered into the matrix correctly. Perhaps the annual salary on the original data sheet was £55,000. You will need to check the coding and the original source material.

(c) Make sure that certain **rules in filter questions** are followed correctly. For example, in Figure 6.4 above, in row N3, the respondent has said that he doesn't holiday in Britain (code = 2) and it therefore follows that the response to variable M8 should be coded 5 (N/A – never holiday in Britain). If the response to variable M8 were coded 1,2,3 or 4, a coding error would have occurred. Statistical analysis programs should be able to pick up errors such as these by running a series of checks on the program.

2.4   Weighting of cases: differential response rates

In some circumstances it may be necessary to apply **different weights** to your data, for example if you have used stratified random sampling to obtain your sample, and have obtained different response rates for each stratum. The following example will show you how to weight your data if you have differential response rates when selecting a sample using stratified random sampling.

We covered stratified random sampling in Chapter 5.

EXAMPLE

Let us suppose that you select a sample for a survey using stratified random sampling and that there are three strata, A, B and C. The response rates for each stratum are as follows.

Stratum	Response rate
A	90%
B	75%
C	60%

The weights to be applied to each stratum are as follows.

Stratum A = 90/90 = 1.0
Stratum B = 90/75 = 1.2
Stratum C = 90/60 = 1.5

Note that the weight for the stratum with the highest response rate will always be 1.

Most statistical analysis software will apply weights to your data if the weights are entered as separate variables in your data matrix. The easiest way to calculate weights is to compare the response rates of each stratum with the response rate of the stratum which has the highest response rate (Stratum A in the above example).

When you have **coded** and **entered** your data into your **data matrix** you will be ready to start your **analysis**. In the next section, we will be looking at ways in which different types of graph can help you to understand more clearly the data you have collected. We shall start by looking at how graphs can be used to show individual results.

3   GRAPHICAL TECHNIQUES – INDIVIDUAL RESULTS

There are a number of ways in which graphs can be used to show individual results.

(a)   Specific values are shown using **frequency distributions**

(b)   Highest and lowest values are shown using **bar charts** and **histograms**

(c)   Trends are shown on **line graphs**

(d)   Proportions are shown on **pie charts**

(e)   Distributions are shown on **frequency polygons, bar charts, histograms and box plots**

We shall be looking at each of these methods of data presentation in turn.

3.1   Frequency distributions

Data sets are generally made up of a limited number of data values. **Frequency distributions** are simply tables that record the **frequency** (number of times) with which a value or characteristic occurs. If there is a large set of data or if there are many different data groups, it is often convenient to **group frequencies** together into **classes**. This is known as a **grouped frequency distribution**. We shall be using frequency distributions extensively in this chapter in order to demonstrate the range of graphical and analysis techniques that are available for presenting your data.

EXAMPLE

The following frequency distribution has been extracted from the results of the 'holiday survey': 1,000 respondents were questioned about their age, annual salaries and holiday preferences. We looked at some of the results of this survey when we demonstrated how data matrices are prepared and how results can be coded.

Age (to the nearest year)	Code	Frequency
18–25	1	120
26–35	2	220
36–45	3	320
46–55	4	190
56–65	5	120
more than 65	6	30
	Total	1,000

Figure 6.6 Frequency distribution showing ages of 'holiday survey' respondents

The frequency distribution in Figure 6.6 above shows the range of different ages of the 1,000 people who were surveyed. This distribution is made up of **discrete data** (ie data which can only take on whole numbers – respondents have been asked to state their age to the nearest year). It also demonstrates how the different ages of the respondents have been grouped together in order to produce a **grouped frequency distribution**.

EXAMPLE

Figure 6.7 below shows a grouped frequency distribution which is made up of **continuous data.** It shows how many of the people surveyed earn salaries that fall within certain bands of income.

Annual Income	Code	Frequency
£		
10,000 or less	1	105
10,001–20,000	2	370
20,001–30,000	3	290
30,001–40,000	4	180
40,001–50,000	5	40
50,001–60,000	6	10
more than 60,000	7	5
	Total	1,000

Figure 6.7 Frequency distribution showing annual incomes of 'holiday survey' respondents

3.2 Bar charts

Bar charts are one of the most common methods of presenting data in a visual form. They are simply charts in which quantities are shown in the form of bars. There are three main types of bar chart.

(a) Simple bar charts
(b) Component bar charts, including percentage component bar charts
(c) Multiple or compound bar charts

Simple bar charts

The results from our 'holiday survey' revealed that the following responses were obtained in relation to Variable M8 (preferred accommodation of those who holiday in Britain).

Preferred accommodation	Code	Frequency
B&B	1	50
Hotel	2	290
Self catering cottages	3	350
Other	4	130
n/a – don't holiday in Britain	5	180
	Total	1,000

Figure 6.8 Frequency distribution showing preferred accommodation of respondents who holiday in Britain

The results shown in Figure 6.8 above could be shown graphically in the form of a simple bar chart. Notice that the data that we are presenting here are **categorical (nominal) data** since they cannot be measured as numerical quantities. It is also evident from the graph that self-catering holidays are the most popular whilst B&B holidays are the least popular.

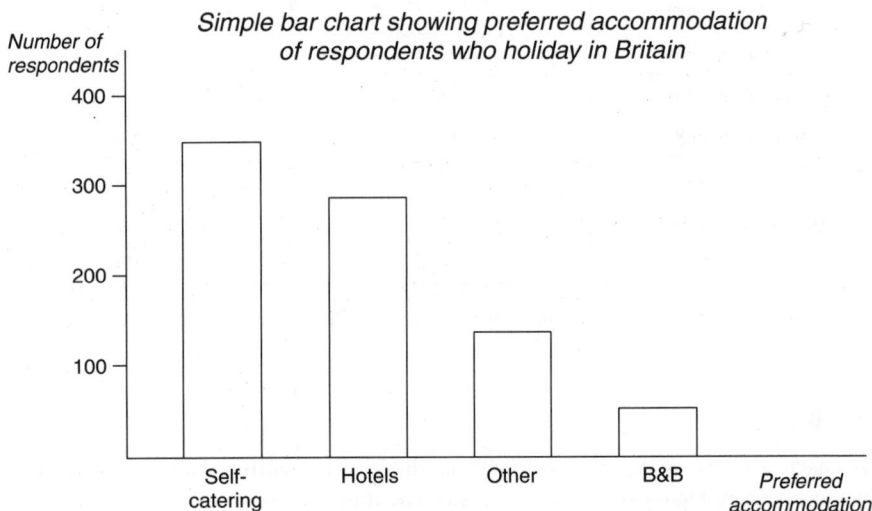

Figure 6.9 Simple bar chart

Note that the results of the 180 respondents who do not holiday in Britain are not included on the graph.

3.3   Histograms

A histogram is a chart that looks like a bar chart except that the bars are joined together. On a histogram, frequencies are represented by the **areas** covered by the bars, and not the **heights** of the bar (as is the case with bar charts). **Histograms** are generally used for **continuous data**, and the continuous nature of the data is indicated by the way in which the bars do not have any gaps between them.

The frequency distribution in Figure 6.7 above could be presented as the following histogram.

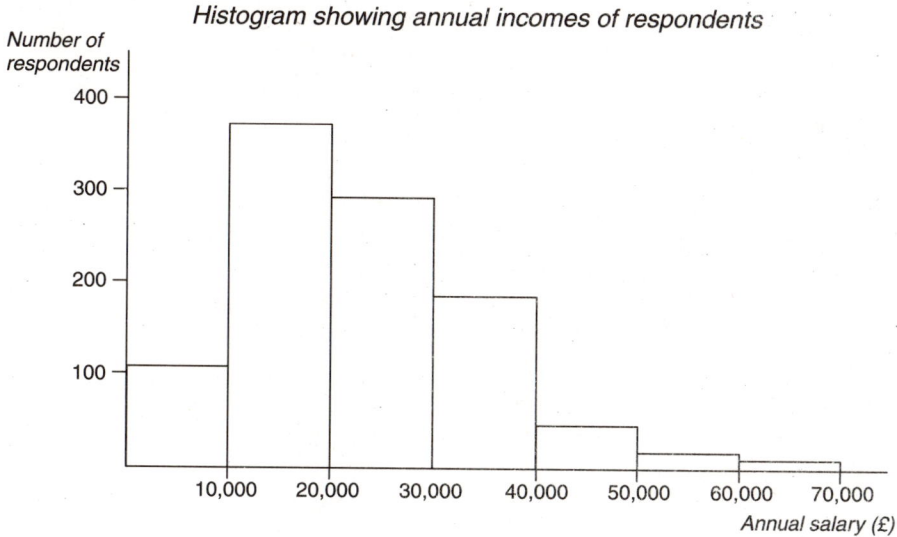

Figure 6.10 Histogram

The graph above has **equal-width class intervals** and so the highest and lowest values are easy to identify (for example, the highest value is the salary band £10,001-£20,000). The heights of the bars still represent the frequencies when the class widths are equal. However, when class widths are unequal, it is the area of the bar which represents the frequencies and not the height. Analysis software is not able to cope easily with drawing histograms with unequal-width classes and therefore treats such histograms as a variation of a bar chart.

Histograms are not a particularly good way of presenting a distribution: they are far better presented by **frequency polygons. Frequency polygons** can be drawn from a histogram by joining up the mid-points of the histogram bars. The histogram in Figure 6.10 could be converted into a frequency polygon as follows.

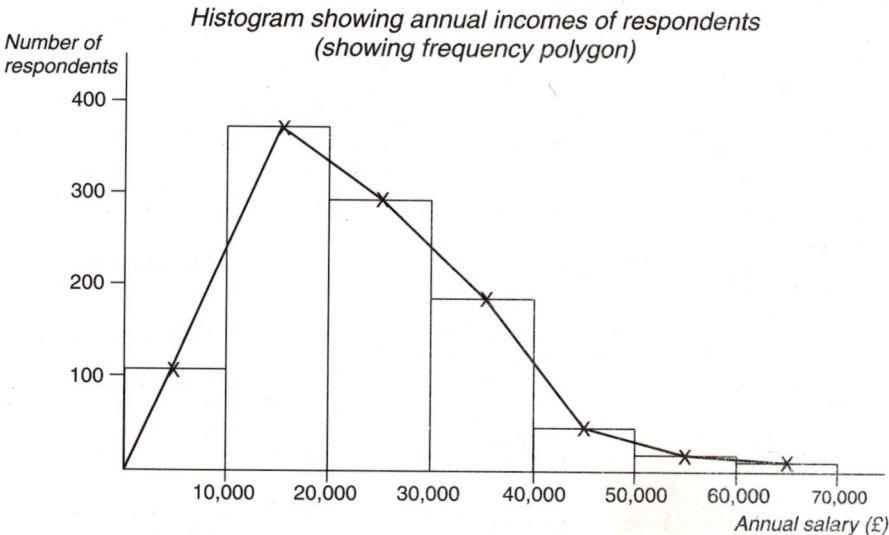

Figure 6.11 Frequency polygon

Note that most analysis software will treat a frequency polygon as a version of a line graph. We shall be looking at line graphs in the next section.

3.4   Line graphs

Line graphs are the most suitable diagrams to draw if you wish to show the **trends of individual results**. For example, if we wanted to compare the average number of holidays taken per year by the general public over the last ten years we could plot our results on a **line graph** such as the one shown in Figure 6.12 below.

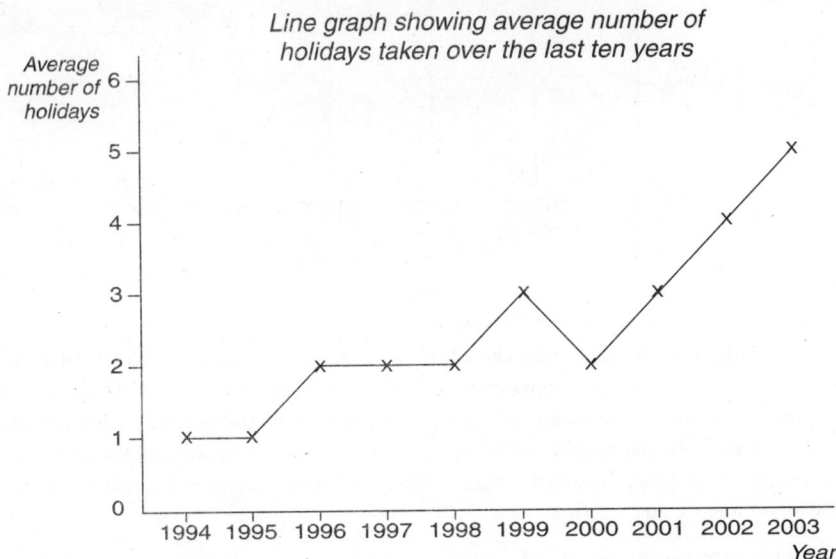

Figure 6.12 Line graph

It is evident from the line graph that the **general trend** in the number of holidays taken by respondents is **increasing** over time.

3.5   Pie charts

A **pie chart** is a chart that is used to show pictorially the **relative size** of component elements of a total. If we wished to show the types of holiday preferred by the respondents in our 'holiday survey', a pie chart would be able to present this data very clearly and would show the proportion of respondents that had a preference for each type of holiday. Suppose our 'holiday survey' revealed the following results.

Preferred holiday type	Code	Frequency	Percentage
Beach	1	350	35%
Skiing	2	290	29%
Sailing	3	280	28%
Other	4	80	8%
	Total	1,000	100%

Analysis software could present these data as follows.

Pie chart showing preferred holiday type of respondents surveyed

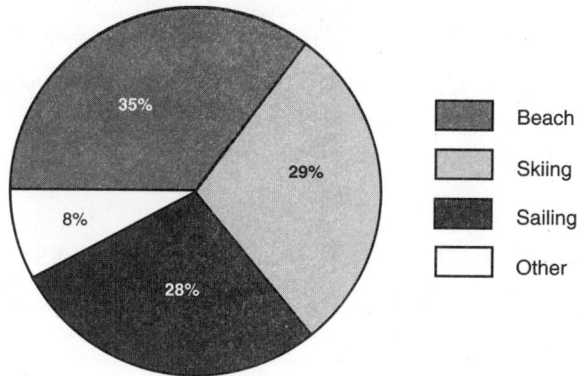

Figure 6.13 Pie chart

Note that a pie chart is a circle and that a circle has 360 degrees. The pie chart is therefore drawn by allocating 35% of the 360 degrees (126 degrees) to beach holidays, 29% of the 360 degrees (104 degrees) to skiing holidays and so on. Don't worry – the data analysis software that you are using will draw your pie charts for you!

3.6   Box plots

Box plots are often included in more advanced statistical analysis software programs. A box plot is a diagram that displays the **distribution of data pictorially** and also identifies the following **statistical values**.

(a) **Median** (middle value of a distribution)
(b) The **range** of the data
(c) **Extreme values** (highest and lowest values in the range of data)
(d) **Inter-quartile range** (the middle 50% of the distribution)

We shall be looking at these terms in more detail when we study statistical techniques in the next section of this chapter.

The annotated sketch below identifies the main features of a box plot.

Diagram to show features of a box plot

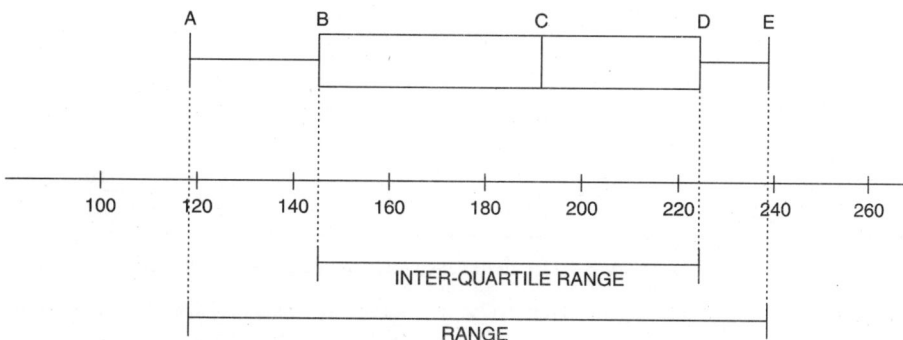

203

A = Lowest value in distribution (118)
B = Lower limit of inter-quartile range (145)
C = Median (192)
D = Upper limit of inter-quartile range (224)
E = Highest value in distribution (238)
A–E = Range (238 – 118 = 120)
A–B = Lower quartile (point below which 25% of distribution lie = 145)
B–D = Inter-quartile range (145 – 224)
D–E = Upper quartile (point above which 25% of distribution lie = 224)

Figure 6.14 Box plot

4   GRAPHICAL TECHNIQUES – COMPARISONS

There are a number of ways in which graphs can be used to show **comparisons** between individual results.

(a)   Specific values and interdependence between values are shown in **contingency tables**

(b)   Highest and lowest values are compared using **multiple bar charts**

(c)   Proportions are compared using **percentage component bar charts and/or two or more pie charts**

(d)   Trends are compared using **multiple line graphs**

(e)   Totals are compared using **component bar charts**

(f)   Distributions are compared using **multiple box plots**

We have already come across some of these data presentation methods when we looked at the most appropriate diagrams to use if we wish to present individual results.

4.1   Contingency tables

Let us return to our 'holiday survey'. Suppose that we wish to determine whether there is any link between the number of holidays taken and whether the respondents are male or female. We could draw up a **contingency table** that details our individual results as follows.

Number of holidays	Male	Female	Total
0	40	80	120
1	100	220	320
2	85	185	270
3	70	120	190
4	18	37	55
5	5	30	35
6	2	8	10
Total	320	680	1,000

Figure 6.15 Contingency table showing number of holidays by gender

Contingency tables are used extensively in statistical analysis. We will return to contingency tables when we study chi-squared tests later in this chapter. These tests are performed in order to determine whether two or more variables are **significantly associated**.

4.2   Multiple, percentage component and component bar charts

We mentioned earlier that there were a number of different types of **bar chart**. We need to use these types of bar chart when comparing the following.

(a)   Highest and lowest values
(b)   Proportions
(c)   Totals

If we wish to make comparisons between the highest and lowest values, the **multiple bar chart** is an ideal tool for doing this. A multiple bar chart is a bar chart in which two or more separate bars are used to present sub-divisions of data. For example, we could explore the type of holiday preferred by men and women by drawing up a multiple bar chart such as the one below.

Preferred holiday type	Male	Female	Total
Beach	40	310	350
Skiing	230	60	290
Sailing	170	110	280
Other	70	10	80
	510	490	1,000

Figure 6.16 Contingency table showing preferred holiday type by gender

Data analysis software would use this information in order to present these results in a multiple bar chart, such as the one shown below in Figure 6.17.

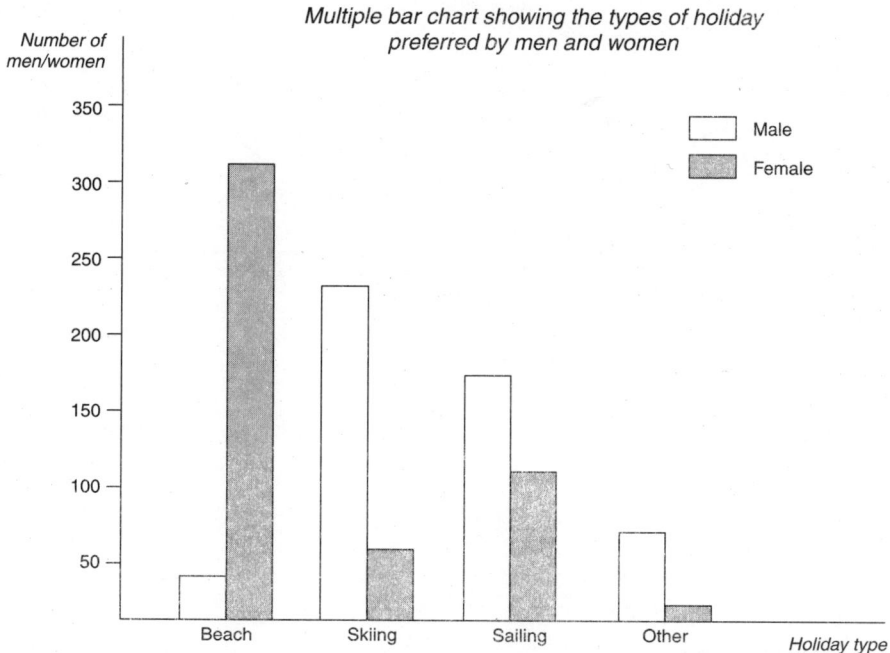

Figure 6.17 Multiple bar chart

Percentage component bar charts

If, however, we wish to make comparisons of the **proportions** between variables, a better tool to use would be a **percentage component bar chart**. A percentage component bar chart indicates the relative sizes of components by the lengths of the sections of the bar. Suppose that we wish to show the number of holidays taken in a year by different nationalities and that the 'holiday survey' revealed the following results. We could easily make comparisons by producing a **percentage component bar chart**.

Number of holidays taken last year	British	American	European (excluding British)	African	Asian	Australian /New Zealand	Total
0	23	40	27	10	12	8	120
1	145	40	70	25	30	10	320
2	130	35	65	10	15	15	270
3	110	15	54	1	9	1	190
4	7	0	45	1	1	1	55
5	3	0	28	1	1	2	35
6	2	0	1	2	2	3	10
	420	130	290	50	70	40	1,000

Figure 6.18 Contingency table showing number of holidays taken last year and nationality

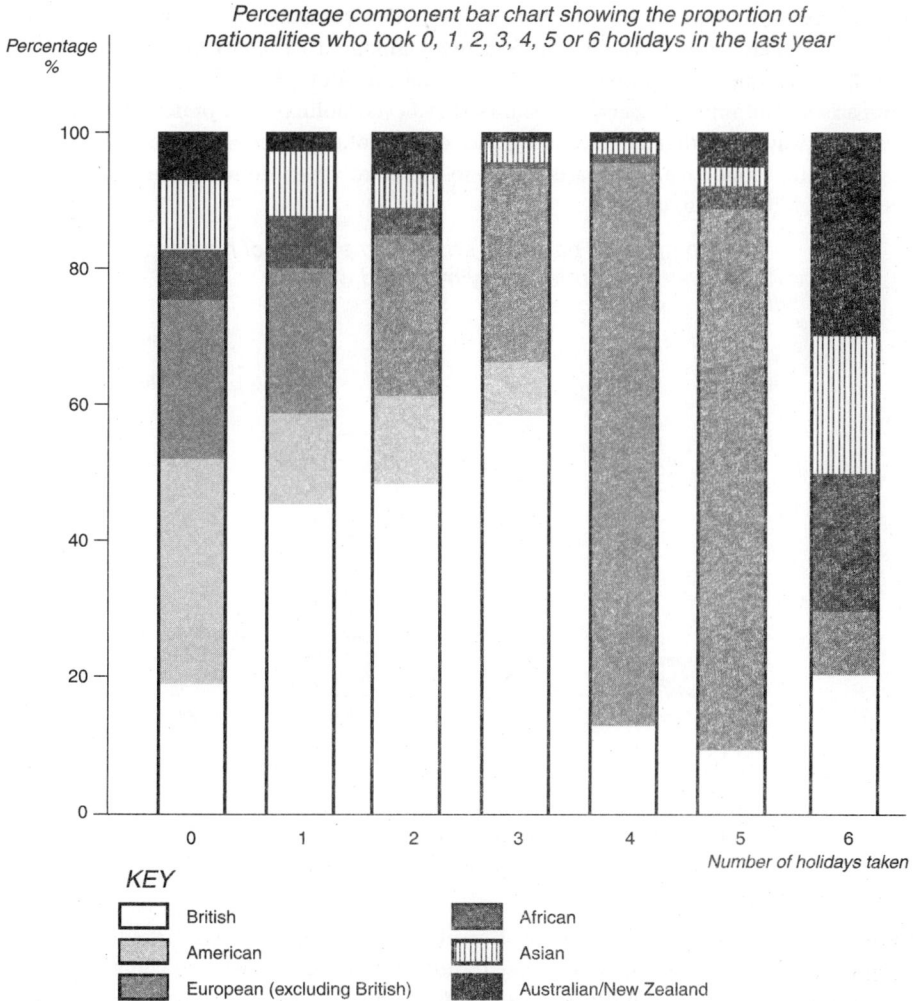

Figure 6.19 Percentage component bar chart

The graph above shows a lot of information and comparisons can be easily made between adjacent bars. Another way of showing this information would have been to have drawn six pie charts with one chart for 0 holidays, one for 1 holiday and so on. Within each chart, the proportion of each of the nationalities having the number of holidays in question would be shown as being coloured or shaded differently.

Component bar charts

If, however, we wish to compare **totals** between variables, we can use a variation on the bar chart known as the **component bar chart** (sometimes called a **stacked bar chart**). A component bar chart is a bar chart that gives a breakdown of each total into its components. The total length of each bar and each component on a bar chart indicates **magnitude**. For example, if we wished to show totals, the information relating to preferred holiday types of men and women that were shown in the multiple bar chart above, could also be shown in a component bar chart. Note how the multiple bar chart indicates whether men or women take the most or least number of beach, skiing and sailing holidays, whereas the component bar chart compares the totals between the different holiday types. It is evident from the component bar chart that beach holidays are the most popular, followed by skiing, sailing and other types of holiday. In comparison, the multiple bar chart shows that beach holidays are preferred by women (by a long way!) and that skiing, sailing and 'other' holidays are more popular with men. Always think about what you are trying to compare when deciding the type of data presentation method to use.

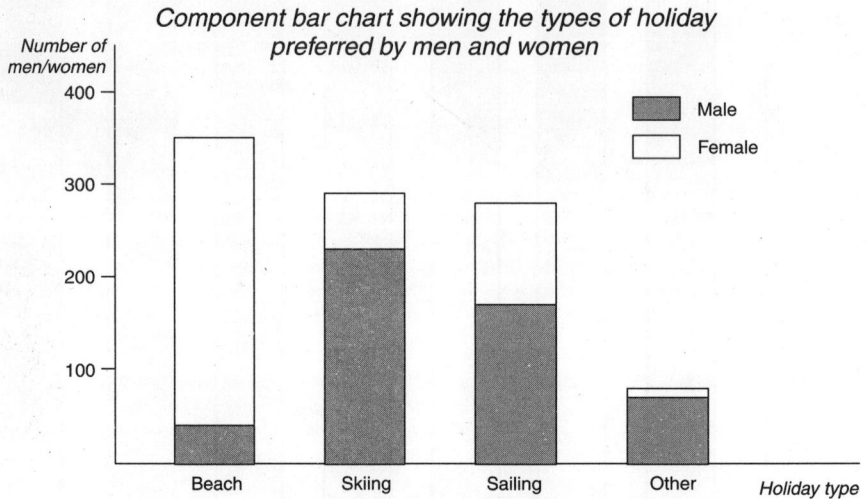

Figure 6.20 Component bar chart

4.3 Multiple line graphs and multiple box plots

Multiple line graphs

When showing the trends of individual results, we have already established that a line graph is the best way of displaying these trends. If, however, we wish to compare trends, we would simply draw a **multiple line graph**. A multiple line graph is simply a graph that displays a number of trend lines on it. The point at which any of these lines cross is known as the **conjunction point**. We shall be looking at line graphs further when we study time series analysis in the next section of this chapter.

Multiple box plots

Distributions may be compared by producing **multiple box plots**. These are similar to the single box plot but show a number of box plots for a number of different variables. Comparisons are easily made because the individual box plots are all on the same diagram.

5   GRAPHICAL TECHNIQUES – RELATIONSHIPS

5.1   Scattergraphs

When considering our data, we may suspect that a relationship exists between two sets of ranked and quantifiable data. A simple example would be that there might well be a link between age and income, in that salary increases tend to come as people get older. To test this idea we can plot data points relating to the two variables under consideration on a **scattergraph**.

- (a)   The **horizontal axis** of a scattergraph represents the **independent** variable x. In our example, this would be age.
- (b)   The **vertical axis** of a scattergraph represents the **dependent** variable y. In our example, this would be income, because we suppose that income **depends**, to some extent, on age

Once the data points have been plotted, a **line of best fit** is drawn and its formula can be determined (the general equation for this is $Y = a + bx$).

- (a)   An upward-sloping line of best fit indicates **positive** correlation.
- (b)   A downward-sloping line of best fit indicates **negative** correlation.

Positive correlation indicates that low values of one variable are associated with low values of the other and high values of one variable are associated with high values of the other.

Negative correlation indicates that low values of one variable are associated with high values of the other, and high values of one variable with low values of the other.

Correlation can be shown graphically on **scattergraphs** as follows.

Perfect correlation

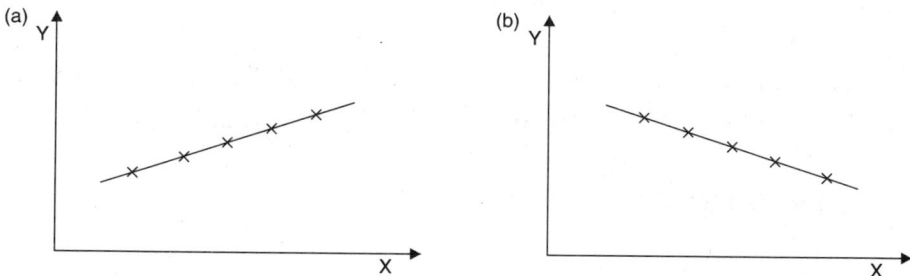

Figure 6.21: Scattergraphs

All the pairs of values lie on a straight line. An exact linear relationship exists between the two variables.

Partial correlation

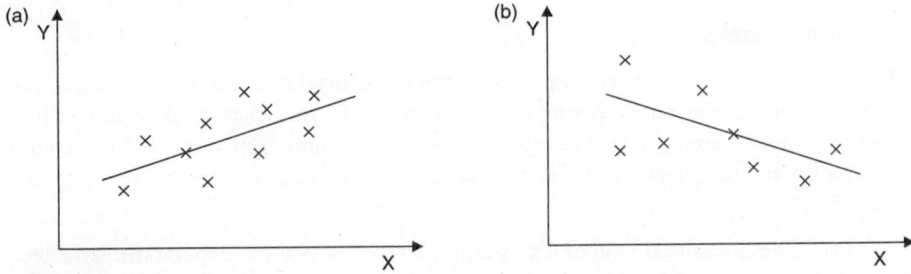

(a) and (b) scatter graphs

In (a), although there is no exact relationship, low values of X tend to be associated with low values of Y, and high values of X with high values of Y.

In (b), again there is no exact relationship, but low values of X tend to be associated with high values of Y and *vice versa*.

No correlation

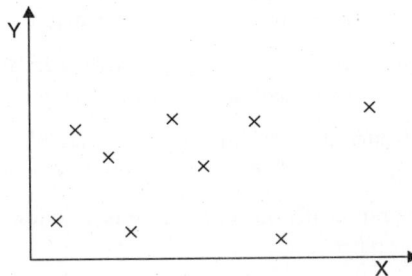

Figure 6.22 Scattergraph showing perfect, partial and no correlation

We shall be looking at relationships between variables in more detail when we look at correlation and regression in the next section of this chapter.

6   STATISTICAL TECHNIQUES

Much of this section will be familiar from Unit 6, Business Decision Making.

So far we have only considered the ways in which your research findings can be presented **graphically**. Statistical techniques allow you to **describe** and **compare** the data that you have collected.

Statistical techniques fall into the following groups.

- (a)   Measures of central tendency
- (b)   Measures of dispersion
- (c)   Existence of relationships
- (d)   Existence of trends

6.1   Measures of central tendency

Measures of central tendency provide a general impression of the most common values of the population or sample. There are three main measures of central tendency.

(a)   Mean
(b)   Median
(c)   Mode

Arithmetic mean

The **arithmetic mean** is calculated by summing all of the values obtained for the variable in question and dividing by the number of values. It is the only measure of central tendency that is calculated by taking all of the data items in a distribution into account. It is usually written as $\bar{x}$. The arithmetic mean has the following advantages.

(a)   It is simple to calculate
(b)   It is universally understood
(c)   It represents the entire data set
(d)   It is used in statistical analysis

Median

The **median** or middle value is found by arranging the data items in your distribution in **order of magnitude**. (A list of data items in order of value is known as an **array**). The **median** value is the value of the central item in the range. In other words, 50% of the remaining values lie above the median and 50% below it. If there are an odd number of items in the array, it will be easy to find the middle item. If, however, there is an even number of items in the array, there will be two middle items and you will need to calculate the arithmetic mean of these two items.

Advantages of the median are as follows.

(a)   It is easy to understand
(b)   It is not affected by extreme values
(c)   It can represent an actual item in the distribution

Mode

The **mode** or **modal value** is the **most frequently-occurring** value or category in the distribution. Unlike the arithmetic mean and the median, it can be used for both categorical and quantifiable data. For example, in relation to the 'holiday survey', the preferred accommodation of those respondents who holiday in Britain is self-catering (refer to the simple bar chart in Figure 6.9 above) and therefore the **modal** holiday accommodation is self-catering.

The mode has the following advantages.

(a)   It is easy to determine
(b)   It is not influenced by any extreme values in the data set
(c)   It can be used for categorical (ordinal) data (unlike the mean and the median)
(d)   It can represent an actual item in the distribution

6.2 Measures of dispersion

In addition to describing a variable's average value it is also useful to describe how dispersed the variables are. The main measures of dispersion are as follows.

(a) Range
(b) Inter-quartile range
(c) Quartiles
(d) Deciles and percentiles
(e) Spread
(f) Standard deviation
(g) Coefficient of variation

Range

The **range** is the difference between the highest and the lowest values in a distribution. For example, in our 'holiday survey', the number of holidays taken by respondents ranged between 0 and 6 (see Figure 6.15). The range of these variables is therefore 6 (6 - 0). Whilst this statistic is not frequently used in research reports, it does give the researcher a good idea of the diversity of the values that he is dealing with.

Inter-quartile range

We had a brief look at the **inter-quartile range** and the **median** when we studied box plots in the previous section of this chapter. The following diagram shows how the range can be divided into a number of different parts.

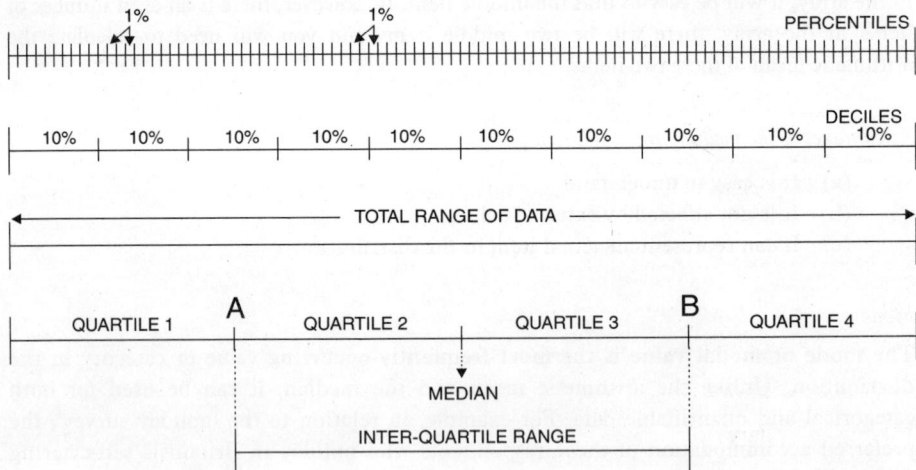

Figure 6.25 Range, percentiles, deciles and quartiles

The **lower quartile** is represented by point A in the graph above and the **upper quartile** is represented by point B.

(a) The **lower quartile** is the point below which 25% of the population lie
(b) The **upper quartile** is the point above which 25% of the population lie

The **inter-quartile range** is a frequently used statistic which identifies the **middle 50%** of the population. As already indicated, the **median** is the middle point in the inter-quartile range.

It is also possible to divide the range into **deciles** and **percentiles**.

(a) ˙**Percentiles** divide a distribution into 100 equal parts
(b) **Deciles** divide a distribution into 10 equal parts

Standard deviation

An important part of your research will involve identifying the extent to which data values for a variable are **dispersed** around the mean. A distribution whose data values are all close to the mean indicate that the mean is more typical of the variable than it is in a distribution in which the data values are more spread out. The **standard deviation** is a statistical value that describes the extent to which data items in a population are spread along the array.

The standard deviation is calculated by taking the square root of the **variance**. The variance is the average of the squared deviations from the mean of each value in a distribution. The standard deviation of data items from a **sample** (rather than a **population**) is calculated using a slightly different formula. If, however, your sample contains more than thirty data items, the statistics calculated are more or less the same.

The computerised analysis software that you are using will automatically calculate the standard deviation of the data that you have collected, so you don't need to worry about any complicated formulae here. You must, however, be able to interpret the statistics that the software calculates for you.

Coefficient of variation

If you wish to compare the dispersion of distributions expressed in different units, you will need to calculate a statistic known as the **coefficient of variation**. The coefficient of variation is calculated by dividing the standard deviation of the distribution by its arithmetic mean. This produces a purely numerical quantity. Mean and standard deviation are expressed in the same units as the variable to which they relate, such as years of age or centimetres of height, but the coefficient of variation is a **dimensionless measure**. Suppose you had collected data on senior management salaries and on the number of days of holiday such managers take in a year. There would not be much point in comparing the means or the standard deviations as they would be expressed in different units. However, the coefficients of variation could be compared. The higher the value of the coefficient of variation, the more spread out the data in the distribution.

The coefficient of variation is also known as the **coefficient of relative dispersion**.

Taking our salary and holiday example a little further, we might obtain results that looked like the table below

	Senior managers	
	£ salary	Days holiday
Mean	62,053	13.72
Standard deviation	9,056	1.76
Coefficient of variation	0.146	0.128

Figure 6.24 Coefficient of variation table

Interpretation of results

Clearly, it is not possible to make meaningful comparisons between salary and holiday means and standard deviations. However, the coefficient of determination of salaries is higher than that of days holiday, indicating that salaries have a greater **relative dispersion** than days holiday. This might cause us to hypothesise on such matters as the relative importance of salary and holiday to senior managers, the time constraints on the work of senior managers in general and the possible existence among senior managers of a felt need to be seen to be present at work.

7 STATISTICAL TECHNIQUES – EXISTENCE OF RELATIONSHIPS

One of the most important uses of statistics is to investigate whether relationships exist between one variable and another. There are a number of ways in which statistics can be used in order to examine this.

(a) Chi-squared (χ^2) test
(b) T-tests
(c) Pearson's product moment correlation coefficient
(d) Coefficient of determination
(e) Regression equations
(f) Spearman's rank correlation coefficient

7.1 Chi-squared test

The χ^2 test is used to compare sets of data. It is used in a procedure that examines a set of observed data points to see if their values **differ significantly** from **what we would have expected them to be**. A significant difference here is a difference that could not have arisen by chance. This kind of testing is known as **significance testing** and to carry it out properly, we must define the chance that a difference will be detected as having a specific numerical value of probability, such as 5% or 1%. This is called the **confidence level**.

For example, we might look at our contingency table of holiday preferences.

Preferred holiday type	Male	Female	Total
Beach	40	310	350
Skiing	230	60	290
Sailing	170	110	280
Other	70	10	80
	510	490	1,000

Figure 6.25 preferred holiday type

In this case we could define an 'expected' set of proportional values for holiday preferences as the values in the total column. We could then use these expected values for comparisons with the preferences expressed separately by men and women. We would proceed by proposing two hypotheses that we would then proceed to test at a given level of probability.

(a) The **null hypothesis** states that there is **no significant difference** between the observed and expected values.

(b) The **alternative hypothesis** states that there is a **significant difference** between the values.

We will not go further into the computation of the χ^2 statistic, since we anticipate that you will use a computer for this purpose. However, we shall explain its interpretation.

In the case of our holiday preference table, we obtain a χ^2 value of 365.54. To assess the importance of this number we must refer to a table of χ^2 values

Chi-squared tables

Most statistics textbooks will contain χ^2 tables. It is important that you are able to read such tables so that you can interpret the results generated by your statistical analysis software.

Chi-squared tables have **confidence level percentage columns** along the top of the table and **degrees of freedom** rows down the side of the table. These two quantities are known as the **entering arguments** for the tables

Degrees of freedom

Degrees of freedom is the name given to the **number of values** that are **free to be varied** when calculating a statistic. For example, if we have a column of five percentages that must sum to 100%, we are free to vary only four of them, since the fifth must always be a balancing figure that causes the column to sum to 100%. In the case of a contingency table that has N rows and M columns, use the following formula.

Degrees of freedom $= (M – 1)(N – 1)$

Thus in our example above, we have M = 4 and N=2 and therefore degrees of freedom $= 3 \times 1 = 3$.

Evaluating the results

If we wish to be 99.9% confident that our survey demonstrates a significant difference between the observed values (the separate preferences of men and of women) and the expected values (the total column values) then we need to look along row three of the table (degrees of freedom = 3) until we reach the column that relates to 0.1%. The 0.1% indicates that there is a 0.1% probability that our results occurred by chance and corresponds to our chosen confidence level of 99.9%.

On consulting our table, the point where degrees of freedom = 3 and desired confidence level = 0.1%, we find a χ^2 value of 16.3. This is the maximum value of χ^2 that would allow us to accept the null hypothesis at our chosen level of probability, 0.1%.

Clearly, our computed χ^2 statistic of 365.54 is much greater than 16.3; this indicates that the probability our results occurred by chance is **less than** 0.001 and that we can be **more than** 99.9% confident that preferred holiday types and the sex of the respondent are **significantly associated**.

Most statistical analysis software will calculate the probability that two variables are **independent**. (In our example, the probability that the variables are independent is less than 0.1%, and we are therefore 99.9% (100 – 0.1) confident that there is a significant association between the variables.) If you are using a spreadsheet, however, you will need to refer to χ^2 tables in order to determine the probability that the two variables are independent.

7.2 T-tests

The t statistic is very useful when we are dealing with small sample sizes. 'Small' in this context means below 30.

Suppose that we wish to investigate whether there is a **significant difference** in the average time taken (in minutes) by small samples of men and women to look up a particular holiday company on the Internet, based on the following results.

	Men	Women
Number in sample	6	8
Mean time (in minutes)	4.26	4.35
Standard deviation	0.0548	0.0424

Figure 6.26 T-test results

Once again, your software will produce the statistic you need: here, the t value = 3.46.

Evaluating the results

As previously, the entering arguments for the t tables are degrees of freedom and desired probability.

With the t statistic, degrees of freedom generally is equal to $n - 1$, where n is the sample size. Here we have two distinct samples, one of 6 men and one of 8 women, so degrees of freedom = (6-1) + (8-1) = 12.

For this example, we will use a probability of 0.05 as our other entering argument. This will give us a confidence level of 95%.

From t distribution tables, where we have 12 degrees of freedom and a probability of 0.05, the t value is 2.18. However, we have a t value from the survey of 3.46 which is much greater. This indicates that the average times taken by men and women to look up the tour company on the Internet were **significantly different** at the 95% confidence level. (In fact, the probability that our t value of 3.46 could have arisen by chance is actually somewhere between 0.005 and 0.0005 and thus extremely remote.)

There are a couple of assumptions associated with t tests that you should be aware of.

    (a)   They assume that the data are **normally distributed**.
    (b)   It is assumed that the two groups have the **same (or very similar) variances**.

Nevertheless, 'although the t test assumes that the data are normally distributed, this can be ignored without too many problems even with sample sizes of less than 30. The assumption that data for the two groups have the same variance (standard deviation squared) can also be ignored provided that the two samples are of similar size.' (Hays, 1994)

7.3 Correlation and regression

We will now turn our attention to the statistical tests that you can use in order to establish whether relationships exist between two variables. The area of statistics that is concerned with this is known as **correlation and regression**.

We have already mentioned correlation in our earlier discussion of **scattergraphs**.

(a) **Regression** locates two variable data in terms of a **mathematical relationship** (the general form is $y = a + bx$) which can be graphed as a curve or a line.

(b) **Correlation,** on the other hand, describes the nature of the spread of the items about the curve or line.

The overall purpose of calculating correlation and regression measures is to ascertain **the extent to which one variable is related to another.**

Degrees of correlation

When the value of one variable is related to the value of another, they are said to be **correlated**. There are varying degrees of correlation.

(a) Perfect positive correlation
(b) Perfect negative correlation
(c) Partial positive correlation
(d) Partial negative correlation
(e) No correlation

We looked at the graphical presentation of correlation (scattergraphs) earlier in this chapter.

If you wish to determine whether a relationship exists between two variables, you will need to run a program that will calculate a statistic known as a **correlation coefficient**. The value of this statistic will enable you to determine the strength of any relationship which might be in existence.

Evaluating results

The correlation coefficient (denoted by the symbol **r**) can take on any value between **–1** and **+1**. The following diagram shows how to interpret the strength of a relationship between two variables once you have calculated a **correlation coefficient**.

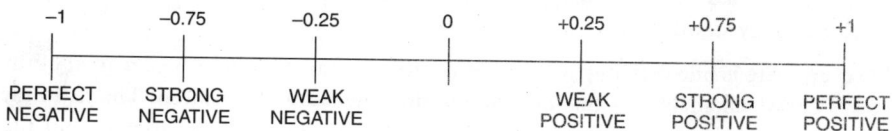

–1	–0.75	–0.25	0	+0.25	+0.75	+1
PERFECT NEGATIVE	STRONG NEGATIVE	WEAK NEGATIVE		WEAK POSITIVE	STRONG POSITIVE	PERFECT POSITIVE

Figure 6.27 Interpreting correlation coefficient values

A correlation coefficient of 0 indicates that the variables in question are **totally independent** of each other and that **no relationship** exists.

7.4 Pearson's product moment correlation coefficient

It is possible to compute several different correlation coefficients for a given set of data. However, **Pearson's product moment correlation coefficient** (PMCC), usually written r, is widely used. If your research results in your collecting **quantifiable data,** this is the coefficient you need to calculate in order to establish whether a relationship exists between two variables and if so, how strong the relationship is.

EXAMPLE

Suppose that we wish to establish whether there is any correlation between the annual salaries of the respondents in the 'holiday survey' and the number of holidays taken per year. The analysis software that you are using will automatically calculate a PMCC for both pairs of variables for you and it will provide the results in the form of a **correlation matrix** such as the one shown below.

	Annual salary	**Number of holidays last year**
Annual salary	1.0000	0.7592★
Number of holidays last year	0.7592★	1.0000
★SIGNIFICANCE<0.01		

Figure 6.28 Correlation matrix

Evaluating results

Note that the values in the correlation matrix are **correlation coefficients**. Therefore the correlation between annual salaries and the number of holidays taken last year is 0.7592. This value indicates that there is a **strong positive** relationship between the annual salaries of respondents and the number of holidays that they took last year.

If the data were collected from a sample (as is the case here) then the software program should also give an indication of the probability that the calculated PPMCC occurred by **chance**. This is the **SIGNIFICANCE** as shown in the table above and this indicates that the probability the PPMCC of 0.7592 occurred by chance is less than 1%. Such statistics can be interpreted as meaning that the correlation between salaries and holidays is therefore **highly significant**.

However, there is one very important consideration to mention here. The maxim of this kind of statistical analysis is that **correlation does not imply causation**. That is to say, there can be a high degree of correlation between the values of two variables, but that provides no evidence at all that the value of one is in any way dependent on the value of the other. Causation requires much more work to demonstrate than simple correlation.

7.5 Coefficient of determination

Unless the correlation coefficient is exactly or very nearly $+1$, -1 or 0, its meaning is a little unclear. For example, if the correlation coefficient for two variables is $+0.7592$ (as in Figure 6.29 above), this tells us that the variables are **positively** (but **not perfectly**) correlated, and that the correlation is **significant**. A more meaningful analysis is available from the square of the correlation coefficient, r^2, which is called the **coefficient of determination** (sometimes known as the **regression coefficient**). This statistic can take on any value between 0 and +1.

The **coefficient of determination, r^2**, measures the proportion of the total variation in the value of one variable that can be **explained** by variations in the value of the other variable. Notice the very precise terminology here: we are still dealing with correlation and, as we know, correlation does not imply **causation**, so we are careful to speak only of **explaining** variation, *not* of causing it.

EXAMPLE

Let us return to our example above in which we investigated the correlation between annual salaries and the number of holidays taken last year. If r = 0.7592, then r^2 = 0.576. This means that approximately 58% of the variations in the number of holidays taken by respondents last year **can be explained** by the annual salaries of those respondents and 42% of variations are probably due to other factors.

7.6 Regression equations

As we have seen, the correlation coefficient measures the degree of correlation between two variables, but, since correlation does not imply causation, it does not tell us how to **predict** values for one variable (y) given values for another variable (x).

If we believe that two variables we are examining do, in fact, have a cause and effect relationship, we refer to the regression equation ($y = a + bx$). We mentioned this when we were discussing scattergraphs. This describes a **causal relationship** in which the value of the **dependant variable** y depends on the value of the **independent variable** x. If we can determine the values of the constants a and b, we will be able to use this equation to predict the value of y for any value of x that might arise. As usual, you will do this using a suitable computer application. You should however be aware of which variable is **dependent** and which **independent**.

Once your software has estimated a and b, it can be used to predict, for example, how many holidays someone earning £20,000 might have taken last year.

EXAMPLE

Suppose that the regression equation linking salaries and number of holidays has the following values for constants a and b.

a = 1
b = 0.00005

If we wished to predict how many holidays (y = independent variable) someone earning £20,000 (x = dependent variable) took last year, we would insert x = 20,000 into the analysis software program in order to predict the number of holidays taken.

Our results would reveal that if someone were earning £20,000 it would be estimated that they took two holidays last year.

Note. You do not need to be able to calculate the result shown above but you might find it helpful to understand how regression analysis works by looking at the equation below.

$Y = a + bx$

Where   a = 1
        b = 0.00005
        x = 20,000
        y = 1 + (0.00005 × 20,000)
        y = 2

7.7   Spearman's rank correlation coefficient

So far we have only looked at degrees of correlation between **quantitative variables** (ie variables which can be measured). Sometimes, however, variables are given in terms of **order** or **rank** rather than actual values (**ordinal data**). When this occurs, a different correlation coefficient, known as the **Spearman's rank correlation coefficient, R,** is calculated.

Spearman's rank correlation coefficient, R is used to measure the correlation between the order or rank of two variables (ordinal data). This coefficient can be interpreted in exactly the same way as the ordinary correlation coefficient (PMCC). Its value can also range from –1 to +1.

8   STATISTICAL TECHNIQUES – EXISTENCE OF TRENDS

In the previous section of this chapter, we investigated the **existence of relationships** between two variables and the **strength** and **significance** of the relationship. We are now going to turn our attention to the relationships that exist between **variables** and **time** and to use these relationships in order to **forecast future values** for the variables. The study of these particular relationships is part of a statistical technique known as **time series analysis**.

8.1   Time series analysis

A **time series** is simply a series of figures or values recorded over time. Time series can also be presented on a graph of a time series known as a **historigram** (not, notice, a *histogram*). The horizontal axis represents time and the vertical axis represents the values of the data recorded.

There are several features of a time series which can be identified.

(a)   A trend
(b)   Seasonal variations
(c)   Cyclical variations
(d)   Non-recurring random fluctuations

Trend

The trend is the most important part of time series analysis that you need to be aware of. The trend is the **underlying long-term movement** over time in the values of the data recorded. Suppose we had conducted a survey over the past ten years that investigated the average amount spent on holidays per annum by 1,000 respondents living in London. We might wish to establish what the trend in annual holiday expenditure was over that period and to use this information in order to predict the estimated annual holiday expenditure over the next year.

Our results could be shown on a historigram such as the one shown in Figure 6.30 below.

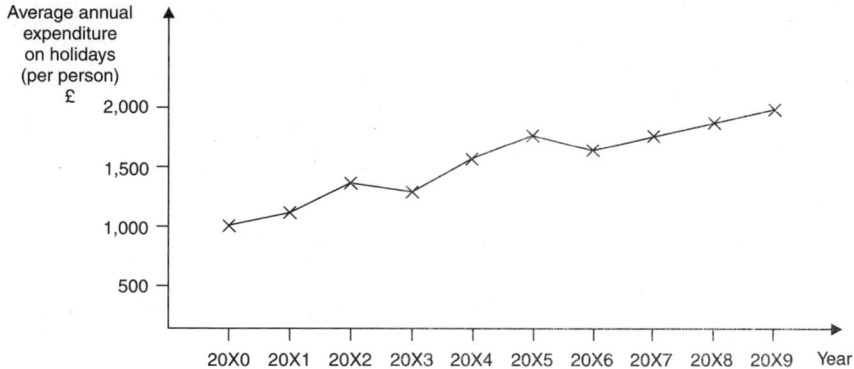

Figure 6.29 Historigram

The time series graph above indicates that the trend is that expenditure is generally increasing over time and that the average annual expenditure on holidays is increasing towards £2,000 per person.

Moving averages

In time series analysis, the trend is found by the calculation of a **moving average**. This removes seasonal and cyclical variations in order to isolate the trend. A moving average is simply a sequence of consecutive averages, each representing a different sub-group of time periods. Moving averages are relatively straightforward to calculate but your analysis software will compute them for you. Seasonal variations can also be computed.

Knowledge of trend and seasonal variations enables us to **forecast future values** by extending the trend line forward into future periods and applying the seasonal variations to it.

8.2   Index numbers

As part of your research, you might wish to compare trends between variables that are not measured in the same **units** or **magnitudes**. For example, you might wish to compare the average cost of a house in England (measured in £ sterling) with the average cost of a house in France (measured in Euros).

Index numbers provide a standardised way of comparing the values over time of prices, wages, volumes and so on. They are used extensively in business, government and commerce. For example, you have no doubt heard of the **RPI** (Retail Prices Index) and **The Financial Times All Share Index**. Another index that you might be aware of is the **Land Registry house price index**. This index illustrates the way index numbers can be used. The index number for the current period provides an indication of the price of houses when compared to a **base period,** which is January 1995. The base period of an index always has a value of 100.

EXAMPLE

If a house cost £37,000 in January 1995 when the house price index was 100, it would be estimated to cost £98,457 in June 2010 when the house price index was 266.1. The following calculation demonstrates how this figure is arrived at.

Index in base month = 100
Index in June 2010= 266.1
Price in base month = £37,000

$$\text{Therefore price in 1997} = \frac{\text{price in base month} \times \text{index in June 2010}}{\text{index in base month}}$$

$$= £98,457$$

We could say that the house price index has risen 166.1 points (266.1 − 100) between January 1995 and June 2010 and that this represents an increase of 166.1%.

---

9   QUALITATIVE DATA ANALYSIS

In the previous sections, we have looked at the analysis of **quantitative data**. Now, we are going to turn our attention to **qualitative** data and the strategies and approaches available for their analysis.

We will start by asking the question 'What are qualitative data?'

9.1   What are qualitative data?

You will remember from the earlier sections of this chapter that quantitative data have the following features.

(a)   They are based on **numbers** (categorical or quantifiable).

(b)   There are a limited number of **standard** responses.

(c)   Analysis of quantitative data involves the use of **graphical** and **statistical** techniques.

Qualitative data, on the other hand, have the following features.

(a)   They are based on **words.**

(b)   There is an **unlimited number** of **non-standard** responses.

(c)   Analysis of qualitative data can involve numerical techniques, but it also involves logical techniques for recognising patterns and relationships.

9.2   Variety of strategies and approaches

The complex nature of qualitative data means that it is difficult to provide a set of rules that should be followed if we wish to analyse and draw conclusions from our research. There are a therefore a great number of ways that this type of data can be analysed.

These sections will provide a brief overview of qualitative data analysis and direct you to other academic texts that you should refer to if you wish to use such techniques to analyse your data. It is for you, the researcher, to adopt whichever strategies or approaches you consider to be appropriate. Before studying this chapter, you could be forgiven for thinking that the idea of analysing qualitative data is quite daunting. You might find yourself asking 'where are the numbers?' or 'what do I do next?' The nature of qualitative data is such that you need to **plan** your work very carefully before commencing, and you will need to approach the analysis in a very **methodical manner**.

9.3   Main approaches to qualitative data analysis

In general, there are three main approaches to analysing qualitative data.

(a)   Deductive
(b)   Inductive
(c)   Quantification

Deductive approach

The deductive approach makes use of theories about your chosen research topic that are **already in existence** in order to analyse data.

We shall be looking at this approach in detail in Section 11.

Inductive approach

The inductive approach is concerned with **the development of personal theories** about your chosen research topic in order to analyse data.

We shall be looking at this approach in detail in Section 12.

Quantification

You will remember from the earlier sections that there is one type of quantitative data that cannot be measured numerically, but which can be placed into **categories** (according to the specific characteristics that it possesses). This type of data is known as categorical data. Categorical data can be **quantified**; that is to say, that they can be **counted** in order to establish the number of times certain categories occur. We saw in the previous chapter how tables and diagrams can be used to show the frequencies with which different categories occur. Now, qualitative data can also be dealt with in this way. **Quantification** of qualitative data can complement the principal methods of analysis that you are using when conducting your research. For example, you could include graphical representations of your data in a supplement or an appendix at the end of your research report.

EXAMPLE

Figure 6.30 below shows the results of a series of semi-structured interviews with twelve managers in an organisation. The objective of this research was to evaluate the extent to which this organisation had adopted the human resources initiatives show below.

In order to **quantify** the results of the interviews, the number of times each of the HR initiatives were referred to were counted and then tabulated as shown.

HR initiatives	HRM practices identified by 12 senior/ line managers													
	1	2	3	4	5	6	7	8	9	10	11	12	Total	%
Developing flexible staff base														
Restructuring			✓										1	8
New style (professional) contracts	✓										✓		2	17
Develop a skills mix														
Effective staff development														
Creation of Professional Development Unit	✓			✓									2	17
Appointment of Professional Development Tutor														
Funding staff development at 2% of payroll	✓			✓									2	17
Performance appraisal for all	✓		✓										2	17
Goal-orientated rewarded and appraisal														
Performance-linked pay scheme			✓		✓						✓		3	25
Generating staff commitment														
Ensuring equal opportunity			✓		✓								2	17
High-quality support staff structure														
Introduce quality improvement programme														
Customer care for personnel department														
Harmonisation of staff terms and conditions														
Identification of HR needs from strategic plan														
Targeted appointments														
Development of robust HR MIS System			✓										1	8
Staff development review scheme	✓	✓	✓	✓	✓	✓	✓				✓	✓	9	75
Devolving staff development budgets										✓		✓	2	17
Investors in People			✓					✓					2	17
Induction programme			✓										1	8
Line management training			✓										1	8
In-house training programmes			✓										1	8
Nurturing staff from within			✓										1	8
Devolvement to line managers											✓	✓	2	17
Personnel/Policy Handbook			✓	✓									2	17

HR initiatives	HRM practices identified by 12 senior/ line managers														
Formal structures to support HR function		✓												1	8
Transfer of payroll to personnel															
Harassment policy			✓											1	8
Grading review and promotion policy									✓		✓			2	17
Direct communication											✓			1	8
Communication audit		✓												1	8
Common Interest Groups		✓												1	8

Figure 6.30 Quantifying qualitative data (Source: Millmore, 1995)

10   FRAMEWORK FOR ANALYSING QUALITATIVE DATA

As there is no standardised approach for analysing qualitative data, we therefore need to establish a **general framework** for dealing with this complex method of analysis. Our suggested framework consists of the following stages.

(a) Categorising data
(b) Unitising data
(c) Identifying relationships
(d) Developing theories/propositions

10.1   Categorising data

The first stage of the framework involves identifying a set of **categories** that are related to the data that you have collected.

If you are adopting a **deductive** approach to your research, you will make use of categories that can be extracted from existing theories. You will be able to specify the main categories **before** you start collecting your data because you will be able to extract them from theories which are **already** in existence.

If, on the other hand, you are adopting an **inductive** approach, you should see the **emergence** of a number of patterns, themes or categories that come from the data that you have collected (or are in the process of collecting). You will not be able to specify the main categories **before** data collection because you will not have built up your own theory at this point.

The categories that you select might be very different from those selected by another researcher since they will be determined by the objectives of **your** research. For this reason, you must have a clearly defined set of objectives at the beginning of your project.

The first stage of the framework will be completed when you have identified the set of categories relevant to your research and produced a description for each one.

10.2   Unitising data

The second stage of the framework involves breaking down the data collected into 'bite-sized' **units** in order that they can be analysed further. A **unit** of data can be any of the following.

    (a) Word(s)

    (b) Sentence(s)

    (c) Paragraph(s)

When units of data have been identified, you will need to attach '**labels**' to them in order to show which category they are being allocated to. This can be done **manually** or by using suitable **qualitative data analysis software**.

10.3 Unitising data manually

On reviewing your qualitative data (or transcripts) manually mark up the margins with the relevant labels. This will enable you to identify to which **category** the different data units belong. When you have labelled all of your data, you can group units of data that have the same labels in order to produce a mass of information relating to individual categories. There are two ways in which this can be done.

    (a) Data can be grouped together by copying units of data from transcripts which have the same labels and entering them onto **data cards.** Each data card will therefore contain a mass of **data units** relating to a specific category.

    (b) Alternatively, **index cards** can be used. A separate index card is needed for each category and each card gives a list of **references** which guide the researcher to all of the transcripts that contain information relating to the category in question.

As with categorisation, it is the objectives of **your** research that will determine the ways in which you break down your data into 'bite-sized' chunks (data units) and subsequently re-group them using data cards or index cards.

We will consider the use of analysis software in order to unitise data in Section 14 at the end of this chapter.

10.4 Identifying relationships

One of the main aims of qualitative data analysis is to identify any **patterns** or **relationships** that may be present within the data that you have collected. The identification of relationships will enable you to build up your own **theories** relating to your research project (if you are using an **inductive** approach). If you are adopting a **deductive** approach you will have developed a set of categories from terms that have emerged from existing theories. As your research progresses and as relationships emerge, you might consider it necessary to re-evaluate the set of categories that you developed originally and modify any that appear to be inappropriate. It is important to keep an **up-to-date** list of categories so that data units are labelled with the correct categories.

When you have identified a possible relationship, you will need to test it in order to prove that it does actually exist. This is the final stage in our framework for analysing qualitative data.

11   DEDUCTIVE APPROACH

If you make use of existing theory in order to analyse your data, you will essentially be adopting a deductive approach.

11.1 Objectives

The research objectives and the questions that you will be asking in order to generate your qualitative data will be influenced by any **existing qualitative research theory** that is available on your chosen research topic. You should use this theory in order to devise a **theoretical framework** around which your data analysis will be organised.

11.2 Advantages and disadvantages of the deductive approach

The main advantages are as follows.

(a) It provides you with a **theoretical framework** on which to base your analysis

(b) The results of your analysis are looked at in conjunction with existing theories and it is therefore easier to make comparisons

The main disadvantage of this approach is that certain (relevant) ideas may not be investigated because they are not part of the existing theory that is being used to develop the theoretical framework.

The two procedures that you need to know about that make use of a theoretical framework are as follows.

(a) Pattern-matching
(b) Explanation-building

11.3 Pattern-matching

Pattern-matching is an analytical procedure that uses a theoretical framework in order to predict a **pattern of possible outcomes**. This theoretical framework is then tested to determine whether it provides a convincing explanation for the results of your research. If the pattern of possible outcomes that were predicted (using the theoretical framework) matches the research results that you obtained, you will have found an explanation for your results. If your results do not match the predicted outcomes, you will need to develop another theoretical framework based on another existing theory.

11.4 Explanation-building

This procedure involves trying to **build up an explanation** during data collection and analysis rather than **testing** a predicted pattern of outcomes (as in pattern-matching). It is a somewhat inductive approach, but it still requires an awareness of relevant theory that may provide the basis for an explanation. It is particularly useful as a **supplement** to pattern-matching or when **competing** relevant theories exist.

The main difference between pattern-matching and explanation-building is this: pattern-matching seeks to **test** a specific existing theory, while explanation-building attempts to **develop and refine** a theoretical framework using research findings during the process of data analysis.

Stages in the explanation-building process

1 Devise a theoretically-based proposition (based on relevant existing theory).

2 Compare the results of your data collection with your proposition.

3 Make adjustments to the original proposition (where necessary) in order to devise a revised proposition.

4 Collect more data.

5   Make further adjustments to the revised proposition (where necessary).

6   Repeat this process until you have built up a satisfactory explanation for the results that you have obtained.

If you consider the deductive approach to qualitative data analysis to be appropriate to your research, refer to the following texts for further information.

(a) Miles and Huberman (1994)
(b) Patton (1990)
(c) Saunders *et al* (2003)

12   INDUCTIVE APPROACH

12.1 Objectives

If you develop your own theory or explanation (rather than making use of existing theory) in order to analyse your data, you will essentially be adopting a **inductive** approach.

One of the main differences between the deductive and inductive approaches to qualitative data analysis is the point at which the main categories are specified. A **deductive** approach is based on existing theory, and therefore allows category specification to take place **before** data collection begins. With an **inductive** approach, the main categories emerge as data is collected and analysed.

One of the most important qualitative research methods that adopt an inductive approach is **grounded theory**.

12.2 Grounded theory

Grounded theory is most accurately described as a research method in which the theory is **developed from the data** (ie the theory is 'grounded' in the data) rather than the other way round. If you wish to use grounded theory in your research, you will need to have a high level of knowledge of your chosen research topic since you will not be making use of any existing theories. You will also need to define your research **objectives** clearly before you start collecting your data. In the grounded theory approach of Strauss and Corbin (1997), the following procedures are identified. Each of these procedures can be related to our framework for analysing qualitative data.

(a) Open coding – linked to 'categorising data' and unitising data'
(b) Axial coding – linked to 'identifying relationships'
(c) Selective coding – linked to 'developing theories/propositions'

12.3 Open coding

Open coding involves breaking down the data you have collected into 'bite-sized' **units** and identifying any **significant categories** or **themes** that emerge from them. Each unit of data is given a label, with similar units being given the same labels. Since grounded theory does not make use of existing theory, categories and themes emerge from the data collected during your research. These codes, as chosen by the researcher, are entirely subjective and are known as **'in vivo'** codes. Once you have identified the main

228

categories, you will have a clearer idea of where you need to focus your data collection in the future.

12.4 Axial coding

Axial coding involves **identifying any relationships** that may have emerged from the open coding process. Once the open coding process has been completed, data is restructured into various patterns in order to try to reveal potential relationships. **Principal categories** and **sub-categories** can also be identified at this stage and you will probably be able to begin constructing **mini-theories** that can be used to aid the development of your own theories and propositions in the **selective coding** process.

12.5 Selective coding

Selective coding involves developing a **grounded theory**.

Once your data collection process has been completed, a number of principal categories and sub-categories will have emerged (in the **axial coding** process). Selective coding involves **identifying the relationships** which exist between these principal categories and identifying one of these principal categories as the **central** or **core** category.

If you are considering using the grounded theory approach in your qualitative research, it is recommended that you consult Strauss and Corbin (1997) in order to study the procedure in more depth. You should also bear the following points in mind if you are considering using this approach in your research.

(a) It is a very time-consuming approach
(b) It is a very intensive research method
(c) It requires a high level of knowledge of the chosen research topic
(d) The final results of your analysis may not necessarily reveal any significant results

If you consider the inductive approach to qualitative data analysis to be appropriate to your research, refer to the following texts for further information.

(a) Strauss and Corbin (1997)
(b) Miles and Huberman (1994)
(c) Palton (1990)
(d) Saunders *et al* (2003)

12.6 Using the deductive and inductive approaches together

You might begin a research project by adopting a deductive approach; that is to say, by using existing theory in order to develop a theoretical framework on which to base your research. As your research progresses, it might become apparent that the framework you have adopted is not sufficiently relevant to your research objectives. If this happens, you can re-analyse your data using an inductive approach in the hope that new, more relevant themes or categories will emerge. By combining the two different approaches to your data analysis, you might find that you are more successful in reaching your research objectives.

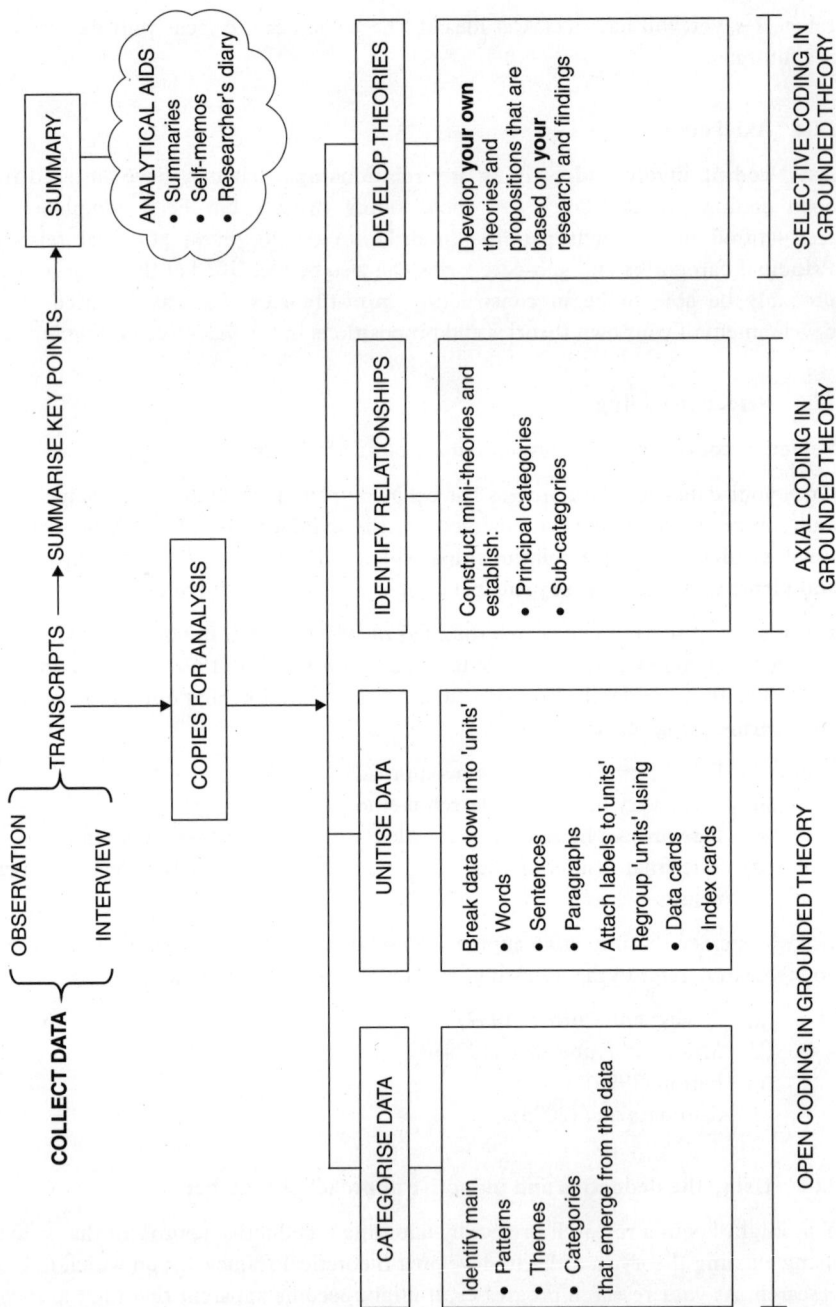

Figure 6.31 Suggested Approach – Inductive Strategy

13   ANALYTICAL AIDS

Whilst analysing your data, you might wish to make a note of any **additional information** that is relevant to your research. This additional information can be recorded using the following **analytical aids**.

(a)   Summaries
(b)   Self-memos
(c)   Researcher's diary

13.1   Summaries

Once you have written up your notes, it is a good idea to produce a **summary** of the key points that have emerged from the data that you have collected. It is also worth making a note of any apparent relationships that you would like to test at a later date in your research. Some of the other items of information that you might wish to note in your summaries are as follows.

(a)   **Comments** relating to the people interviewed or observed

(b)   Anything **unusual** or seemingly **significant** that happened during the interview or observation

(c)   The **setting** of the interview or observation

(d)   Details of any **other documents** that may be referred to in your analysis, for example, minutes of meetings and internal reports

13.2   Interim summaries

An **interim summary** may be produced if you wish to summarise your research findings at a certain point. They are a good way of **consolidating** the information that you have gathered and any initial conclusions that you may have drawn. The information contained in an interim summary includes the following.

(a)   Your findings at a certain point in your research

(b)   How confident you are in your findings and initial conclusions

(c)   Ways in which you might be able to improve subsequent data collection and analysis (based on your findings to date)

When you have produced your **summary** and/or **interim summary,** it is a good idea to attach a copy of it to your primary research documents (written-up notes or transcripts) so that it can be referred to as you continue with your analysis.

13.3   Self-memos

As you progress with your research, you will undoubtedly think of ideas relating to the data collection and analysis techniques that you are using. It is good practice to make an **official note** of the ideas you have in the form of a **self-memo**. It is also important to make a note of these ideas **at the time** you have them, since it is all too easy to forget an idea if you do not write it down as soon as possible.

As ideas come to you, you might wish to record them in a **reporter's notebook** or in the margin of a transcript that you are reviewing. Notes contained within self-memos should be **dated** and **referenced** back to the original source documentation. It is also important to update your memos regularly so that as your research progresses, your memorandums are up to date.

13.4 Researcher's diary

A **researcher's diary** is an alternative to a **self-memo** and is used to record ideas relating to your research project (although these analytical aids are not mutually exclusive, and you may use both methods at the same time). The main purposes of a researcher's diary are as follows.

    (a) To record ideas about your research

    (b) To record the ways in which you intend to direct your research

    (c) To help you to identify categories

    (d) To help you to identify possible relationships and ways in which they can be tested

14   USE OF COMPUTERS IN QUALITATIVE DATA ANALYSIS

14.1 Using computers

Qualitative data analysis is enhanced by computers in the following ways.

    (a) Small (but significant) pieces of data can be quickly and easily isolated from the mass of information collected during research. If this process were conducted manually, this would be a very tedious and time-consuming task.

    (b) Computers are time-saving devices.

    (c) Researchers can spend more time and energy analysing data rather than performing routine, mechanical tasks.

    (d) The widespread availability of email allows for the speedy transmission of data to anywhere in the world.

    (e) Their flexibility allows new data to be inserted into the appropriate place **after** data collection.

    (f) **Coding**. New codes can be added as new categories emerge and data can also be coded in several ways at the same time.

Qualitative data can be analysed using the following software.

    (a) Databases
    (b) Word processing packages
    (c) Computer-assisted qualitative data analysis software

14.2 Databases

The large amounts of qualitative data that need to be analysed during your research can easily be stored in a **database**. It is essential that your database has the following features.

    (a) It is **complete**
    (b) It is **up-to-date**
    (c) It allows **easy access** to all of the documents contained within it

A necessary feature of the software program that you choose is that it includes a **comprehensive indexing system** which will enable you to access selected items of data quickly and easily.

Most software programs will be capable of searching databases and attaching **labels** to specific units of qualitative data text. We can compare this to the much slower manual method of reviewing data and marking up the margins with the appropriate labels or codes. It is worth pointing out that the researcher has the advantage of familiarising himself with his research material when he manually codes his data units and that some of this familiarity is lost when computers are used to aid the process of unitising data.

14.3 Word processing packages

Word processing packages can also be used to store your research notes and have the advantage of enabling data to be entered at the same time interviews or observations are taking place.

Word processors have the following features.

(a) They enable large volumes of qualitative data (textual) to be easily **stored**

(b) They have **search** and **retrieve** options which enable the researcher to locate items of data and group data around the main categories that have been identified

(c) **Hypertext** programs allow units of data to be **tagged** with invisible markers thus aiding data retrieval and coding

14.4 Computer-assisted qualitative data analysis software

There are a number of advantages associated with using **computer-assisted qualitative data analysis software (CAQDAS)** when you are faced with large volumes of qualitative data that require analysing. There is however, no statistical package that can replace the interpretation skills of a researcher and so CAQDAS are most usefully employed to carry out the following functions.

(a) Project management
(b) Coding of data units
(c) Retrieval of data units
(d) Data management
(e) Testing theories and propositions

Information relating to CAQDAS is constantly changing and can become **out-of-date** very quickly. We would recommend that you visit the websites of some of the most popular CAQDAS in order to obtain the most **up-to-date information** relating to these programs. We suggest below details of **websites** relating to some of the more sophisticated software programs.

(a) http://www.atlasti.de (English version available)
(b) http://www.qsrinternational.com//default.aspx

14.5 A final word ...

If you are considering using computers to aid your qualitative data analysis, you should bear the following points in mind.

(a) Computers are **not a substitute** for the researcher's judgement and skills.

(b) The researcher must to select the computer program that is **appropriate for the research** being undertaken.

(c) Sometimes it may be easier to **analyse qualitative data by hand.**

(d) The skills and experience of the researcher may be lost if too much reliance is placed on computer programs for analysing qualitative data

Chapter roundup

- Data analysis differs depending on whether the data is quantitative or qualitative.

- Before analysis, data must be prepared for analysis by various means such as data coding.

- You may be able to use graphical techniques as part of your data analysis: for individual results, for the purpose of comparison and to establish relationships.

- Statistical techniques enable you to describe and compare the data that you have collected, establish relationships and identify trends.

- Qualitative data analysis is different as qualitative data are based on words, there is an unlimited number of non-standard responses and conceptualisation is required.

- If you make use of existing theory in order to analyse your data, you will be using a deductive approach.

- If you develop your own theory or explanation you will be using an inductive approach.

Chapter 7 :

PROJECT PRESENTATION

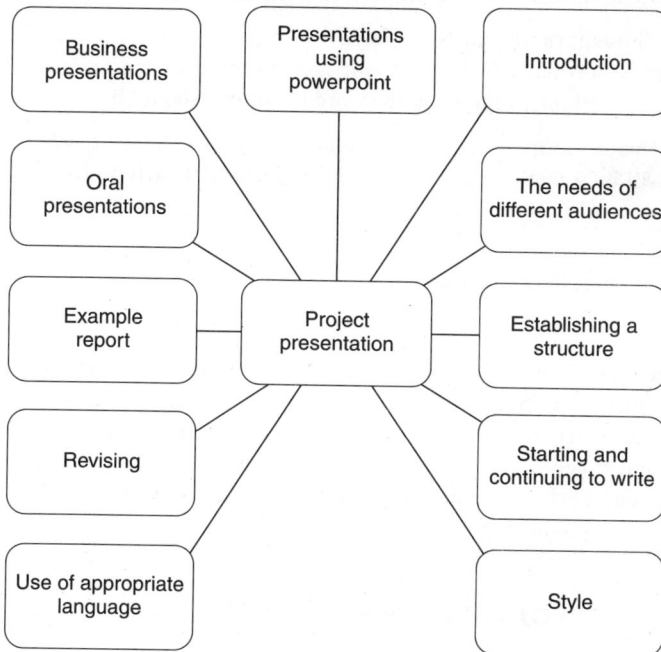

```
┌──────────────┐   ┌──────────────┐   ┌──────────────┐
│   Business   │   │Presentations │   │ Introduction │
│ presentations│   │    using     │   │              │
│              │   │  powerpoint  │   │              │
└──────────────┘   └──────────────┘   └──────────────┘

┌──────────────┐                      ┌──────────────┐
│     Oral     │                      │ The needs of │
│ presentations│                      │ different    │
│              │                      │ audiences    │
└──────────────┘                      └──────────────┘

┌──────────────┐   ┌──────────────┐   ┌──────────────┐
│   Example    │   │   Project    │   │Establishing a│
│   report     │───│ presentation │───│  structure   │
└──────────────┘   └──────────────┘   └──────────────┘

┌──────────────┐                      ┌──────────────┐
│   Revising   │                      │ Starting and │
│              │                      │continuing to │
│              │                      │    write     │
└──────────────┘                      └──────────────┘

┌──────────────┐                      ┌──────────────┐
│Use of        │                      │    Style     │
│appropriate   │                      │              │
│language      │                      │              │
└──────────────┘                      └──────────────┘
```

Your objectives

In this chapter you will learn about the following:

   (a)   The needs of the different audiences you will be writing for

   (b)   How to establish a structure for your report

   (c)   Writing style and language

   (d)   Editing and synthesising skills

   (e)   The skills needed to deliver an oral presentation

1   INTRODUCTION

1.1   The format required

The Guidance for the Research Project unit specifies the learning outcome for this section as

- Present and evaluate the finding with regard to the initial proposal

The Edexcel Guidelines do not provide any formal guidance as to the length of the research project report but around 5,000 words would probably be a good target at which to aim. Most institutions will tell you the word count you should be aiming for.

A sheet of A4 paper contains on average about 300 words per page, which means that your project will be something in excess of 15 pages long. It will probably be the largest piece of writing you have ever done.

1.2   Why is it perceived as difficult?

'Writing is joined-up thinking'. (Luck, 1999).

When you are committing your thoughts to paper you can feel very exposed. You are revealing the inner workings of your mind to a potentially highly critical audience, who will be able to unravel any weakness in your thinking and logic process. Coupled with this, in this context you cannot justify what you have said as there is no opportunity for a viva examination. You will be judged purely on what you have written, so you must write exactly what you mean.

2   THE NEEDS OF DIFFERENT AUDIENCES

2.1   Who are you writing for?

There are two main groups at whom your research project may be addressed:

- The assessors at your college

- The management or staff of the company around which you have based your research, either your own company or a company which has agreed to grant you access to information in return for access to your report findings.

We explored the idea of acknowledging the needs of different audiences in Chapter 4 on the development of the Research Project proposal. In some cases you could end up effectively writing two projects, one to submit to your college and one to present to the company you have researched. You will remember that the needs of the academic audience may differ significantly from those of the corporate audience.

In both cases, however, you will find certain factors in common.

> '.....whatever structure has been selected, your readers will wish to be quite clear why you carried out the investigation, how you conducted it, what methods you used to gather your evidence and what you found out.'
>
> (Bell, 1999)

The main feature of a report to the company that you would not expect to include in your project to be submitted for your degree or diploma is a section recommending future action. An academic project does not necessarily seek to change the situation that has been found: rather it states what that situation is and then draws conclusions from it.

2.2   The needs of different audiences

Your tutor at college, as an audience, has different needs from those of the potential readers of your research project in the company you are researching.

FOR DISCUSSION

Identify the different needs and wants (or the 'wish list') of the two different entities that will be assessing or reviewing your Research Project.

Feedback

Tutor at college

- Around 5,000 words, even if there is more to be said

- An identification of a problem or a statement of a current situation, possibly with a recommendation of action

- Evidence that you have undertaken the necessary research and that you went through the appropriate thought processes in devising your research strategy

- Evidence of the breadth of your literature review

- Clear and accurate referencing, acknowledging all sources exactly following the Harvard system

- The cost of your research and the time taken (as long as you meet the relevant deadlines within your HND programme) are irrelevant to your college. You set your own budget.

Employer/company researched

- Less interested in why you undertook the research in a particular way; a short, sweet background section might be more appropriate here

- More interested in the identification of problems/pitfalls and suggestions as to how to resolve them

- Would like to see a feasible, economical and time efficient solution

- Length of dissertation is not prescribed; fewer words may do, or you may need to go above the expected 500,000 or so

- If the research was funded by the company, a budget will have been imposed on you

In essence, your tutor as an audience needs to know that you have fulfilled the HND requirements and produced a Research Project worthy of the qualification. The company needs you to solve a problem enabling it to benefit.

3   ESTABLISHING A STRUCTURE

3.1   The importance of establishing a structure

The outline structure we include here is suggested by Marshall (1997) but you will find this basic structure, albeit with some minor modifications, in all of the key authorities on research methodology.

Your report should broadly follow this pattern.

1.   Title page
2.   Acknowledgements
3.   Contents page
4.   List of tables, figures and illustrations (if appropriate)
5.   Abstract
6.   Introduction
7.   Review of the literature
8.   Methodology (how you did the research)
9.   Findings
10.   Discussion
11.   Summary
12.   Conclusions
13.   Appendices
14.   Bibliography

You should be aware, however, that this structure is not necessarily prescriptive. The structure you choose will depend on the type of research you are doing and hence the type of report you will produce. The structure shown above would fit the deductive approach, as the assumption is that the literature is reviewed to establish the current state of knowledge. You then relate this to the research you have undertaken. (Saunders *et al* 2003).

If you have adopted the inductive approach in your research, you may prefer to present your findings and conclusions earlier in the report and then go on to explain the methodology adopted.

Jankowicz (2000) suggests that

> *'If your study is an empirical one and your material is complex, involving several different issues, then, after an introduction and overall description of methodology and literature review, you might prefer to devote subsequent chapters to presenting each issue in turn, each one containing its own literature review, methodology, data presentation and discussion, the whole being followed by concluding chapters of discussion, conclusions and recommendations.'*

3.2   The title page

This should contain:

- Name of the awarding body
- Title
- Author
- Date
- Word count

Here is an example.

Anonymous College

Higher National Diploma in Business

Research Project

The effects of technological change on staffing levels and costs

James Hudson

June 2008

5,547 words

3.3   The contents page

You should produce a formal contents page. Given the required length of your report, you should set it out in chapters, rather than in the shorter sections which you may have used in previous reports or large scale projects.

Here is an example:

Contents		Page
Abstract		x
Chapter 1	Review of the literature	x
Chapter 2	Methodology	x
Chapter 3	Findings	x
Chapter 4	Discussion of findings	x
Chapter 5	Summary and conclusions	x
Appendix A	Questionnaire	
Appendix B	Sampling techniques employed	
Appendix C	Spreadsheet	
Bibliography		

3.4   Acknowledgements

You can acknowledge the help of anyone you like, and thank them publicly in the acknowledgements. You might want to thank collectively the company you have researched, or mention specific individuals within it who helped you. You may also want to acknowledge the help of people who helped you administratively or people who read through your final manuscript checking for errors. Members of your family may also come in for a grateful mention, especially if you think that you were rather more difficult to live with while you were researching and writing your project!

3.5   The abstract

The abstract sets out the objectives of your Research Project, your reasons for choosing to research the area you have chosen and an initial summary of your findings. In the context of a business report, you may see this document split into two, called the 'terms of reference' (the reason and the objective) and the executive summary (the overall conclusion). The abstract is a critical part of the project, as it is one of the first things the reader will read and will therefore give rise to strong initial impressions that may not easily be subsequently dispelled.

Although you may start to draft the abstract quite early on in proceedings, the final refining of it will probably be one of the last pieces of work that you do on your Research Project.

Opinions differ as to the necessary length of the abstract, and indeed as to whether or not it is a compulsory element of your project. Hussey and Hussey (1997) maintain that it is *a very short summary of the entire document of about 100 words*' and imply that it is not essential. Saunders *et al* (2000) envisage it as being a little longer, perhaps up to two sides of A4, and refer to it as *'probably the most important part of your report'*. The authorities do however agree as to what it should contain:

- An introduction to the topic
- A brief description of the research you have done
- A brief résumé of your results
- A brief indication of the implications of the results.

Luck (1999) suggests that the abstract should be completely stand alone, and should ideally contain no citations or abbreviations. The reader should not need to refer to anything else while reading the abstract: it should provide the absolute core of your research project.

Try not to confuse the abstract with the introduction, which we cover in the next paragraph.

Executive summary

The executive summary should consist of just a few paragraphs summarising your main findings and recommendations. Although this appears early in the Report, forming part of the Introduction, you should not actually write it until the end.

Here is an example, which is taken from a research project on company environmental data.

EXAMPLE: EXECUTIVE SUMMARY

Demands for environmental information from companies are increasing. However, there are no standard methods for company disclosure of such data. This dissertation attempted to answer how and why companies are currently communicating environmental data, via an analysis of both environmental publications and a questionnaire I devised and sent to thirty companies.

It was found that methods and extent of data disclosure vary immensely between firms with little actual concrete information detailed. Environmental data is offered in both company annual reports and separate environmental publications. Both infer that environmental concern does not prevail over business benefits as the cause for such disclosure.

With a view to implementing standardisation, I constructed a set of activity based costing (ABC) environmental accounts and environmental performance indicators (EPIs) for the cereal manufacturer Weetabix Ltd, focusing on waste disposal costs.

Environmental disclosure can progress via implementing a standard disclosure methodology, together with independent verification procedures. These efforts will, hopefully, increase the seriousness of the issue and enable inter firm comparisons. However, success of standardisation revolves around the introduction, if possible, of a common interpretation framework for environmental costs and issues. Without this, environmental disclosure will never be placed on a level equal to other business concerns.

Again, it is common for executive summaries to be presented as a numbered list of points, and this is very much a case of personal preference. An example of this style is given here, drawn from the project on reward systems.

EXAMPLE

Summary of findings

(1)   A change in a reward system will result in changed objectives for individuals and ultimately changed objectives for the organisation.

(2)   The new pay scheme for salesmen changes their objective to maximising contribution rather than sales turnover.

(3)   The new pay scheme for managers changes their objectives to maximising profit rather than contribution.

(4)   Target setting is made very much more important by the introduction of the new pay scheme. For this reason more participation in the target setting process is required and the importance of truthful statements of sales managers' expectations needs to be stressed.

(5)   To ensure the maximum benefit is gained from the new pay scheme more information needs to be given regarding the commission earned on different products; namely more information about margins.

(6)   Other rewards, such as competitions, training, cars and promotion should not be forgotten, but instead should be integrated into the reward system so as to optimise motivation of the salesforce.

(7)   Effectively planned and controlled reward systems do contribute to company success.

3.6 The introduction

Hussey and Hussey (1997) suggest that this chapter be written right at the end, at the same time as the conclusion. This will help you to include the correct elements in each and avoid the temptation of including your conclusions in the introduction. It may contain these elements:

- The central theme or issue in your research project

- Why it was sufficiently important to you to warrant your researching it

- How your research fits in to the general field of research in this area

- An explanation of your research question or hypothesis (which may have become refined from your original research proposal: Hussey and Hussey (1997))

- A guide to the content and purpose of the chapters in the dissertation, described by Saunders *et al*(2000) as a 'route map' through the rest of the document

Here is an example.

EXAMPLE

Introduction

1.1 The extent of the subject area

This project will focus on environmental impact disclosures made by companies to external audiences. I will achieve this by analysing the current state of environmental reporting which will then be taken one step further by introducing two methods of disclosing such information and the benefits they may achieve.

I chose to study the topic of environmental disclosure because I am aware of 'green' issues gaining increasing importance through media exposure and environmental events. This is filtering through to businesses where a rise in interest and concern about the environment has been reflected in new demands for information (Butler, 1992). The Advisory Committee on Business and the Environment (1996) explain:

'Deeper knowledge of a business's environmental performance would help analysts, fund managers and other key players to form more accurate judgements of its risk profile and worth.' (pp36). However, the 'Business and the Environment' journal (August 1997) indicates that this is not as straightforward as may first appear: 'In less than a generation, society will look back at the availability of environmental performance information today and be amazed at the gaps, clutter and noise.' (pp 4) This hints that a study in this area will provide several issues for discussion.

1.2   Aims and objectives of the research project

My project will attempt to solve the following concerns.

- How and why companies currently disclose their environmental impact information, including a consideration of:

  (1)   The methods utilised

  (2)   The extent of the data content

  (3)   The vehicle of communication used for this distribution and its effectiveness

  (4)   The audience they are aiming at

  (5)   Their motivations for disclosing

  (6)   The influence wider accountability has on their motivations – if any

- Does the management cost accounting tool of activity based costing lend itself to be adapted to environmental cost disclosure and help external readers understand a company's environmental situation?

- Do environmental performance indicators, as a form of environmental reporting, help external readers understand a company's environmental situation?

- Which of ABC or EPIs offer a better foundation for company environmental disclosure?

- Is a standard environmental disclosure methodology possible? If so, what barriers will be incurred?

Note that this is just an example: terms of reference can be set out in a more tabular style, or could be a numbered list of points. Here is an example of a slightly more 'chatty' style, taken from a project on the contribution of reward systems to company success.

EXAMPLE

Introduction

This project evolved from a year's work in the statistics and finance department in Q Ltd. During the year I spent much of my time analysing sales and contribution figures for individual areas and for the whole company. The other half of my job was to calculate commission payments each month and to authorise bonuses.

I was particularly interested in how the accounting and control systems within Q Ltd influenced behaviour and in turn what result these changes in behaviour had on the firm. At the same time as this it was clear that Q Ltd was experiencing deteriorating sales and declining contribution.

Therefore I set myself the aim to explore how effective different reward systems (which require accounting and control systems to operate) have been and could be used in improving sales performance, contribution and ultimately the profit of the company. Conclusions are hard to prove but theory, opinion and logic can lead to some recommendations.

Structure of the report

Initially a chapter on the theory of reward systems will set the foundation for comments made throughout the text. Next, a short chapter on the structure and performance of Q Ltd should help the reader to understand and appreciate later references to the company in the main body of the project.

Rewards for salesmen will then be analysed in the next chapter. This will include a section on targets, due to their function as a basis for rewarding salesmen. Several pay schemes will be analysed in chapter 6 followed by a short chapter on competitions and incentives.

Chapter 8 will discuss how managers and executives are rewarded. After a short introduction, a section on the theory of truth inducing incentives will help reveal the behavioural problems which can arise in setting targets. Management pay schemes within Q Ltd will then be looked at followed by a longer section on executive incentives.

All these points will be brought together in the concluding chapter.

3.7 The literature review

The main purpose of the literature review is to discuss the previous research that has been done into the area of your Research Project, and to show how your own research will fit into it. It will contain the content and background of the study (Bell, 1999).

You should try to avoid the temptation of simply listing and describing everything you have read. You must be selective, and only include material that relates directly to the topic.

In summary, you should set the scene, place your own work in context and prepare the reader for what is to follow (Bell, 1999).

Hussey and Hussey (1997) suggest this guide to writing the literature review.

- Only select relevant material
- Group the material into categories and comment on the most important features
- Compare the results of different studies, picking out those which have the most important bearing on your research
- Set the context for your own study
- Be critical. Do not merely record or describe other people's work: provide a critique by pointing out the strengths and weaknesses of other research and evaluating other studies and theories by reference to your own.

Bell (1999) suggests that you can write the literature review first, even before you start your own data collection. It may subsequently need some revision, but at least you won't have to go through every note you have made and decide what to include and what to discard.

Remember:

    (a)   Primary information is data which is collected specifically for a given project, for example the management accounts of the particular company you are writing about.

    (b)   Secondary information is that which can also be used for some purpose other than the specific task in hand, for example statistics for an industry in general. Secondary information can be regarded more as background information.

You need to consider in what order you will present the information you have obtained. If you need to set the scene and provide background information for the industry you are dealing with, and then move on to the precise results of the company under scrutiny, you should discuss your secondary information first. If, however, you are taking specific information relating to one company, and extrapolating or applying it elsewhere, then it may be better to present the primary information first.

We set out here an example, taken from a dissertation on performance measurement, which shows what information gathering techniques were used.

EXAMPLE

Description of methods used to gather information

This describes in detail the procedure under which the research into this project was carried out. The research was broken down into two distinct sections – secondary research and primary research.

(a)   **Secondary research**

    The secondary research consisted of two different methods.

- **Conventional library research**. Reading through both books and journals, sorting out materials which covered operations management and management accounting areas, and following up references with various libraries. Facilities used for obtaining this data included: Oxford Brookes University, public libraries (ie Slough Central Library) and inter-library loan facilities (ie Thames Valley University).

- **Electronic research**. Searching through a variety of business related databases such as Searchbank, Financial Times, Economist and ABI. This initially proved to be a relatively quick way of finding and providing up-to-date information. However, it took considerable time to find articles with relevant data. The search yielded approximately fifty articles (1996-1999) drawn from journals in five disciplines: performance, measurement, dealer performance measurement (motor industry), forklift truck industry, balanced scorecard and customer satisfaction measurement. Once the information was found, this proved to be a very successful research method. Consequently, secondary research enabled the writer to achieve the project objectives in several ways.

    Firstly, it helped guide the writer in building up a good knowledge of the subject. An effective performance measurement model therefore could be devised.

    Secondly, it was also used as justification to evaluate the HDPMS critically in the Data Analysis section.

(b) **Primary research**

Primary data were obtained through the company's internal materials and interviews.

- **Internal materials.** Corporate literature and internal reports were kindly provided by a number of Z PLC departments such as Dealer Development, Finance, Marketing and Credit Control. The internal materials consisted of Z PLC Annual Reports, Z PLC Dealer Annual Business Plan, Z PLC European Project List Reviews, Customer Support Surveys and Monthly Awareness Reports.

  The internal data was utilised to examine the present HDPMS. This information was the foundation of the findings chapter.

3.8 Methodology

Saunders *et al* (2000) say that

'This should be a detailed chapter giving the reader sufficient information to make an estimate of the reliability and validity of your methods'.

It should explain how the problem was investigated and why particular methods and techniques were employed (Bell, 1999). This might include:

- Details of procedures (eg questionnaires, surveys, interviews, focus groups and so on: when and where they were carried out)
- Sample sizes and justification
- Methods of selection of sample and justification
- Methods of dealing with refusals to participate or non-replies
- Statistical analysis carried out

Hussey and Hussey (1997) argue that your approach to the methodology will differ according to the type of study you are engaged in, positivistic or phenomenological. The only feature they have in common is an introductory paragraph, briefly describing the main features of the methodology and giving an outline of the chapter.

A positivistic study

The different types of research methodology are described in detail in Chapter 2.

Hussey and Hussey (1997) suggest that if you are carrying out a positivistic study your methodology chapter should contain these five main sections.

1. A general description of the study, an explanation of the structure and main contents and chapters. This introductory section is a good place to discuss the limitations and delimitations of your study, if you have not done so in the first chapter.

2. A description of the source and number of subjects in the study. This will require a description of the population and your sampling procedure.

3. An explanation of the appropriateness of the research instruments or measures you have used and their reliability and validity as discussed in the

literature. If you have designed your own research instruments, you will need to justify this and discuss the issues of reliability and validity in some depth.

4   A description of the data collection methods you have adopted: how, where and when you collected the data. It is sometimes helpful to incorporate a chronological flowchart in this section.

5   A description of the methods of data analysis you have used, why they were appropriate given the nature of your hypotheses, the number of independent and dependent variables and the level of measurement of each of the variables.

In a positivistic approach, you are likely to be using well-known procedures and tests, and you would not need to explain them in great depth. However, if you have modified or adapted any of the standard tests you will need to explain in detail what you have done (Hussey and Hussey, 1997).

A phenomenological study

Hussey and Hussey (1997) say that in a phenomenological study the methodology section should stress the nature and rationale for the chosen methodology and then lead on to discuss the methods of data collection and analysis.

Hussey and Hussey (1997) then suggest the sections that should appear in the methodology chapter of a phenomenological study.

1   Explain how your paradigm is appropriate to the research topic.

2   If you have a theoretical framework explain how it relates to the research problem and guides the research.

3   Explain the place of the methodology within your paradigm, its nature and development, making reference to any similar studies which have adopted it. As there are variations within a phenomenological approach, it is useful to quote a number of definitions of the methodology you are using, explain the main features and justify your choice.

4   Describe the data collection methods you have used, their strengths and weaknesses, and justify your choice by referring to the alternatives you considered but thought were unsuitable. You should state where the data was collected, from whom and why. Data collection will normally have taken place over a period of time, so it is helpful to include a timetable showing when specific activities took place and any critical events which occurred.

5   Describe the data analysis methods you have used at a very general level. This is sometimes difficult, but you should emphasise the main features and leave the discussion of the details until the 'Results' chapter.

6   In some studies you will also need to include a discussion on validity and reliability. There are differences of opinion on this and you should seek guidance from your supervisor. If there is uncertainty, we consider it prudent to discuss issues of verification, generalisability and the limitations of the study.

3.9   The results chapter

The results chapter is for the presentation of your findings. Analysis and discussion of those results will then normally take place in a subsequent chapter.

However, Hussey and Hussey (1997) make the point that although this is true of a positivistic study, where the facts of the results are stated, in a phenomenological study the results and analysis may be too mixed up for this to be possible.

Because you are trying to make sense of the data collected, you will have to discuss the data and its meaning simultaneously.

If you are having difficulty deciding what should go into the results chapter and what should go into the analysis and discussion chapter (ie the difference between findings and conclusions) you could follow the advice of Saunders *et al* (2000). They suggest that you draw up a table with two columns in it. They should be headed up thus:

What I found out	*What judgements I have formed or decisions I have reached as a result of what I found out*
In a questionnaire 83% of respondents said that money was their prime motivator at work	Rates of pay are one of the main factors contributing to employee satisfaction

The first list will contain facts; the second list will contain your interpretation of those facts to reach a conclusion.

Saunders *et al* (2000) also maintain that drawing up a table like that will *'lead you to a consideration of the way in which you present your findings'*. If you list your findings and thoughts about them in a tabular style like this, it will help you to produce a clear and logical structure within the report itself.

3.10   Analysis, discussion and conclusions

Opinions differ as to whether discussion and conclusion constitute the same thing and should therefore be included in the same chapter, or whether they are separate and should be kept apart.

Hussey and Hussey (1997) for example regard analysis and discussion as one element and the conclusion as something different. Saunders *et al* (2000) on the other hand, think that conclusion and discussion are the same.

In any event, the conclusion section should start with a reiteration of the purpose of the research and a restatement of the research question or hypothesis, so that the two can be linked.

Activity 1   **(30 minutes)**

Here is a paragraph containing some facts about Carnelian Ltd, in no particular order. This paragraph illustrates two things.

(a)   It will show you quite how irritating unstructured and unformatted data is to read and make sense of. The marker may be under time pressure, so don't annoy him or her.

(b)   It introduces you to the concept of format and structure.

Carnelian Ltd was founded in 1872. 50% of its sales are exports to Germany. It has two principal shareholders, Ms Underwood and Mr Mongrove, who each own 50% of the issued share capital. Net assets are £150,000. The company specialises in making artificial flowers for sale. The Finance Director is Mr Mace. There are 20 employees, of whom five are employed in marketing (reporting to Ms Underwood). The production department report to Mr Mongrove. Turnover per annum is £1m. Issued share capital is 1,000 ordinary shares of £1 each. The company used to market by mail order, but now mainly promotes itself through its website. The two people who work in accounts and the IT expert report to Mr Mace. The best selling flower is the silk orchid accounting for 30% of turnover. Profit before tax was £50,000 in 20X1. No one customer accounts for more than 1% of turnover.

Required

Produce a report about Carnelian Ltd incorporating all the data above.

4   STARTING AND CONTINUING TO WRITE

4.1   Writing as a continuous process

All of the authorities on research methodology stress the importance of regarding the writing of your project as an ongoing activity. If you leave the writing until late in the day and try to treat it as a discrete operation, you run a higher risk of failure. Your perception of the task will also become increasingly difficult the longer you leave it making it harder for you to start.

Judith Bell (1999) says

> 'Report and thesis writing is not, or should not be, a frantic activity carried out at the end of the project. It is a process of varied stages all of which need to be recorded at the time they are completed. Your first drafts will almost certainly need to be revised and in some cases completely rewritten, but the foundations for the report should have been established at the planning stage.'

Given the importance attached to drafting and redrafting (which can happen as much as half a dozen times) which is discussed later in this chapter, you will see that committing your thoughts to paper from the outset is critical.

You may find that the process of putting pen to paper (or fingers to keyboard) is the most difficult part of the entire research project. Students will find almost any reason for putting off the moment of starting to write, whether by allowing themselves to be distracted and not allowing themselves the required degree of peace and quiet, or by postponing indefinitely the conclusion of their research and data analysis.

4.2   Making it easier

There are two ways in which you can ensure that the writing phase is as straightforward as possible.

- Allow enough time in your overall plan to do it. Luck (1999) says that you should allocate about one third of the total time allowed for your research project to the writing of it; and

- Start writing early in the course of your work on the project; do not leave it until a mad scramble at the end. As we have already said, writing is an ongoing process that can be constantly refined.

Here are some suggestions as to how to start writing and then keep going:

Starting writing

1 Put all your ideas down in a mindmap. Write down the original idea (it really doesn't matter in what form) and then your other trains of thought springing from it (Hussey and Hussey, 1997). This will enable you to clarify the principle issues (Easterby-Smith *et al* (1991)

2 If you find the idea of committing your thoughts to paper daunting, start off by speaking into a tape recorder. (Easterby-Smith *et al* 1991 and Luck, 1999)

3 Start with a chapter that you think you will find easy: you do not have to write your project in the exact order in which it will finally appear. Many students find it helpful to start writing the literature review at a very early stage, even if it will then need some redrafting.

4 If you are having trouble with a specific section, consider writing your concluding sentence first. You can then either write the section backwards from that, so that you end up with the initial points, or, having written the concluding sentence, build up to it in a logical way using the other points you want to make.

Keeping going

1 Set aside regular blocks of time for writing, so that it becomes routine.

2 Try to organise yourself so that you can write on successive days (Saunders *et al*, 2000). This will mean that you will not run the risk of losing the thread of your writing, and should find it relatively easy to resume.

3 Avoid stopping for the day in the midst of a complex part of your writing, or when you are next embarking on a difficult section. It is much easier to start the next work session with something straightforward to ease yourself back in to the work (Bell, 1999 and Saunders *et al 2000*).

4 Try to write only when your mind is fresh, for example at the beginning rather than the end of the day.

5 Maintain the same location for your writing. This will make you feel comfortable, confident and secure. It is also useful not to have to move all your books and papers around too much.

6 Try to minimise distractions. Move anything that is likely to tempt you (for example computer games, the television). Such basic aids as a do not disturb notice or an answerphone can be useful here (Saunders *et al*, 2000). Make sure that your family or other people around you understand the importance of what you are trying to do.

7 Reward yourself! After a certain number of words or a fixed period of time or the completion of a topic, give yourself a few minutes off for a walk round the garden, a cup of coffee, a glance at the newspaper. You will probably achieve more by working in short sharp bursts with breaks, rather than plodding on for hours on end.

5   STYLE

5.1   The importance of style

You might wonder why developing and using an acceptable style is important.

FOR DISCUSSION

Think about the reading that you have been doing while researching for your project. Think specifically in terms of books or articles that you have found it easy to read and material that you have found very turgid. Try to identify what it is that causes them to be one or the other.

You will see that one critical feature is the style. Where the material had a very heavy and stodgy style it will have taken you longer to read, understand and digest the contents; it probably seemed like very hard work. If the style was easier to read, making it easier to assimilate the contents, even if they are very technical, you probably found it was quicker to identify the gist of the argument and understand the conclusion.

So how can you ensure that you adopt a similarly 'easy' style?

Writers on this area tend to agree that it boils down to 'readability' (Sharp and Howard, 1996 p. 193) and 'imperceptibility' (Luck, 1999 p. 125). It is a generally accepted principle that clear and readable prose is far more user-friendly than its counterpart. In the UK there is an organisation called the Campaign for Plain English, which seeks to encourage organisations from the Government downward to use plain and simple language. It even awards prizes each year for the best examples of the use of plain English, as well as announcing which entities it regards as failing dismally in the use of plain language.

5.2   Using plain English

There are two key components in the use of plain English:

- Language
- Use of paragraphs

Language

Luck (1999) uses the word 'imperceptible' when describing the desired style of language. By this he means that

> *'.....the reader is allowed to concentrate on what is being said, not on the way in which it is written.'*

He likens reading to listening to an orchestra, because if all the players in the orchestra are performing as they should, you are not aware of that fact and can only hear the music as a single item. Similarly when you are reading you are generally unaware of the specific words being used; you are just aware of the content. You only notice the language when there is something wrong with it, such as poor grammatical construction or bad spelling. Such factors often have the effect of acting as irritants, and detract from the value of what is actually being said.

Look at some of the material you have read as part of your research. Pay particular attention to the style of the items that have been informative, *but easy to read*. Read them this time not from the point of view of their technical content and relevance to your research, but in terms of what they tell you about writing style. What makes the style attractive? Is it:

- Usage of shorter words rather than longer ones?

- The use of a 'chatty' rather than a formal style?

- The use of the first person (eg 'I discovered that.....') rather than the third person ('it was discovered that.....)?

- The use of adjectives and adverbs to make the writing more descriptive?

- The use of features such as repetition, to add emphasis to a point, or quotations, to add authority?

- The degree to which technical jargon and concepts are explained?

- The pace of the writing: does it sustain your interest and keep moving briskly, or does it dwell on points and adopt a more leisurely approach?

It may not be appropriate for you to utilise all of the features that you identify as contributing to the style of the writing, for example it may be just too casual always to use the first person. However, if you have positively identified certain features as being particularly attractive, you should be able to weave them in to your writing from time to time to contribute to the overall style.

Basic principle: 'Less is More'

Rule	Example	
	No	**Yes**
Keep words simple	Expenditure vs	Cost
	Aggregate vs	Total
Short words are quicker to write	Terminate vs	End
Avoid words you don't need to write	I would be grateful	Please
	Due to the fact that	Because
	In the not too distant future	Soon (better: give a time scale)
	At this point in time	Now (or currently)
	In the majority of instances	In most cases (or usually)
	It is recommended that A Ltd should consider	A Ltd should consider
	36 words (55 syllables)	14 words (18 syllables)

Jargon

Be **careful** of jargon: jargon is **technical language with a precise meaning** and therefore has its uses. Keep in mind the needs and likely response of your audience. Do not try to blind the assessor with technological jargon. If you do, the assessor may question whether you understand it yourself.

Be precise. Be careful of 'very' 'fairly' 'partly', unless you are unable to state facts.

Avoid patronising language

(a) There is a fine line between explaining technical vocabulary or situations which may not be familiar to the reader, and 'dumbing down'. By that we mean reducing the level of your writing to something well below the assumed competence of your audience.

(b) You do not need to explain routine technical terms. You can assume that your audience has a reasonable awareness of factors such as the current state of the domestic and international economy, the debate over the UK's adoption of the Euro, the advance of e-commerce, the now tempered enthusiasm for dot.com start ups and so forth.

(c) Your meetings with your mentor and your peer group presentation could provide a suitable forum for you to discuss the style of language which you have adopted. You could receive some constructive feedback.

Spellcheckers

The spellchecker is one of the most useful elements in a word processing package, and can help both the poor speller and the clumsy typist. It is similar in most packages. If you are working in Word, click on Tools and then Spelling, and Word will work right through your document seeing if the spelling matches the spelling of words in the computer's dictionary. If not, it will suggest alternatives from which you click on the best one to replace what you have typed.

For example, if you have typed 'drp' the choices you are offered include 'drip', 'drop', 'dry' and 'dip'. You also have the option to add what you have typed to the computer's dictionary, so that unusual technical or foreign words are not thrown up repeatedly.

You must bear in mind, however, that the **spellchecker will only pick up words which do not match an entry in the computer's dictionary**: it will not recognise the fact that you have merely typed in the wrong word, for example 'from' instead of 'form'. Take care also if you are an overseas candidate whose spellchecker is set to another language, including one of the nine variations of English included in many standard word processing packages. As the report must be written in English, you should set the spellchecker to UK English.

You still need to read through what you have written, for sense and correct language. Some people like to do this on the screen at the end of each section or paragraph, while others prefer to print out at intervals and read the hard copy. It really does not matter which you do, as long as you do one of them.

Grammar checkers

Having reached the stage you have in your academic and professional careers, your standard of grammar should be quite high. It is still worth running the grammar check over your report, however, as it enables you to stand back and see the wood from the trees.

The grammar check will perform tasks such as:

(a) Detecting sentences where you have omitted the verb

(b) Detecting sentences where you have used mixed singular and plural subject and verb (for example 'two of the main reasons for the development of the multinational company is ....'.)

(c) Indicating sentences which are unduly long or have too many clauses, potentially confusing the reader

You can specify in the grammar check what style of language you are using, such as 'casual' 'technical' and 'standard'. You can also use a grammar option that gives the readability statistics of your work. This is a useful tool in that it can indicate when your language is becoming over obscure.

Thesaurus

If you think your use of words is becoming repetitive, try the thesaurus. This will suggest alternatives and can also supply meanings.

Use of paragraphs

Paragraphs should not be too long. There are few things more off-putting than starting to read a page on which the writing is totally uninterrupted by a single paragraph break. A page that is broken up into a few paragraphs is far easier on the eye and seems less intimidating to the reader. However, neither should they be too short. Sharp and Howard (1996) maintain that paragraphs should be long enough to do justice to a particular idea. They go on to say that if paragraphs are very short they will not be easy on the eye, and will have a staccato effect, making the reader switch too rapidly from one topic to another, thus running the risk of losing the flow.

5.3   An effective writing style

Luck, (1999) identifies four goals to aim at to achieve effective writing. They are:

- Simplicity
- Clarity
- Accuracy
- Precision

Simplicity

The point to remember is that by the time you come to write your Project you will be an expert on your subject, and you may have forgotten the fact that at the outset you had little detailed knowledge. When writing, you will have to explain your work to readers who may know far less about it. Luck (1999) suggests these ways of simplifying your style.

- Try to recall the lack of knowledge (what Luck calls the 'uninitiated state') you had when you started the research, and think in terms of writing for the benefit of readers who are in that position now. Make your writing accessible.

- Try using the technique of précis, that is summarising a long piece of writing into its key components. You will end up with writing in which there is no wastage: everything will contribute to the sense of what you are saying.

- Ask someone to read what you have written and to tell you honestly whether your style is understandable and your message is coming across

Clarity

Luck (1999) says that you must try to make your writing as readable as possible. This will help it to stand out from the crowd of other research projects that the assessor will be marking. Clarity can be achieved by techniques like these.

- Well-structured chapters, broken up into manageable and digestible sections by the use of headings, subheadings and numbered paragraphs (rather like the style of this book)

- The use of short easily-understood words and sentences

- A statement of clear aims, objectives and hypotheses

- Avoiding jargon and clichés

- Providing an explanation for abbreviations and acronyms

- Using the simplest words possible in the circumstances and eliminating unnecessary words

- Avoiding the use of what Luck (1999) describes as 'over-frequent or unwanted reference citations, quotations, footnotes etc.'

Accuracy

You must present your readers with the current view of the facts (Luck, 1999) giving them all the information that they need to know. When you put forward an argument, make sure that you justify it with evidence. Luck (1999) says that there are three ways of doing this:

(a) By referring to the source from which you have acquired the material
(b) By developing the logic of a previous statement
(c) By evidence that you have obtained yourself

Precision

Your information must be precise; not vague. You must demonstrate to the reader that you are confident about your research and your conclusions. Luck (1999, p. 128) suggests that you should do this by

(a) Retaining detail
(b) Avoiding exaggeration

(c) Pointing out important distinctions and differences

(d) Avoiding unwarranted generalisations

(e) Saying what you mean

(f) Avoiding colloquialisms, similes and metaphors.

If you are presenting numerical data, you should bear in mind these issues:

(a) Use an appropriate number of decimal places

(b) State your confidence limits in your tests

(c) Use statistical tests to distinguish significant events from chance variation.

6   USE OF APPROPRIATE LANGUAGE

6.1   The active and passive voice

It is increasingly the case that the use of the active voice is encouraged rather than the use of the passive voice.

What's the difference between the two?

- The **active voice** uses the I or we construction (the first person singular). For example 'I examined the ways in which the motivation of employees can be improved by the offering of additional non-salary benefits'.

- The **passive voice** uses the impersonal third person singular. It is more formal, and therefore sometimes regarded as more old fashioned. For example 'The ways in which the motivation of employees can be improved by the offering of additional non-salary benefits were examined'.

The use of the passive voice is still largely expected in research work and projects such as this, especially in the sections where you are describing issues such as work carried out, tests done and the selection of statistical samples.

Lester and Lester (2002) think that the passive voice is preferable as it keeps the reader's attention on the subject of the research, not the identity of the writer, as would be the case were the first person to be used throughout.

However, it can be argued that it is appropriate to revert to the active voice and use the first person if you really want to emphasise a point. This could happen where you are writing the conclusion on a specific aspect about which you feel very strongly. The use of the first person would stress that strength of feeling. Think carefully about this, and use it sparingly.

6.2   Sexist, racist and other offensive language

It is now generally accepted that anyone writing for publication, for whatever purpose, should avoid the use of language which is in any way offensive to any group of people. Although you may know that you are the last person to harbour racist, sexist or any other offensive views, it is easy inadvertently to use inappropriate language when writing.

Here are some words and phrases that you should think carefully about.

Word	*Suggested alternative*
Businessman/business woman	business executive
Headmaster/headmistress	head teacher
Policeman/policewoman	police officer
Chairman/chairwoman	chair/presiding officer
Manpower	staff levels/workforce
Mankind	humanity/human race
Best man for the job	best person for the job
Man in the street	average person
Spokesman	representative/spokesperson

Be careful if you find yourself describing people by race or national characteristics. It will almost certainly not be relevant in the context of this research project. The same is true if you find yourself referring to someone's disability.

7   REVISING

7.1   Revising

We have already made the point that writing your research project is an ongoing process that you will start early on in the whole procedure. Revising and editing, therefore, are techniques that you will be using throughout. Since the word processor has become ubiquitous, this process has become much easier.

Revising and editing will happen on an ongoing basis, as you work through each section of the project, and also at the end of the first complete writing, when you will be faced with the task of editing the whole document. Some students prefer to spend a lot of time editing each chapter on an ad hoc basis, but you will not be able to do this exclusively, as you may find that aspects of one particular chapter can only be finally edited once you have dealt with another aspect of a later chapter.

Revising individual chapters

- After each paragraph or group of paragraphs, read through and eliminate anything which does not add value or weight to the argument. At this point you should have the time to consider carefully the words you have used, and whether there is any alternative way of making the point.

- You can also look at paragraph lengths and consider combining short ones together or breaking up longer ones.

- As you deal with each paragraph, ask yourself what point it is making and what justification (in terms of evidence or logical thought progression) you have for that point.

- Consider the linkages that you have made from one paragraph to another: is there a natural 'flow' or do you need to rewrite some of the connecting material?

7.2   Looking for errors

There are different schools of thought as to whether it is helpful to have the spelling and grammar checkers on while writing, so that errors are noticed immediately, or whether it is preferable to run them at the end of a section, so that the hunt for errors is a specific task. It really is a case of personal preference, as long as you ensure that you do use the spelling and grammar checker at some point.

However, the one rule to remember about this is that you must not rely solely on your computer's tools: there is no substitute for reading the final draft and getting at least one other person to do the same thing.

The best spell checker in the world will not detect the fact that you have used the wrong word, but spelt it correctly, for example the use of 'form' instead of 'from'.

8   EXAMPLE REPORT

This is an example of a report compiled from given data. It is obviously shorter than the one you will be expected to produce, and there is far less data to deal with, but it will give you a good illustration in miniature of the way in which information can be used to produce a report.

You are the management accountant of a company which specialises in producing dairy products for the slimming market. The results of your latest research have just been published.

EXAMPLE

Data

Market Research Results

This research was carried out from January to June 2002, using in-depth interviews in the respondents' homes, recorded on tape and interpreted by ourselves, 'The XYZ Research Agency', specialists in market research for the food industry.

Sample size: 500
Age range: 15-55
Socio-economic groups: ABC1★
Locations: Bristol, Manchester and Greater London
Sex: Males and Females

Three broad categories were tested and the results are as follows:

Motives for wanting to lose weight	% of respondents with weight problems mentioning
To feel good physically	68
For health reasons	67
To stay fit	43
Because I want to live longer	25
To stay mentally alert	23
To be more attractive	21
To be more popular	15

Methods for weight control	
Avoid certain foods, eat 'slimming items'	32
Eat and drink less	23
Play sports, keep 'fit'	22
'Have certain diet days'	7
Take medicines, stimulants	3
Food which people dislike giving up	
Cakes, pies, bakery products	31
Sweets, sugar	23
Beer, alcoholic beverages	17
Meat, sausages etc	15
Chocolate	13
Cream	9
Fruit juices	9
Potatoes	9
Pasta	9

In general, the comments also revealed that dieting means a loss of pleasure at mealtimes, causes problems when one can't eat the same as the family and also one is regarded as being 'ill' when dieting.

* Socio-economic groupings:

A   Higher managerial, Chief Executives etc.
B   Managerial, Executives etc
C1   Higher clerical, Supervisory etc

Required

Write a short formal report to the Marketing Director, Mr David Forsythe, highlighting the conclusions drawn from this research. Your recommendation will be used to help identify new products for possible development in this market

Suggested answer:

To: Marketing Director
From: Management Accountant
Date:

REPORT ON NEW PRODUCT DEVELOPMENT

1   Executive summary
2   Methods of research
3   Findings

EXECUTIVE SUMMARY

This report highlights the conclusions drawn from market research into the 'slimming market' conducted by The XYZ Research Agency between January and June 2002. The report, to include recommendations for possible new product development and new promotion methods was requested by Mr David Forsythe, Marketing Director.

METHOD OF RESEARCH

This report has been compiled from research findings designed to show:

(a) Respondents' motives for losing weight
(b) Respondents' methods of weight control
(c) Foods which respondents were reluctant to give up

Respondents were a sample group of 500 ABC1s aged 15-55 of both sexes in the Bristol, Manchester and Greater London areas. In-depth interviews were recorded in the respondents' homes, and analysed by XYZ Research: see Appendix A.

FINDINGS

Motives for losing weight (see Appendix A)

Most respondents expressed their motives for losing weight as the desire for physical well-being (68%), health (67%) and fitness (43%), with related concerns, such as longevity and mental alertness, also scoring over 20%.

Perhaps unexpectedly, the motives most commonly associated with 'slimming' – increased attractiveness and popularity – scored comparatively low, with 21% and 15% respectively.

Methods of weight control (see Appendix B)

The most frequently-stated method of weight control (32%) was based on food selection: consuming 'slimming items' and avoiding certain foods. Reduced consumption in general (23%) and increased physical activity (22%) featured strongly, however, compared to the use of medicines and stimulants, mentioned by only 3% of respondents.

Foods respondents disliked giving up (see Appendix C)

A significant proportion of respondents were reluctant to give up foods in the high-calorie 'snack' categories: cakes, pies and bakery products (31%), sweets and sugar (23%). Alcohol (17%), meat (15%) and chocolate (13%) also featured significantly, compared to the more 'healthy' food groups such as fruit juice, potatoes and pasta (9% each). Cream was the only dairy product mentioned, (9%)

General comments

Respondents experienced 'dieting' as a loss of pleasure, an inconvenience when it comes to family meals, and a social stigma.

CONCLUSIONS

The prime reason for losing weight was health and fitness, mainly achieved through regulated food intake and increased activity. However, respondents felt deprived in general by the dieting process, and particularly disliked giving up snack foods and food generally regarded as 'unhealthy': processed foods, high in fats and sugars, low in fibre.

APPENDIX A: MOTIVES FOR WEIGHT LOSS

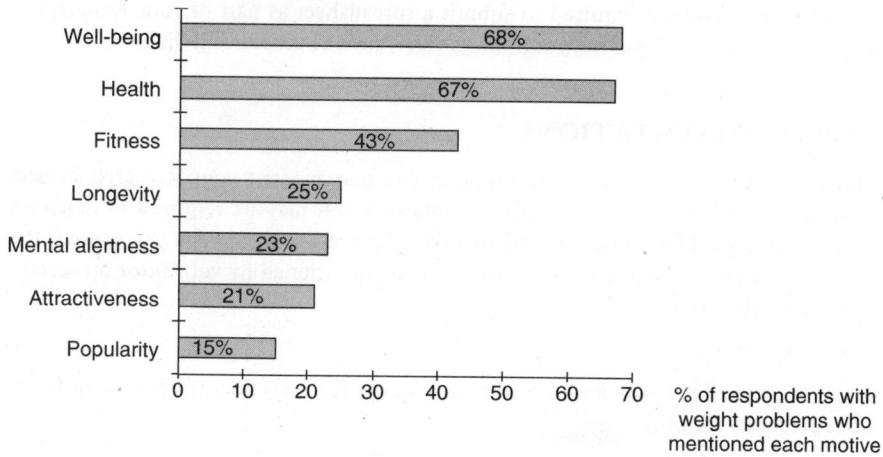

% of respondents with weight problems who mentioned each motive

APPENDIX B: METHODS OF WEIGHT CONTROL

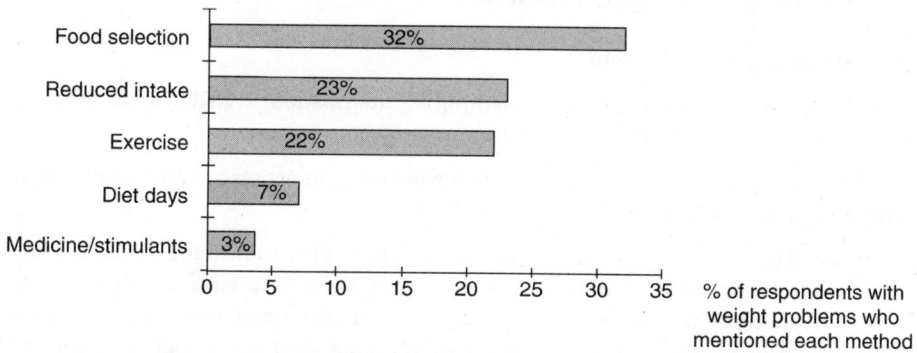

% of respondents with weight problems who mentioned each method

APPENDIX C: FOODS WHICH PEOPLE DISLIKE GIVING UP

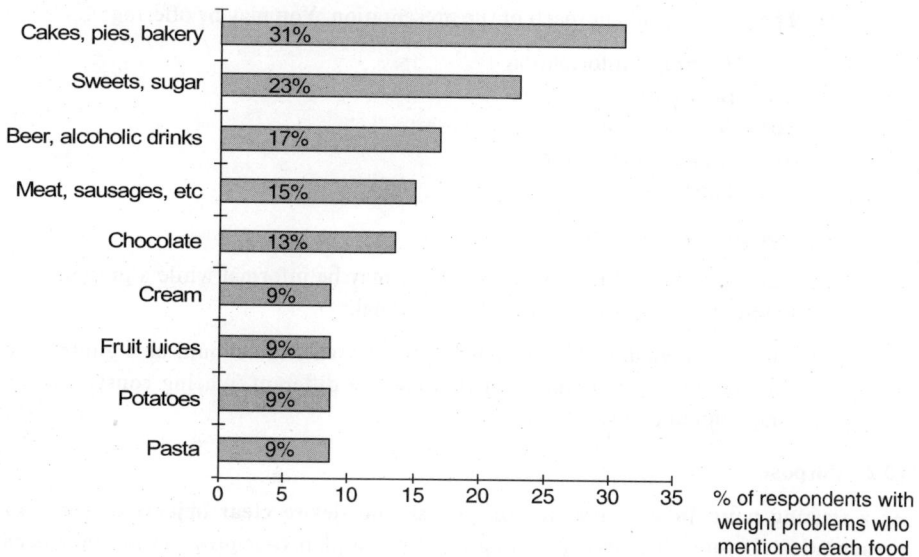

% of respondents with weight problems who mentioned each food

Debrief. What did you think of the report? Note that the report writer had constructed a graph of the data. You are required to submit a spreadsheet as part of your Report, but don't forget other ways of making your points clear, such as graphs and diagrams.

9 ORAL PRESENTATIONS

The Edexcel Guidelines suggest that although you may present your Research Project report as a written document, it is also possible that you may be required to deliver a formal presentation. This could take the form of a presentation whereby you present the report to an audience, or a *viva voce* whereby you are questioned by your tutor on certain aspects of your Report.

These are skills that you may have already seen in the Business Essentials Course Book, Business Decision Making

10 BUSINESS PRESENTATIONS

10.1 Preparing a presentation

A **presentation** is the act of making something (eg information) available to an audience. Presentations are usually planned acts of communication.

A **business presentation** could be made in a wide range of contexts, which may vary in terms of a number of aspects.

(a) The size and composition of the audience. This could range from a single manager to a small group of decision-makers or a large conference. The audience may be known to you or be complete strangers. They may have prior knowledge of the area you are speaking about or be complete 'laymen'. All these factors will affect the audience's ability to accept your message.

(b) The purpose and approach of the presentation. You may be offering:

    (i) Technical information

    (ii) Instruction

    (iii) A comparison

    (iv) A recommendation

    (v) Persuasion

(c) The complexity of the subject matter

(d) The level of formality. A staff briefing may be informal while a presentation to senior management is likely to be formal.

(e) The time available. The purpose of the presentation should be a guide as to time required – but time available may be different, placing constraints on your content and style.

10.2 Purpose

As a starting point in your preparation you should devise **clear objectives for your presentation**. If your objectives are going to help you plan your presentation they need to be **specific** and **measurable**.

Your objectives should be stated in terms of what the audience will do, or how they will be changed, at the end of the presentation: eg they will believe, be persuaded, agree, be motivated, do, understand, be able – or something similar.

Start with your primary objective, then move on to secondary objectives you will need to achieve along the way. This hierarchy of objectives provides a useful aid to planning the content and structure of your presentation.

10.3 Audience

You are likely to have a fair idea of the audience composition – from senior decision-makers to trainees.

The **audience's motivations and expectations** will influence their perceptions of you and your message. Why might they be at your presentation?

(a) Attendance may be compulsory. Unless interest can be stimulated by the presentation, compulsory attendance may create resistance to the message.

(b) Attendance may be recommended by a superior. Participants may be motivated because they perceive it to be in their own interest to do so.

(c) They are interested in the topic of the presentation. This often means there is a fine line to tread between telling the audience what they already know, and losing them by assuming more knowledge than they possess.

(d) They need specific information. An audience that is deliberately seeking information, and intending to use it to further their own objectives, is highly motivated.

Taking into account audience needs and expectations, your message needs to have the following qualities.

(a) **Relevance**. It should be relevant to the audience's needs and interests, eg making a difficult decision easier, or satisfying a need.

(b) **Credibility**. It should be consistent in itself, contain known facts, apparently objective, and from a source perceived to be trustworthy.

(c) **Accessibility**

    (i) It should be audible and visible. Do you need to be closer to the audience? Do you need a microphone? Enlarged visual aids?

    (ii) It should also be understandable. What is the audience's level of knowledge of the topic? What technical terms or 'jargon' will need to be avoided or explained?

10.4 Developing content

Armed with your clearly stated objectives and audience profile, you can plan the content of your presentation.

One approach, which may help to clarify your thinking, is as follows.

Step 1. **Brainstorm**. Think laterally about the subject, noting down your thoughts. Do not worry about the order or relevance of the ideas – just keep them coming, until your brain 'dries up'.

Step 2. **Prioritise.** Select the **key points**, and a **storyline** or theme that gives your argument a unified sense of 'direction'. The fewer points you make (with the most emphasis) and the clearer the direction in which your thoughts are heading, the easier it will be for the audience to grasp and retain your message. Discard – or de-emphasise – points which do not further your simple design.

Step 3. **Structure / Outline.** Make notes that show the selected main points and how they link to each other. Then flesh out your message. The outline should include an introduction; supporting evidence, examples and illustrations; notes of where (and what) visual aids will be required; signals of logical progressions and a conclusion.

Step 4. **Practise.** Learn the basic outline, or sequence of ideas, rather than a word-for-word 'script': if you repeat a speech by rote, it will sound stilted and mechanical. You should attempt **at least one full, timed 'dress' rehearsal**, preferably in front of a mock audience.

Step 5. Develop your cue and visual aids. Your outline may be too unwieldy to act as a cue or aide for the talk itself. Cards small enough to fit into the palm of your hand are ideal memory 'joggers'. If you are using slides, either on an overhead projector or via a PC and presentation software (eg Microsoft PowerPoint), these will also guide you and the audience. They should contain very brief, clear notes (verbal or pictorial), which provide:

- Key words for each topic and the logical links between them, and
- The full text of any (brief) detailed information you wish to quote

10.5 The introduction

You only get one chance to make a good first impression!

Purpose of the Introduction	Suggested approach(es)	Example
Establish your credibility on the subject	Very briefly (eg two sentences) outline your qualifications and / or experience, emphasising the parts most relevant to the topic. An 'old' **un**successful anecdote may demonstrate the need for proficiency in the subject.	'My first experience of an accounting package was not an enjoyable experience – due in equal measures to the quality of the package and the quality of my skills! However, the last decade has seen rapid developments in accounting packages, and hopefully a steady development of my knowledge and skills.'
Gain the audience's attention and interest	Establish the relevance of the topic to the audience – problems or opportunities they may be able to apply the material to. Surprise them with an interesting fact.	'In 1985 60% of management accountants used a computer less than three times a week!'

Establish a rapport with the audience	Anecdote, humour or identify with them.	
Prepare the audience for the content and structure of your presentation	Define and describe the topic. Make it clear why the presentation is being made. What are the objectives? Set the scene, introduce the topic and state your 'theme'.	'The techniques explained in this session have the potential to save you on average ten hours a week.'

10.6 The 'body' of the presentation – clarifying the message

Your structured notes and outline should contain cues that clarify the shape and progression of your information or argument. This will help keep you 'on track' and enable the audience to:

(a) Maintain a sense of purpose and motivation
(b) Follow your argument, so that they arrive with you at the conclusion.

Logical cues indicate the links between one topic or statement and the next. Here are some examples.

(a) You can simply begin each point with **linking words or phrases** like:

This has led to...

Therefore ... [conclusion, result or effect, arising from previous point]

So...

As a result...

However...

But ... [contradiction or alternative to previous point]

On the other hand...

Similarly ... [confirmation or additional example of previous point]

Again...

Moreover ... [building on the previous point]

(b) You can set up a **framework** for the whole argument, giving the audience an overview and then filling in the detail. For example:

'There are three main reasons why ... Firstly ... Secondly ... Thirdly....'

'So what's the answer? You could take two sides, here. On the one hand.... On the other hand....'

'Let's trace how this came about. On Monday 17th.... Then on Tuesday....'

'Of course, this isn't a perfect solution. It has the advantages of.... But there are also disadvantages, in that....'

'You might like to think of communication in terms of the 5 C's. That's: concise, clear, correct, complete, and courteous. Let's look at each of these in turn'.

(c) You can use devices that **summarise or repeat the previous point** and lead the audience to the next. These have the advantage of giving you, and the listener, a 'breather' in which to gather your thoughts.

Other ways in which content can be used to clarify the message include the following.

(a) **Examples** and illustrations – showing how an idea works in practice.

(b) **Anecdotes** – inviting the audience to relate an idea to a real-life situation.

(c) **Questions** – rhetorical, or requiring the audience to answer, raising particular points that may need clarification.

(d) **Explanation** – showing how or why something has happened.

(e) **Description** – helping the audience to visualise the setting you are describing.

(f) **Definition** – explaining the precise meaning of terms that may not be understood.

(g) The use of facts, **quotations** or **statistics** – to 'prove' your point.

Your **vocabulary** and style should contribute to the clarity of the message. Use short, simple sentences. Avoid jargon, unexplained acronyms, colloquialisms, double meanings and vague expressions.

Adding emphasis

Emphasis is the 'weight', importance or impact given to particular words or ideas. This can be achieved through delivery – the tone and volume of your voice, eye contact and gestures. Emphasis can also be provided through the following techniques:

Technique	Comment
Repetition	'If accuracy in income estimation is vital to our investment decisions, then accurate income estimation techniques must be developed.'
Rhetorical questions	'Do you know how many of our departmental heads are unhappy with the management information we provide? Fifty percent. Do you think that's acceptable?'
Quotation	'Information overload is the number one issue in the information we are producing. That's the conclusion of our survey.'
Statistics	'One in two of our internal customers have complained this year: that's 20% more complaints than last year. If the trend continues, we will soon have more complainers than satisfied customers!'
Exaggeration	'We have to look at our quality control system, because if the current trend continues, we are going to end up without any customers at all.'

Adding interest

Simple, clear information may only be interesting to those already motivated by the subject. You should strike a balance between the need for clarity and the need to make your message vivid, attention grabbing and memorable.

Here are some further suggestions.

(a) **Analogy.** Comparing something to something else which is in itself more colourful or interesting.

(b) **Anecdote or narrative.** Telling a story that illustrates the point, using suspense, humour or a more human context.

(c) **Curiosity or surprise.** For example, 'If you put all the widgets we've sold this year end to end, they would stretch twice around the equator.'

(d) **Humour.** Used well, this will add entertainment value, and serve as a useful 'breather' for listeners. Be careful, humour may not travel well; the audience may not be on the speaker's wavelength. Use with caution!

(e) **Emotion.** You may wish to appeal to the audience's emotions. As with humour you have to be sure of your audience before you attempt this. Your appeal may come across as patronising, manipulative or just irrelevant. Emotion does add human interest, and can be used to stress the humanity and involvement of the speaker.

'When I first heard about this technique, I was sceptical about it: *surely* it couldn't be as effective as they were trying to claim? But when I tried it for myself – Wow! I was just ... so excited. So impressed. Perhaps I can share some of that with you today.'

Activity 2 (10 minutes)

You are preparing a presentation to management on the benefits of flexitime hours. What techniques might you use?

---

11 PRESENTATIONS USING POWERPOINT

11.1 Visual aids

Visual aids use a visual image to aid communication. The purpose of visual aids is not to look good for their own sake, but to support the message. Michael Stevens (*Improving Your Presentation Skills*) notes:

'The proper use of aids is to achieve something in your presentation that you cannot do as effectively with words alone. They are only *a means to an end*, for instance to clarify an idea, or prove a point. A good aid is one that does this efficiently.'

Slides (Used with an overhead projector or PC and projector)

Slides may include photographs, text, diagrams and other images projected onto a screen or other surface. Slides have several useful features.

(a) They allow the use of images that can be used to create a mood or impression. As they are perceived as an image of reality, they are also powerful tools if you wish to 'prove a point'.

(b) They are pre-prepared. The slides for a business presentation would now usually be prepared using presentation software. This allows careful planning and execution, and slides can be finished to a very high degree of style, quality and 'professionalism'.

(c) The sequence and timing of slides is controlled by the presenter, allowing the synchronisation of images with relevant points in the presentation. Slides are therefore flexible in keeping pace with the presenter and audience.

(d) The swiftness with which one image follows another is particularly suited to messages of contrast or comparison: two products, say, or before and after scenarios.

Before you start up the presentation software, you need to review your speech outline and identify the points that can be illustrated with PowerPoint:

- Definitions
- Charts
- Graphs
- Statistics etc.

11.2 What is a PowerPoint presentation?

A PowerPoint presentation is a selection of slides, handouts, speaker's notes and your outline.

(a) **Slides** – these are the pages of a presentation and can contain text, images, graphs and sounds. As well as being used as a PowerPoint slide show the slides can be printed as overhead transparencies.

(b) **Handouts** – these are smaller printed versions of your slides with 2, 3 or 6 slides on an A4 page.

(c) **Speaker's notes** – you can produce these to be used alongside your presentation.

(d) **Outline** – this shows the title and main text of the whole presentation but not images

There are five views you can use when creating a PowerPoint presentation. You can switch between views using the buttons in the **bottom left** corner of the PowerPoint window. Each view gives you different editing capabilities and a different way of looking at your work.

(a) **Slide view** – Working on one slide at a time you can add text, draw shapes, add graphics and change the layout of your slide.

(b) **Outline view** – This can be used to organise your presentation. You work only with slide titles and the main text.

(c) **Slide Sorter view** – This gives you an overall view of all the slides in your presentation. You can rearrange the order of the slides, add transitions and set timings for electronic presentations

(d) **Notes Page view** – You can add speaker's notes to any of the slides in your presentation.

(e) **Slide Show view** – This gives you an overall view of all the slides in your presentation. You can rearrange the order of the slides, add transitions and set timings for electronic presentations.

PowerPoint has four toolbars – standard, format, draw and common tasks (shown in this order below)

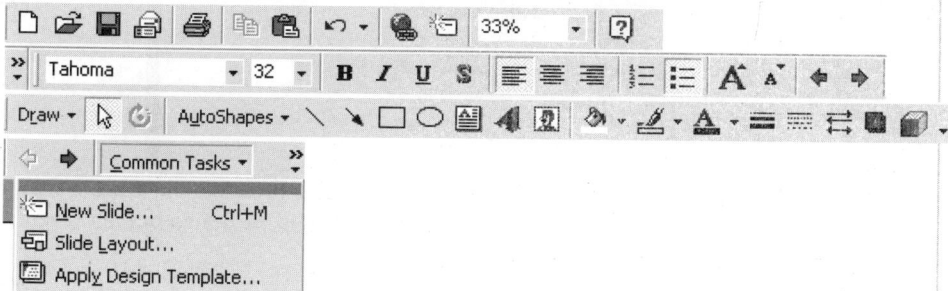

To give an idea of how efficient this presentation media is, here's an example. A traditional text heavy report may contain 100 pages of text and graphics, and wading through this material can be time-consuming and hard to understand. However when organized in a slide format, this massive amount of information can be reduced down to a 20-50 page slide presentation, with concise bullet points and compelling visuals.

11.3 Creating a basic PowerPoint presentation

We are going to begin by creating and viewing a basic PowerPoint presentation and then go on to add some embellishments. Like any creative package, once you have the confidence to explore, there are many extras that you can do on your own. This section in a study pack will only be sufficient to get you started.

1. Open Microsoft PowerPoint by either double-clicking on the PowerPoint shortcut on the Windows desktop or select it from the Start Menu

2. Select 'Design Template' from the PowerPoint window (we will look at the AutoContent Wizard later in this section) and click the Slide Design button on the Formatting toolbar. PowerPoint displays a gallery of designs that include co-ordinated colours, fonts, and layouts Scroll through the gallery to find a design you think you would like and click the design to apply it to your slide show.

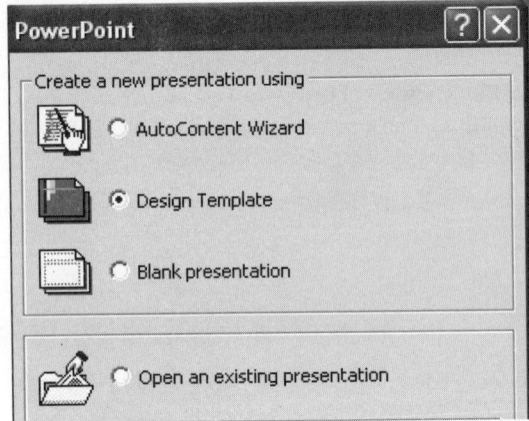

A template can be applied to a new or existing presentation. Once a design has been applied to a presentation you can change the design but not revert to using no design.

You can change the design any time, even after you have created an entire slide show. However, by default PowerPoint changes the design for all slides in the presentation, and changes later may make it necessary to edit the slide show to make text and other objects fit the new layout. For example, a title that fits nicely in one design layout might be too long for another. If possible, try to select a design that you will stick with for the entire presentation.

3. PowerPoint will take you directly to choose an AutoLayout for your new slide. You need to choose a slide layout from those offered in the preview box. Helpfully the default is a title slide. Click on OK. A template for your first slide appears to which you can add a title and sub title.

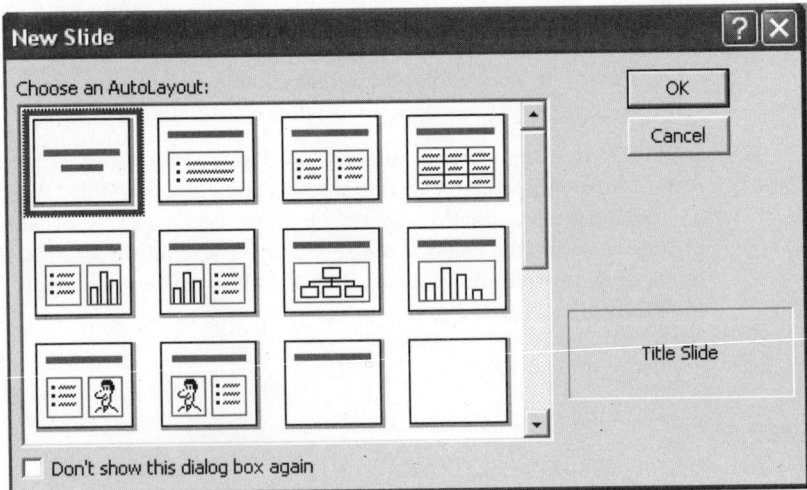

The other options are:

Title Slide	Bulleted list	Bulleted list with 2 columns	Table
Bulleted list + chart	Chart + bulleted list	Organisational chart	Chart
Bulleted list + image	Image + bulleted list	Blank with title	Blank

4.   Enter your title ***Introduction to PowerPoint*** and subtitle – this can be your name or the date that you (or someone else) will be showing the presentation. If you do not want the subtitle you can click on it and delete it.

Introduction to PowerPoint

Practice moving, removing and resizing a body box. Click on it once and grab the edges to make it a different size. The text will reset itself to match the size and shape you create. Move the title and sub-title boxes wherever on the page you want them. Practice changing the characteristics of the title and text – this could be the title, the body or all of the text – highlight what you want to change. Choose Format from the Menu bar and then Font. In this window, you can change the face, style, size and colour of the font. Click on the Colour bar and choose More Colours if none of the standard colours appeal to you.

You can use Undo to reverse nearly anything. But Undo is not only a tool that you use to correct mistakes. Because creating PowerPoint slides is akin to an artistic experience, consider the Undo tool as a way to try things out. You can do, undo, and do again until you get just what you want.

You can also delete slides or slide information. To delete information from a slide, simply click the object you want to remove (for example, a graph or graphic image) and press Delete. To delete an entire slide, click the slide icon in the outline area at the left and press Delete. PowerPoint does *not* warn you that you're about to lose an entire slide. If you accidentally delete a slide, simply click the Undo button on the toolbar.

When saving a presentation for the first time from the file menu select Save As. Choose where you want your file to be saved in, give your file a name and select the type of file you want in the save as type box (this is set to presentation by default).

5.   Add a new slide to the presentation by going to the Insert menu and select New Slide.

Every slide should have a title. They clarify the message of the slide and ensure coherence within your presentation. Clear titles will help you organise the material. You will find them useful in Slide Show View when you navigate within your presentation. They are also essential in PowerPoint if and when you convert your presentation for delivery on the Web, as they become the Web menu names.

It is a good idea to make a preview slide to let your audience know what is in store for the session so, in the New Slide window, select the 'bulleted list' layout and do the following:

Elements of a Presentation

> - What a PowerPoint presentation contains
> - PowerPoint toolbars
> - PowerPoint views

Save the presentation by selecting Save from the File menu.

You can change the design of the bullet points using Format > Bullets and Numbering. To avoid a cluttered look, try to limit slides to the title line and six lines per slide and a maximum of six words per line. If your main idea or theme requires more than this, add an additional slide (or two or three) rather than trying to fit all the necessary text onto one slide. A good rule of thumb is to leave 10-15% around all edges of the slide free of text and graphics. Only use key words or phrases when making titles and sub-headings on your slides.

6. Add a new slide by clicking on the New Slide button on the Standard Toolbar. In the New Slide window, select the 2 column text layout and do the following:

What a PowerPoint presentation contains

- Slides
- Presentations
- Handouts
- Outlines

7. Add a new slide as before and in the New Slide window, select the Text & Clip Art layout, and do the following:

PowerPoint Toolbars

- Standard
- Formatting
- Drawing
- Common tasks

To insert ClipArt – double click on the image on the slide. Select the one you want and then click the grey 'Insert' button on the right. ClipArt images can be moved and re-sized just like AutoShapes.

8. Add the last new slide as before and in the New Slide window, select the Chart & Text layout, and do the following:

PowerPoint Views

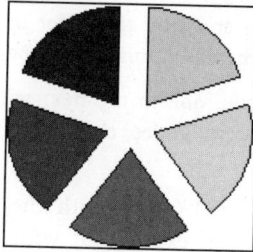

- Outline view
- Slide Sorter view
- Notes Page view
- Slide Show view
- Slide view

Graphs can be inserted by double clicking on the chart image on the slide. A Datasheet will also appear which you can edit to include your own graph information. If you right click within the chart area, but not on the chart itself, a menu appears, allowing you to edit your chart. The chart will be automatically inserted into your presentation and can be edited similar to graphs.

Tips on formatting your slides:

- Experiment with type styles, sizes and colours. Don't be afraid to bold text, underline or italicise if you are trying to emphasize a point.

- Keep titles short. About 5-7 words will get your point across.

- Make good use of the space available on the slide. Enlarge the graphs and have the text large enough that it is easy to read across a room.

- Format your slides horizontally (landscape) and not vertically (portrait). You don't want part of your slide to be below eye level.

- Try not to put too much data on one slide. One idea per slide is ideal. If you have many graphs and data in one place, the audience may lose interest. In addition, the increased amount of text will most likely require you reduce your font size, which will make it harder to read from a distance.

- Two graphs maximum per slide. This will make your data easier to understand. If you must have two visuals, make sure the text accompanying it is simple.

- Avoid busy slide backgrounds. Multiple colours or gradients can make text hard to read.

Activity 3 *(pencil icon)*   **(20 minutes)**

Produce a presentation slide and supporting notes that could be used to start a presentation entitled 'What is the Internet?'

11.4 Viewing and testing your PowerPoint presentation

After completing all your slides, select *View Show* from the *Slide* show menu to review your presentation. This menu gives you control over all aspects of the slideshow, and allows you to use animation, slide transition and alter the order in which items appear on slides. Transitions occur *between* slides, whereas animation happens *on* the slides.

By default, the slides in your show snap from one to the next without any transition between them. To add a transition between two slides, click on Slide Show – > Slide Transition.

Note that 'No Transition' is currently selected (underneath the picture) but arrows indicate choices of transitions, which you can experiment with. You can apply the transition to one of the slides, or apply it to all your slides. Just as with colour schemes, it is a good idea to use transitions in a consistent manner – for example, use one or two throughout the presentation to help create visual unity. Also notice that the slides can advance when you click the mouse or you can set them to automatically advance every set number of seconds. This latter option is especially good for looping slides used for advertising or public information.

If you wish you can even add sound effects – but these will only play if a sound output has been connected up when giving the presentation. Press Escape button on keyboard to end slide show.

To add animation, choose the text you want to animate and select Preset Animation from the Slide Show menu, and click on one of the different styles. For a more comprehensive choice of animation, right click on the highlighted text you want to animate, and select custom animation. This will give you endless options with the facility to preview the animation itself.

Testing is one of the most important parts of making a successful presentation, and, often one of the things that is overlooked. You should test your slide show to make sure that everything is just the way you want it. At any point it is possible to change the way the whole show looks by using the options in the Format menu. Don't forget to save your work afterwards.

Printing

You can print your entire presentation – the slides, outline, speaker's notes, and audience handouts – in colour or in black and white. All printing features are available from the File >Print menu. No matter what you print, the process is basically the same. You open the presentation you want to print and choose whether you want to print slides, handouts, notes pages, or an outline.

Then you identify the slides to be printed and the number of copies you want.

You can make colour or black-and-white overhead transparencies from your slides. When you print audience handouts, you can print one, two, three, or six slides on a page.

Creating speaker's notes

To type notes while working on a presentation:

- On the View menu, click Notes Page.
- Click the notes box, and then enter your notes for the current slide.
- Use the scroll bar to move to other slides you want to add notes to.

To enlarge the view of the notes box, click the Zoom box. You can also add notes by entering them in the Speaker Notes dialog box. Click Speaker Notes on the View menu, and then type your notes. The notes are added to your notes page.

11.5 AutoContent Wizard

Instead of going the route of Blank Presentation or Design Template, we can opt for letting the Wizard do most of the work.

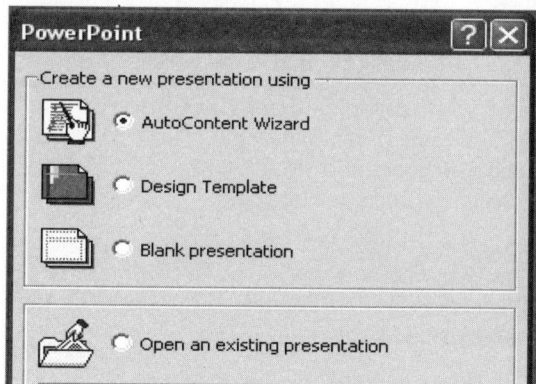

Click on AutoContent Wizard, and PowerPoint displays the AutoContent Wizard dialog box. Click Next to get started. The AutoContent Wizard leads you through the steps required to prepare presentations with specific content.

The first step is to select a presentation type. You can choose from various categories, or you can select All to see all the templates you can choose from. When you find the one you want, select it and then click Next.

The second step is to choose the presentation style. Typically, you'll be making an onscreen presentation, but you can also create a presentation targeted for the Web, for printed overhead transparencies, or for 35mm slides. Stick with the onscreen presentation for now. After you select it, click Next.

The third step is to choose certain basic options, which include the following:

- Title

- Footer – this is text that appears at the bottom of each slide. An example might be your company logo or department name.

- Date – by default, PowerPoint automatically generates the date your slide show was last updated (that is, saved) and places it at the bottom of each slide. Uncheck the Date Last Updated box if you don't want it

- Slide numbers – PowerPoint assumes that you want slide numbers. Uncheck the Slide Number check box if you don't.

After you make your choices, click Next, and then on the final wizard screen, click Finish. PowerPoint displays the title slide with the options you chose.

You can scroll through the outline to get a sense of suggested elements for a successful presentation on the topic you chose. For example, if you chose a marketing plan, you see slides showing market summary, production definition, competition, and so on. You may or may not use all the sample slides, and you'll likely add others. To change a slide's text content, you go to the left side of the screen and select the slide that you want to change by clicking on it.

Chapter roundup

- In presenting your thoughts in paper, you are submitting yourself to a critical audience without any opportunity for justifying or modifying your assertions. You are judged purely on what you have written, so you must present yourself professionally and make yourself clearly understood.

- The needs of you academic audience may differ from your corporate audience to the extent that you may need to produce two reports. Understanding the needs of your audience will help you adopt an appropriate style and choice of language.

- The structure of your report will depend on the type of research you are doing and the type of report you intend to produce. However, there are a number of established conventions,: be aware of the these to help organise your thinking.

- All the authorities on research methodology stress the importance of writing as an ongoing activity. Effective time management, reviewing materials and establishing a regular writing routine are good habits to get into.

- You may present your thought through an oral business presentation, supported by visual aids, such as a power point presentation.

Answers to activities

1   You could have chosen a number of different formats. At the very least, you could have organised the data in logical order.

Report

To: The marker
From: A Candidate
Date:
Re Carnelian Ltd

Contents

1   Executive summary
2   Products and markets
3   Organisation and management
4   Financial position

Appendix A: customers

Appendix B: financial position

1   Executive summary

1.1 Carnelian Ltd is a long established, privately owned company specialising in the manufacture of artificial flowers for sale worldwide, employing a functional departmentation structure.

2   Customers and markets

2.1 Turnover from artificial flowers is £1m per annum.

2.2 £300,000 derives from one product, the silk orchid.

2.3 Exports to Germany account for 50% of turnover.

2.4 No one customer accounts for 1% of turnover. See Appendix A for a list of customers.

2.5 The main marketing activity is the website, which has replaced mail order.

3'   Organisation and management

3.1 The company employs 23 people, including the directors.

3.2 The company is divided into three departments.

- Marketing – 5 personnel reporting to Ms Underwood.
- Production – 12 personnel reporting to Mr Mongrove.
- Finance and IT – three personnel reporting to Mr Mace.

4   Financial position and capital structure

4.1 The company makes a profit margin of 5% and a return of assets of 33%. See Appendix B for workings.

4.2 The sole shareholders are Ms Underwood and Mr Mongrove, each of whom own 500 of the issued share capital of 1000 ordinary shares of £1 each.

Appendix A

List of customers

Appendix B: financial position

B.1 Profit margin

Profit £50,000/turnover £1m = 5%

B.2 ROCE

£50,000/£150,000 —=-33% Turnover: £1m

Net assets £150,000

2   Some options are outlined below. The **techniques** listed below are applicable to a range of presentations.

(a) As part of your **introduction**, **explain** what flexitime is and the philosophy behind it.

(b) Include **statistics** on staff absenteeism and turnover to support your argument.

(c) Offer a **case study** of another organisation that introduced flexitime to their benefit.

(d) Present **quotes and opinions** of staff who are working 9-5, and others in a flexitime scheme.

(e) Present a **series of scenarios** (from the organisation's and employees' points of view) in which a problem – seasonal demand, dentist's appointment, travel delays etc – would be solved by flexitime.

(f) Compare flexitime, in **an analogy**, with a school day of fixed hours, with pupils completing homework outside those hours.

Comment on the answer

You will note that the very requirement to produce a report structuring the data suggested some useful analysis such as calculating ROCE and profit margins. We are not saying that this is perfect by any means, but you can tell that the data about Carnelian Ltd is much easier to grasp than it was before. You may have chosen a different structure of course.

3

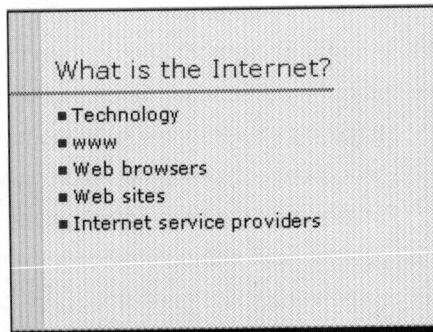

Technology. The Internet is the name given to the technology that allows any computer with a telecommunications link to exchange information with any other suitably equipped computer.

The Internet is also called the **World Wide Web** (**www**), information superhighway or cyberspace, although technically it is the 'Web' that makes the Internet easy to use.

Web browsers are the software loaded on Internet-enabled computers to allow them to view information from the Internet.

Internet information is contained on ***Websites***, which range from a few pages about one individual to large sites offering a range of services such as Amazon.co.uk and Lastminute.com.

Access to the Internet is provided by ***Internet Service Providers***. An Internet connection may be made via a telephone line (or an ISDN or ASDL line) to the ISP and then onto the www.

Bibliography

Aaker, DA. Kumar, V & Day, GS. (1995) Marketing Research. New York: Wiley. Cited in Adamantios Diamantopoulos & Bodo B Schlegelmilck. (2000) *Taking the Fear Out of Data Analysis.* London: Business Press.

Bell, J. (1999) *Doing Your Research Project.* (3rd ed.) Buckingham: Open University Press.

Brown, S, McDowell, L, Race, P (1995) *500 Tips for Research Students,* Abingdon, Routledge

Buchanan, D., Boddy, D, and McCalman, J. (1988) 'Getting in, getting on, getting out and getting back',˜ in Bryman, A. (ed.) *Doing Research in Organisations.* London: Routledge, pp. 53-67.

Buzan, A. (1989) *Use your Head.* London: BBC Publications. Cited in Sharp, J.A. and Howard, K. (1996) *The Management of a Student Research Project.* (2nd ed.) Aldershot: Gower.

Buzan, A. (1995) *The Mind Map Book.* London: BBC Books.

Catalogue of British Official Publications Not Published by HMSO. Chadwyck-Healey: Cambridge. Cited in Sharp, J.A. and Howard, K. (1996) *The Management of a Student Research Project.* (2nd ed.) Aldershot: Gower.

Cohen, L. and Manion, L. (1994) *Research Methods in Education.* (4th ed.) London: Routledge. Cited in Bell, J. (1999) *Doing Your Research Project.* (3rd ed.) Buckingham: Open University Press.

Denscombe, M. (1998) *The Good Research Guide.* Buckingham: Open University Press.

Directory of British Associations. CBD Research Ltd: Beckenham. Cited in Sharp, J.A. and Howard, K. (1996) *The Management of a Student Research Project.* (2nd ed.) Aldershot: Gower.

Educational Enterprises. (3rd ed) Buckingham: Open University Press.

Easterby-Smith, M., Thorpe, R. and Lowe, A. (1991) *Management Research: an Introduction.* London: Sage.

Fielding, N. G. and Lee, R. M. (1993) *Using Computers in Qualitative Research.* London: Sage.

Gill, J. and Johnson, P.(1997) *Research Methods for Managers* (2nd ed.) London: Paul Chapman.

Gummesson,E. (1991) *Qualitative Methods in Management Research.* Newbury Park, California: Sage.

Hays, W. L. (1994) *Statistics* (4th ed.) London: Holt-Saunders.

Hussey, J. and Hussey, R. (1997) *Business Research.* Basingstoke: Macmillan Press.

Jankowicz, A.D. (2000) *Business Research Projects.* (3rd ed.) London: Business Press.

Johnson, J.M. (1975) *Doing Field Research.* New York: Free Press. Cited in Saunders, M., Lewis, P. and Thornhill, A. (2000) *Research Methods for Business Students.* (2nd ed.) Harlow: Financial Times Prentice Hall.

Kervin, J.B. (1999) *Methods for Business Research* (2nd ed.) New York: Harper Collins.

Luck, M.(1999) *Your Student Research Project.* Aldershot: Gower.

Marshall, C. and Rossman, G.B. (1999) *Designing Qualitative Research*. (3rd ed.) Thousand Oaks, California: Sage. Cited in Saunders, M., Lewis, P. and Thornhill, A. (2000) *Research Methods for Business Students*. (2nd ed.) Harlow: Financial Times Prentice Hall.

Marshall, P. (1997) *Research Methods*. Oxford: How To Books Ltd.

Millmore, M. (1995) *HRM in C & GCHE?: Assessing the Current State of Play*. MA dissertation, Cheltenham, Cheltenham & Gloucester College of Higher Education.

Miles, M. B. and Huberman, A. M. (1994) *Qualitative Data Analysis: an Expanded Sourcebook*. (2nd ed.) London: Sage.

Open University Course EIII 1998) *Educational Evaluation*. Milton Keynes. Open University Educational Enterprises. Cited in Bell, J, (1999).

Palton, M. Q. (1990) *Qualitative Evaluation and Research Methods*. (2nd ed.) London: Sage.

Raimond, P. (1993) *Management Projects*. London: Chapman and Hall. Cited in Saunders, M., Lewis, P. and Thornhill, A. (2000) *Research Methods for Business Students*. (2nd ed.) Harlow: Financial Times Prentice Hall.

Robson, C. (1993) *Real World Research: a Resource for Social Scientists and Practitioner Researchers*. Oxford: Blackwell.

Saunders, M., Lewis, P. and Thornhill, A. Cited in Hays (1994).

Saunders, M., Lewis, P. and Thornhill, A. (2000) *Research Methods for Business Students*. (2nd ed.) Harlow: Financial Times Prentice Hall.

Saunders, M., Lewis, P. and Thornhill, A. (2003) *Research Methods for Business Students*. (3rd ed.) Harlow: Financial Times Prentice Hall.

Sharp, J.A. and Howard, K. (1996) *The Management of a Student Research Project*. (2nd ed.) Aldershot: Gower.

Stevens, M (1987) *Improving Your Presentation Skills*, Kogan Page Ltd

Stewart, D.W. and Kamins, M.A. (1993) *Secondary Research: Information Sources and Methods* (2nd ed.) Newbury Park: Sage. Cited in Saunders, M., Lewis, P. and Thornhill, A. (2000) *Research Methods for Business Students*. (2nd ed.) Harlow: Financial Times Prentice Hall.

Strauss, A. and Corbin, J. (1997) (eds) *Grounded Theory in Practice*. Thousand Oaks: Sage.

The Times (2002) 'In Brief'. *The Times MBA Supplement*. 28th January, p.2

United Nations Statistical Yearbook. United Nations: New York. Cited in Sharp, J.A. and Howard, K. (1996) *The Management of a Student Research Project*. (2nd ed.) Aldershot: Gower.

Verma, G.K. and Beard, R.M. (1981) *What is Educational Research? Perspectives on Techniques of Research*. Aldershot: Gower. Cited in Bell, J. (1999) *Doing Your Research Project*. (3rd ed.) Buckingham: Open University Press.

Index

Abstracts, 115, 240
Academic needs, 66
Access, 85, 138
Accuracy, 255
Acknowledgements, 239
Action research, 43
Active listening, 14
Active v passive honesty, 58
Active voice, 256
Ad hoc surveys, 141
Analogy, 77
Analysis, 23
Analysis, discussion and conclusions, 248
Analysis, synthesis and accurate communication, 108
Analytical aids, 231
Analytical mind, 14
Anonymity, 54
Applied research, 6
Approach to the work, 29
Arithmetic mean, 211
Attributes of a good project, 2
Attributes of a successful project, 2
Audiences, 236, 263
AutoContent Wizard, 275
Axial coding, 229

Backing-up your work, 124
Balance, 3
Bar charts, 199
Bibliographical software, 123
Bibliographies, 118
Bookmarking, 121
Books, 117
Books and journals, 142
Boolean operators, 116
Box plots, 203
Brainstorming, 77, 263

Case studies, 41
Categorical (nominal) data, 188, 200
Categorising data, 225
Category, 165
Census, 140
Central office edit, 190
Change management, 15
Chi-squared (χ^2) tables, 215
Chi-squared test, 214
Citation, 125
Citation indexes, 115
Clarity, 255
Clear vision, 29

Closed, 164
Cluster sampling, 180
Code books, 192
Coding errors, 196
Coding the responses, 172
Coefficient of determination, 218
Coefficient of variation, 213
Communication, 14
Component bar charts, 207
Computer databases, 144
Computer-assisted qualitative data analysis software, 233
Computerised catalogues, 117
Computers, 232
Conclusion, 30
Confidence, 177
Confidentiality, 54
Consistency, 174
Contents page, 239
Contextual evaluation, 30
Contingency tables, 204
Continuous and regular surveys, 140
Continuous data, 189
Convenience sampling, 183
Correlation, 217
Correlation and regression, 217
Courtesy, 49
Creative thinking techniques, 72
Creativity, 14
Creeping expectations, 88
Critical literature review, 11, 106
Critical review, 71
Cross-sectional studies, 45
Cultural influences, 55

Data, 132
Data analysis, 12
Data cards, 226
Data coding, 192
Data collection, 12
Data editing and data cleaning, 190
Data matrix, 191
Data protection regulations, 55
Databases, 116, 232
Deception of participants, 52
Deductive approach, 20, 223, 226
Deductive research, 100
Definition, 266
Degrees of correlation, 217
Delivery and collection questionnaire, 160
Delphi technique, 82
Description, 266
Descriptive study, 149

Designing the questionnaire, 164
Differential response rates, 197
Dignity, 56
Discrete data, 189
Discussions, 69
Dispersion, 212
Documentary secondary data, 139

E-mail mailing lists, 121
Embarrassment and ridicule, 55
Emotional maturity, 14
Emphasis, 266
Empirical investigation, 6
Empirical testing and development, 7
Epistemology, 36
Errors, 258
Establishing a contract, 65
Ethical codes of practice, 60
Ethical issues, 4
Ethical standards, 51
Ethics, 49
Evaluating literature sources, 121
Evaluating results, 215-218
Evaluation criteria, 79
Executive summary, 240
Existing code books, 194
Experiments, 40
Explanation, 266
Explanation-building, 227
Explanatory study, 149
Exploratory review, 71
Exploratory review of literature, 70
Exploratory study, 149

Fabrication of evidence, 58
Face to face questionnaire, 158
Filter questions, 196
Flexibility, 14
Focus, 29
Focus groups, 153
Frequency distributions, 198
Frequency polygons, 201
Fully structured, 147

General search engines, 120
Generalisability, 21, 48
Generality, 2
Grammar checkers, 254
Graphical techniques, 198
Grid or matrix, 167
Grounded theory, 228

Habituation, 54

Handouts, 268
Harvard method of citation, 126
Histograms, 200
Homogeneity, 174
Husserl, 37

Identifying research questions, research
    objectives or hypotheses, 96
Illegitimate codes, 196
Illogical relationships, 196
Independence, 14
In-depth interviews, 149
Index cards, 226
Index numbers, 221
Indexes, 115
Inductive approach, 20, 223, 228
Inductive research, 100
Ineligibles, 160
Information gateways, 120
Informed consent, 51
Insertion of data into a data matrix, 191
Integrity of evidence, 58
Interest, 267
Interim consistency method, 174
Interim summaries, 231
Inter-library loans, 121
Internet, 119
Interpretation of results, 214
Inter-quartile range, 212
Interval data, 189
Interview skills, 151
Interviewer bias, 150
Interviewer effect, 150
Interviewing, 15
Interviews, 147
Introduction, 242

Jargon, 253
Judgmental sampling, 182

Key words, 99, 114

Language, 256
Learning outcomes, 18, 19
Likert scale, 166
Line graphs, 202
List, 165
Literature review, 106, 244
Literature search, 106
Logical cues, 265
Longitudinal studies, 45

Making notes of literature read, 123
Management power, 87
Management problem, 8
Margin of error, 177
Mean, 211
Measures of central tendency, 211
Measures of dispersion, 212
Median, 211
Meta search engines, 120
Methodology, 246
Missing data, 190
Missing data codes, 195
Mixed methods approach, 135
Mode, 211
Motivation, 14
Multiple bar chart, 205
Multiple box plots, 208
Multiple dichotomy method, 195
Multiple line graphs, 208
Multiple response method, 195
Multiple source secondary data, 141
Multiple, percentage component and
    component bar charts, 205
Multi-stage sampling, 181

Negative correlation, 209
Negotiation, 15
Nominal data, 188
Non-probability sampling, 181
Non-responses, 160
Non-sale of respondent details, 55
Non-symmetrical projects, 98
Notebooks, 74
Numerical codes, 192
Numerical measurement, 189

Objectivity, 58
Offensive language, 256
Official publications, 143
Ongoing review, 71
On-line questionnaire, 160
Open coding, 228
Open-ended, 164
Ordinal data, 188
Organisational conflict, 87
Organisational needs, 65
Organisationally-generated research
    ideas, 84
Originality, 2

Paradigm, 38
Parallel form method, 174
Parsimony, 36

Partial correlation, 209, 210
Participant observation, 53
Participants' rights, 54
Passive voice, 256
Past projects and dissertations, 75
Past research projects and dissertations, 68
Patronising language, 253
Pattern-matching, 227
Pearson's product moment correlation
    coefficient, 218
Percentage component bar charts, 206
Personal skills, 22
Persuasion and influencing, 15
Phenomenological paradigm, 155, 162
Phenomenological study, 247
Phenomenology, 37
Pie charts, 202
Piloting the questionnaire, 171
Planning, 11
Planning the literature review, 112
Population, 177
Positive correlation, 209
Positivism, 36
Positivistic paradigm, 155
Positivistic study, 246
Postal questionnaire, 159
Power and research approach, 50
Power and structure, 50
Power relationships, 87
PowerPoint, 267, 268
Practise, 264
Practitioner sources of literature, 111
Pragmatism, 3, 38
Precision, 177, 255
Preliminary search, 70
Preliminary studies, 83
Preparation of data for analysis, 190
Presentations, 262
    accessibility, 263
    analogy, 267
    anecdote, 267
    content, 263
    credibility, 263
    emotion, 267
    emphasis, 266
    exaggeration, 266
    humour, 267
    introduction, 264
    message, 265
    purpose, 262
    quotation, 266
    relevance, 263
    repitition, 266
    rhetorical questions, 266

slides, 267
statistics, 266
visual aids, 264, 267
Presentation of findings, 60
Previous research projects and
    dissertations, 118
Primary data, 4, 133, 147
Primary research, 246
Primary sources of literature, 110
Printed articles, 116
Printing, 274
Prioritising, 264
Privacy and dignity, 55
Probability sampling, 175
Problem solving, 15
Problem-oriented approach, 136
Project management, 15
Proposal preparation and refinement, 11
Pulling all the ideas together, 79
Pure research, 5
Purpose of the work, 29
Purposes of a research proposal, 64
Purposive sampling, 182

Qualitative analysis, 23
Qualitative data analysis, 222
Qualitative data analysis software, 226
Quality of evidence used, 4
Quantifiable data, 188
Quantification, 223
Quantitative analysis, 23
Quantity, 167
Questionnaires, 155, 156
Questions, 164, 266
Quota selection, 182

Range, 212
Ranking, 166
Ratio data, 189
Rational thinking techniques, 67
Reasoning and critical thinking, 30
Re-coding, 193
Reductionist approach, 36
Refereed academic journals, 111
References, 226
Referencing your literature, 125
Refining research ideas, 82
Refining research topics, 95
Refusals, 160
Regression, 217
Regression equations, 219
Relationship building, 15
Relevance, 121, 138
Relevance trees, 75

Reliability, 21, 47, 138, 154, 173
Replicability, 59
Report writing, 16
Research philosophies, 36
Research proposal, 64
Research strategies, 39
Research symmetry, 98
Research trail, 60
Researcher behaviour, 52
Researcher's diary, 232
Researcher's power, 87
Researcher's reputation, 49
Researcher's responsibility, 54
Response rates, 178
Results chapter, 248
Retention of research records, 59
Revising, 257

Sampling, 175
Sampling technique, 179
Scale, 166
Scattergraphs, 209
Scope of the project, 17
Search engines, 119
Search parameters, 113
Secondary analysis, 135
Secondary data, 4, 133, 136, 191
Secondary research, 245
Secondary sources of literature, 111
Selective coding, 229
Self-awareness, 14
Self-memos, 231
Self-selection bias, 161
Self-selection sampling, 183
Semi-structured, 148
Semi-structured interviews, 149
Simple random, 179
Simplicity, 254
Slides, 268
Snowball sampling, 183
Solve a management problem, 8
Sources of secondary data, 141
Speaker's notes, 268
Spearman's rank correlation coefficient,
    220
Specialised search engines, 120
Spellcheckers, 253
Split halves method, 174
Standard deviation, 213
Statistical techniques, 210
Strategies to gain access, 89
Stratified sampling, 179
Strengths, weaknesses and interests, 68
Structure, 238

Style, 251
Subject directories, 120
Sufficiency, 122
Summaries, 231
Survey approach, 107
Survey-based secondary data, 140
Surveys, 39
Symmetrical projects, 98
Systematic sampling, 179

Team working, 15
Technical publications, 143
Telephone questionnaire, 159
Tertiary literature sources, 112, 115
Test-retest method, 174
Thinking techniques to generate ideas, 67
Time management, 15
Time series analysis, 220
Timing of approaches, 57
Timings, 31
Title page, 238
Topic search, 11
Topic selection, 71
Trade association data, 144
Trends, 220
Triangulation, 38, 136
T-tests, 216

Unavailables, 160
Unitising data, 225
Unitising data manually, 226
Unstructured, 148

Validity, 21, 46, 149
Vancouver System, 126
Volume, 32

Ways to record, 123
Websites, 119
Word processing packages, 233
World Wide Web, 119
Writing, 249
Writing research questions and objectives, 94
Writing your research proposal, 10